"Dr. Johnson's compilation offers both breadth and depth to any reader interested in mental health for active-duty service members, veterans, and their families. Their unique symptom landscape and related evidence-based treatments are explained with a cultural competence that only becomes more essential as the military population keeps growing in diversity. I highly recommend this book to anyone who works with veterans. It is a valuable resource that will help you provide effective and culturally responsive care as well as support others in doing so."

      Dr. Daniel Levinson, *Licensed psychologist serving veterans, USA*

"This book is a cogent and comprehensive examination of the clinical mental health issues experienced by diverse active-duty service members and veterans. Practitioners and researchers working with these populations will gain considerable insight from the work of Dr. Johnson and the experts assembled to craft this culturally responsive clinical resource. The integration of empirically-based practices along with cultural factors is very timely. The dual focus on the military and veterans is quite instructive. I strongly recommend this book to anyone working with military or veteran clinical populations."

      Dr. R. Lee Brown, *Chief Executive Director of Risks & Crisis Solutions, San Diego State University-Homeland Security Department, USA*

First-Line Clinical Approaches with Active Duty Service Members and Veterans

This book offers a culturally responsive and empirically based approach to working with active-duty service members, veterans, and their families.

It examines the assessment and evidence-based treatment of sexual trauma, alcohol and substance abuse, depression, insomnia, intimacy issues, and OCD in service members and veterans and the major ethical and clinical challenges for licensed independent providers. The chapters are written by distinguished scholars and experienced healthcare providers who deliver health-focused interventions and integrate relevant cross-cultural factors for working with diverse patients.

Loaded with clinical examples and up-to-date research, this book is essential for all mental health professionals working or in training to serve military personnel or veterans in the United States.

Ronn Johnson, Ph.D., ABPP, is a tenured full professor and Senior Associate Dean for Diversity, Inclusion & Belonging at Creighton University School of Medicine, Nebraska, USA. He is also Director of Team-Based Care in the Department of Family Medicine at the Creighton Medical Center, Omaha, Nebraska, USA. Previously, he was the lead clinical psychologist at the mental health clinic at the Nebraska-Western VA Healthcare System (NWI) and has worked in several VAs and active-duty military stations. Dr. Johnson is board certified in Group and Clinical Psychology by the American Board of Professional Psychology.

First-Line Clinical Approaches with Active Duty Service Members and Veterans

EDITED BY RONN JOHNSON

NEW YORK AND LONDON

Designed cover image: SDI Productions @ Getty Images

First published 2024
by Routledge
605 Third Avenue, New York, NY 10158

and by Routledge
4 Park Square, Milton Park, Abingdon, Oxon, OX14 4RN

Routledge is an imprint of the Taylor & Francis Group, an informa business

© 2024 selection and editorial matter, Ronn Johnson; individual chapters, the contributors

The right of Ronn Johnson to be identified as the author of the editorial material, and of the authors for their individual chapters, has been asserted in accordance with sections 77 and 78 of the Copyright, Designs and Patents Act 1988.

All rights reserved. No part of this book may be reprinted or reproduced or utilised in any form or by any electronic, mechanical, or other means, now known or hereafter invented, including photocopying and recording, or in any information storage or retrieval system, without permission in writing from the publishers.

Trademark notice: Product or corporate names may be trademarks or registered trademarks, and are used only for identification and explanation without intent to infringe.

Library of Congress Cataloging-in-Publication Data
Names: Johnson, Ronn, editor.
Title: First-line clinical approaches with active duty service members and veterans / edited by Ronn Johnson.
New York, NY : Routledge, 2023. | Includes bibliographical references and index. | Identifiers: LCCN 2023024771 (print) |
LCCN 2023024772 (ebook) | ISBN 9781032029269 (paperback) |
ISBN 9781032029436 (hardback) | ISBN 9781003185949 (ebook)
Subjects: LCSH: Soldiers--Mental health services--United States. |
Veterans--Mental health services--United States. | Families of military personnel--Mental health services--United States. | Psychology, Military. | United States--Armed Forces--Medical care. |
Veterans--Mental health--United States. | Combat--Psychological aspects.
Classification: LCC UH629.3 .F57 2023 (print) | LCC UH629.3 (ebook) |
DDC 355.3/45--dc23/eng/20230831
LC record available at https://lccn.loc.gov/2023024771
LC ebook record available at https://lccn.loc.gov/2023024772

ISBN: 978-1-032-02943-6 (hbk)
ISBN: 978-1-032-02926-9 (pbk)
ISBN: 978-1-003-18594-9 (ebk)

DOI: 10.4324/9781003185949

Typeset in Dante
by SPi Technologies India Pvt Ltd (Straive)

This book was crafted to honor the diverse active-duty service members and veterans who made life-altering sacrifices for their country. The book is also dedicated to licensed mental health providers who tirelessly serve those who served this country.

Contents

Acknowledgements	xii
Preface	xiii
List of Contributors	xv

1 Clinical Perspectives on the Delivery of Psychological Health Services to Diverse Active-Duty Service Members, Veterans, and Their Families   1
  Ronn Johnson

2 Culturally Responsive Psychological Treatment for Military Sexual Trauma   13
  Kari A. Weiterschan and Vanessa Tirone

3 Culturally Responsive Approaches for LGBT+ Active-Duty Service Members and Veterans   25
  Natasha A. Schvey, LTJG Shannon L. Exley, and Arielle T. Pearlman

4 Assessment and Treatment of Intimacy Issues and Sexual Disorders in Active-Duty Service Members and Veterans   38
  Chandra E. Khalifian, Katerine T. Rashkovsky, and Kayla Knopp

5 Evidence-Based Practices for Psychotherapy with Active-
   Duty Service Members and Veterans   55
   Maria C. Crouch, Jennifer M. Loya, and Joan M. Cook

6 Alcohol and Substance Abuse Services for Active-Duty
   Service Members and Veterans   75
   *Jeremiah A. Schumm, Anthony R. Kelemen, and
   Lily K. Taplin*

7 Cannabis Use Disorder in Active-Duty Service Members
   and Veterans   90
   *Anthony H. Ecker, Julianna Hogan, Jennifer L. Bryan, and
   Katharine L. Thomas*

8 Treating Nightmares, Sleep, and Insomnia Disturbances in
   Active-Duty Service Members and Veterans   101
   Elaine Boland and Katharine E. Miller

9 Couples Therapy with Active-Duty Service Members
   and Veterans   113
   *Amber M. Jarnecke, Jessica H. Kansky, Karen Petty, and
   Jenna B. Teves*

10 Family Therapy with Active-Duty Service Members
   and Veterans   129
   *Angela L. Lamson, Florence J. Lewis, Natalie M. Richardson,
   and Krysttel C. Stryczek*

11 Treating Depression and Persistent Depressive Disorders
   in Active-Duty Service Members and Veterans   164
   *Alan L. Peterson, Chelsea J. Sterne, Anthony A. Cesare,
   and Brittany Hall-Clark*

12 Obsessive-Compulsive Disorder and Related Disorders in
   Active-Duty Service Members and Veterans   178
   Nathaniel Van Kirk, Rose Luehrs, and Elizabeth McIngvale

13 Psychotherapy Training of Predoctoral Psychology Interns,
    Postdocs, and Psychiatric Residents   194
    Kathryne S. Marinchak, Suzanne Spinola, and
    Howard R. Steinberg

Index   208

Acknowledgements

Special acknowledgement to my family and extended family for support during the crafting of this book. Birdie, I love you and Sapphire. There is an impressive collection of colleagues at Creighton Medical School that I especially want to express a heartfelt appreciation for their friendship and wise counsel offered during this book journey. In no order they are Doctors Renuga Vivekanandan, Joann Porter, Sade Kosoko-Lasaki, Amy McGaha, Maureen Tierney, Claudia Chambers, Cassie Eno, and Tom Svolos. I single out Dr. Robert "Bo" Dunlay for the confidence, sage advice, and encouragement extended to me as we tirelessly work as a team to make Creighton University Medical School an exemplar global academic medicine center. Finally, to my mentor Dr. Jim Poteet for the unwavering Christ-like love you have graciously given me over decades. Thank you seems inadequate to convey my appreciation for what you have done for me, Coach.

From the beginning of this book project an extremely dedicated group of editorial assistants worked tirelessly to make this critical publication happen. Not in order of contribution, Stephen Seyler's cogent spreadsheets and organizational structures functioned as the invaluable scaffolding for guiding the development of this book. Dianne Dalzell was a constant source of encouragement. Douglas Helling brought decades of legal work into this publication process that greatly facilitated contributor relationships. Christine Helling wisely functioned as a communication hub between editorial assistants, editor, and contributors. Thank all of you for your unwavering support during this arduous process.

Preface

Millions of U.S. service members have participated in various military campaigns and continue to serve globally in various active-duty stations. I always say that if you want to see the cost of freedom, sit in the lobby of any active-duty or VA healthcare center for an hour. There you will easily observe the painful life realities for active-duty service members, veterans, and their families. The deployments and post-military adjustments are primary sources of biopsychosocial stress that results in the need for mental health services. Fitness-for-duty issues for active-duty service members is an added human factor. Veterans experience bureaucratic VA barriers and long lines to be seen to secure disability ratings that financially compensate them for injuries sustained in connection with their military service. The strong clinical need to offer prompt and culturally responsive services in the wake of a large influx of patients is further thwarted by a gaping disconnect between VA administrators and a dedicated collection of healthcare providers. For example, at the height of COVID, one VA chief of staff clumsily directed doctoral-level health service providers to conduct COVID screens at the hospital entrance after they failed to anticipate the contract staffing needs for the screening tables. Nationally, the VA is hemorrhaging qualified healthcare providers, and recruitment efforts are insufficient to address the chronic staff shortages.

Active-duty service members and veterans report experiences with military sexual trauma (MST), xenophobia, sexual harassment, and blatant acts of racism. Suicidal behavior and substance abuse are pervasive challenges for active-duty military personnel and veterans. Veterans in rural settings and Native Americans must confront their unique health disparity challenges as they seek access to care. While the stated goal is to provide high-quality care through the Department of Veterans Affairs (VA) health system, this occurs in uneven clinical pockets during transitions in the care of diverse veterans.

As someone who clinically worked at five VA facilities and active-duty military settings, I have a culturally informed sense of understanding the mental health–related needs of ADSMs and veterans. The primary aim of this book is to offer the first of a comprehensive series that guides the process of delivering evidenced-based care that addresses the issues presented by active-duty service members, veterans, and their families. The book also integrates ethnoracial factors into each chapter because of its relevance in providing care to diverse ADSM and veteran patients. The chapters are written by distinguished scholars and experienced healthcare providers. They have effectively converted research into health-focused interventions for ADSM and veterans.

Contributors

Elaine Boland (PhD, DBSM) is a clinical psychologist at the Corporal Michael J. Crescenz VA Medical Center. She is also an assistant professor in the Department of Psychiatry at the University of Pennsylvania.

Jennifer L. Bryan (PhD) works in the Menninger Department of Psychiatry and Behavioral Sciences at Baylor College of Medicine. She also works in the Center for Innovations in Quality, Effectiveness and Safety at the VA South Central Mental Illness Research, Education, and Clinical Center.

Anthony A. Cesare (MA) is a graduate research assistant in the Department of Psychiatry and Behavioral Sciences at the University of Texas Health Science Center at San Antonio.

Joan M. Cook (PhD) is a Clinical Psychologist and Professor in the Department of Psychiatry at the Yale School of Medicine.

Maria C. Crouch (PhD) is a clinical-community psychologist and postdoctoral fellow in the Department of Psychiatry at the Yale School of Medicine.

Anthony H. Ecker (PhD) works in the Menninger Department of Psychiatry and Behavioral Sciences at the Baylor College of Medicine. He also works in the Center for Innovations in Quality, Effectiveness and Safety at the VA South Central Mental Illness Research, Education, and Clinical Center.

LTJG Shannon L. Exley (MS) is a doctoral candidate at the Uniformed Services University of the Health Sciences.

Brittany Hall-Clark (PhD, ABPP) is an associate professor in the Department of Psychiatry and Behavioral Sciences at the University of Texas Health Science Center at San Antonio.

Julianna Hogan (PhD) works in the Menninger Department of Psychiatry and Behavioral Sciences at the Baylor College of Medicine. She also works in the Center for Innovations in Quality, Effectiveness and Safety at the VA South Central Mental Illness Research, Education, and Clinical Center.

Amber M. Jarnecke (PhD) is an assistant professor at the Medical University of South Carolina.

Ronn Johnson (PhD, ABPP) is Professor and Senior Associate Dean for Diversity, Inclusion, and Belonging at the Creighton University School of Medicine. He is also Director of Team Based Care and Interprofessional Education at the Department of Family and Community Medicine at Creighton Medical Center.

Jessica H. Kansky (Phd) is a postdoctoral fellow in the Ralph H. Johnson Veterans Affairs Medical Center.

Anthony R. Kelemen (PsyM) is a doctoral student in the School of Professional Psychology at Wright State University.

Chandra E. Khalifian (PhD) is a research psychologist for the VA San Diego Healthcare System (VASDHS).

Kayla Knopp (PhD) is a research psychologist for the VA San Diego Healthcare System (VASDHS).

Angela L. Lamson (PhD, LFMT) is the Nancy W. Darden Distinguished Professor of Human Development and Family Science in the College of Health and Human Performance at East Carolina University.

Florence J. Lewis (PhD, LFMT) is the Founder of Upside Health Research Network.

Jennifer M. Loya (PhD) is a clinical psychologist and postdoctoral fellow in the Department of Psychiatry at the Yale School of Medicine.

Rose Luehrs (MA) is a clinical supervisor at Rogers Behavioral Health.

Kathryne S. Marinchak (PsyD) is a staff psychologist at the VA Connecticut Healthcare System. She is also an assistant professor at the University of Connecticut School of Medicine.

Elizabeth McIngvale (PhD) is the Director of the OCD Institute of Houston.

Katharine E. Miller (PhD, DBSM) is a staff psychologist in the Minneapolis VA Health Care System.

Arielle T. Pearlman (MS) is a doctoral candidate at the Uniformed Services University of the Health Sciences.

Alan L. Peterson (PhD, ABPP) is a professor in the Department of Psychiatry and Behavioral Sciences at the University of Texas Health Science Center at San Antonio. He is also a professor in the Department of Psychology at the University of Texas at San Antonio.

Karen Petty (PhD) is a staff psychologist at the Ralph H. Johnson Veterans Affairs Medical Center. She is also an assistant professor at the Medical University of South Carolina.

Katerine T. Rashkovsky (BS) is a research coordinator for the VA San Diego Healthcare System (VASDHS).

Natalie M. Richardson (PhD, LFMT) is a member of the Core Faculty in the School of Social and Behavioral Sciences at Capella University.

Jeremiah A. Schumm (PhD, ABPP) is a professor and the Director of Clinical Training in the School of Professional Psychology at Wright State University.

Natasha A. Schvey (PhD) is an associate professor at Uniformed Services University of the Health Sciences.

Suzanne Spinola (PhD) is a staff psychologist at the VA Connecticut Healthcare System. She is also a clinical instructor at the Yale University School of Medicine.

Howard R. Steinberg (PhD) is the Director of the Mental Health Firm at the Newington Campus in the VA Connecticut Healthcare System. He is also an associate professor of Clinical Psychiatry at the Yale University School of Medicine.

Chelsea J. Sterne (MS) is a doctoral candidate in the Department of Psychology at the University of Texas at San Antonio.

Krysttel C. Stryczek (MA) is a research health scientist at the VA Northeast Ohio Healthcare System.

Lily K. Taplin (PsyM) is a doctoral student in the School of Professional Psychology at Wright State University.

Jenna B. Teves (PhD) is a staff psychologist at the Ralph H. Johnson Veterans Affairs Medical Center. She is also an assistant professor at the Medical University of South Carolina.

Katharine L. Thomas (BA) works in the Trauma Research Consortium at Baylor, Scott, and White Health.

Vanessa Tirone (PhD) is a licensed clinical psychologist and owner of Good Neighbor Psychology PLLC.

Nathaniel Van Kirk (PhD) is an instructor in the Department of Psychiatry at Harvard Medical School. He is also the Director of Psychological Services in the OCD Institute at McLean Hospital.

Kari A. Weiterschan (PhD) is a licensed clinical psychologist and owner of Evolve Healing and Wellness Center in Palatine, Illinois.

Clinical Perspectives on the Delivery of Psychological Health Services to Diverse Active-Duty Service Members, Veterans, and Their Families

Ronn Johnson

According to the Department of Defense, there were 1.195 million active-duty military and more than 778,000 reserve forces. The number of U.S. veterans has increased over the years, and as of 2014, there are over 21.8 million veterans in the United States. Male veterans comprise 93% of the veteran population with 20.2 million. Female veterans comprise 7% of the total veteran population with 1.6 million (U.S. Census Bureau, 2014). The numbers of active and reserve duty military personnel and veterans in the United States comprise over 23 million individuals. Psychological issues of service members and veterans, including suicide, are higher than ever experienced in the United States, with epidemic levels of suicide, posttraumatic stress disorder (PTSD), traumatic brain injuries (TBIs), and other mental health–related injuries.

The publication of a clinically oriented book devoted to collectively advancing evidence-based mental health services to diverse active-duty service members, veterans, and their families comes at a valuable time. The contributors were encouraged to integrate cultural, gender, and ethnoracial factors whenever possible as they examined critical issues in working with diverse active-duty service members (ADSM), veterans, and their families. Complicating the care of active-duty members is a pervasive sense of anxiety related to concerns about the career ramifications of seeking mental health treatment, which can negatively affect their advancement. Even though the ADSM is concerned that mental health treatment recommendations from providers can harm one's career trajectory, the prevalence of psychological disorders in the military remains troublesome. An entrenched traditional male military culture punctuates this unwanted perception of mental health. In this case, seeking and receiving mental health services is historically viewed as an unwanted symptom of weakness within the military and degrades the confidence of other ADSMs (Zinzow et al., 2013).

Other obstacles to care relate to the military command structure and healthcare providers. In this case, concerns about confidentiality and trust are much harder to accomplish when military readiness is inextricably linked to an ADSM's readiness (fitness for duty). This fitness for duty includes physical and mental domains (Miggantz, 2013; Quartana et al., 2014; Zinzow et al., 2013). Under these practice-demand situations, ADSMs might feel less inclined to disclose what they erroneously perceive as a liability. Their distorted misperception is further compounded by a decision to rely more on personal resources that could include a form of denial of the symptoms with the irrational belief that they will magically subside over time (Dabovich et al., 2019a Miggantz, 2013). The prevalence data tell a different story in this area for ADSM.

It has been reported that for the U.S. Armed Forces, the numbers ranged from about 6.8% to 10.0% across service lines for those receiving some type of mental health diagnosis in the year 2019. Regarding services, that number represents 1.9 million outpatient encounters (Department of Defense [DoD], 2019). Drilling down further on these numbers reveals that 3.8% in that initial range were determined to meet the diagnostic criteria for PTSD. This number was followed by 7.3% with anxiety, 7.5% with depression, and 2.6% with alcohol and substance-related disorders (DOD, 2019). Even more disturbing was a finding that a sizable group of military personnel chose to not disclose mental health or drug-related symptomatology (Dabovich et al., 2019b). As a result, their access to care is thwarted because their clinical difficulties are not timely assessed for the possible benefits of evidence-based treatment options.

Still, what is known about ADSMs is alarming. The military conflicts in the wars in Iraq, Afghanistan, and other locations have produced worrisome health and mental health problems for ADSMs. ADSMs present with increased rates of dysphoria and PTSD. Service members also exhibit alcohol and other substance use disorders, behavioral difficulties, and other clinical consequences stemming from military sexual trauma (Andrews et al., 2007; APA, 2007; Calhoun et al., 2008; Ender, 2009; Finley, 2011; Hoge et al., 2004; Institute of Medicine, 2010; Tanielian & Jaycox, 2008; Wang et al., 2005; Watkins et al., 2011). The psychological sequelae of military service are reflected in high suicide rates. While the suicide rates indicate fewer service members died from suicide in 2021 than in 2020, the rates are nonetheless a concern. In 2021, there were 24.3 suicides per 100,000 service members.

The consequences of military service may be observed in declines in comorbid health, psychological functioning, and interpersonal relationships. ADSMs returning from Operation Enduring Freedom and Operation Iraqi Freedom reported trauma symptoms, sleep problems, and dissociation. They also experienced reduced levels of relationship satisfaction (Goff et al., 2007). To little surprise, clinical reports of PTSD symptoms coincided with a lower rating of marital satisfaction (Allen et al., 2010).

It should come as no surprise that the mental health issues found in ADSMs flow seamlessly into diverse veterans. The United States Census Bureau reported that as of June 2020, roughly 18 million Americans, or about 7 percent of the adult population, were veterans of the U.S. Armed Forces in 2018 (U.S. Census Bureau, 2020). The patterns of need for psychological services experienced by ADSMs are like some of those observed in diverse veterans. Veterans are at disproportionate risk for mental health issues due to service in combat zones (Institute of Medicine, 2010). In this case, PTSD, depression, and suicide are sometimes the residual clinical effects of military service. Veterans with a history of MST are at increased risk for severe mental health issues including PTSD, mood disorders, substance misuse disorders, and suicide (e.g., Kimerling et al., 2007, 2016; Sexton et al., 2017; Surís et al., 2004). Fiscally, MST is linked to increased healthcare costs (Brignone et al., 2017) and higher mental healthcare utilization rates within the VHA (Surís & Lind, 2008).

While the Veterans Health Administration (VHA) is the most extensive integrated healthcare system in the United States, which was founded to provide mental health care to U.S. military veterans (U.S. Department of Veterans Affairs, 2021), there are lingering service delivery barriers (e.g., chronic healthcare staff shortages in rural areas, non-competitive salary structures for psychologists, expanding loss of providers, and poor V.A. administrator disconnect from service providers). All these unwanted healthcare circumstances occur at a time when ADSMs and veterans confront a range of mental health issues that includes posttraumatic stress disorder, traumatic brain injury, depression, and substance use disorders (SUD). For ADSMs, post-deployment adjustments remain a critical area of concern. It is evident that organizational changes must address individual diversity challenges and system-level factors that function as barriers associated with ADSMs and veterans receiving evidence-based and culturally responsive mental health treatments.

All the above transitions in care matters buttress a need for mental health resources that shape the practice trajectory of healthcare providers. This book series was crafted to extend the knowledge base of evidence-based cultural competencies for working with active-duty service members, veterans, and their families. The chapter overviews the assessment and treatment-relevant considerations for working with these highly diverse military service populations.

Overview of the Book

Military Sexual Trauma

The 12 additional chapters of this book include Chapter 2 regarding culturally responsive psychological treatment for military sexual trauma. Military sexual trauma (MST) is a prevalent issue in the U.S. military, as it touches every demographic of service members and veterans. To no surprise, MST is associated with significant psychological consequences for survivors. Certain underrepresented groups within this broader population are at increased risk for adverse health outcomes. Mostly, they often experience unique barriers to treatment (e.g., self-stigma, institutional betrayal). This chapter relies on the existing literature to first provide an overview of common psychological sequala associated with MST. The discussion includes PTSD, depression, substance abuse, and suicide as comorbid clinical issues. The empirical evidence on effective treatments for MST–related mental health concerns among ADSM and veterans, specifically PTSD, is also examined. Through the lens of intersectional theory, the chapter highlights aspects of diversity, military culture, and sexual trauma that are important for providers to consider when working with MST survivors. Clinical case examples and recommendations for culturally responsive interventions at various levels of the therapeutic process are also outlined. The overarching goal of this chapter is to assist mental health providers in developing awareness and cultural competence that enhances their clinical capacity for introducing psychological interventions for diverse MST survivors.

LGBTQIA+

The MST chapter is followed by Chapter 3, which addresses culturally responsive care with lesbian, gay, and bisexual military personnel. It should come as no surprise that mental health providers are critical in supporting and optimizing the health and wellbeing of their LGBTQIA+ patients. This is especially pertinent given the well-documented and avoidable mental health disparities facing persons with LGBTQIA+ identities. These disparities stem from societal stigma, marginalization, and systemic inequities and are compounded by a lack of access to timely, affirming care. The U.S. military's historical exclusion of those with diverse sexual orientations and gender identities punctuates the need for timely, affirming, and culturally responsive care for LGBTQIA+ service members and veterans. Although as of January 2021, all LGBTQIA+ persons are eligible for military service, inequities in access to and quality of healthcare may persist. By ensuring skilled, affirming, and culturally responsive services, mental health providers can help to attenuate these inequities. This LGBTQIA+ chapter provides an overview of culturally responsive approaches for this population of active-duty service members and veterans. Considerations related to the therapeutic environment, assessment, and intervention are discussed, as well the importance of acknowledging and addressing the role of intersecting identities. The limitations of existing literature and recommendations for future research to inform best practices are reviewed. In the end, the message is that providing affirming, welcoming, and supportive mental healthcare is critical to mitigating avoidable mental health disparities and enhancing health among LGBTQIA+ service members and veterans.

Intimacy and Sexual Disorders

Chapter 4 addresses the assessment and treatment of intimacy issues and sexual disorders. This chapter covers the existing literature on assessing and treating intimacy issues and sexual dysfunction in the military and veteran population. The authors describe the prevalence and risk, and protective factors for sexual dysfunction among women, men, and LGBTQ+ military service members and veterans. They also describe current psychological and medical approaches to treating sexual disorders, including couple-based approaches. Current research suggests high rates of sexual dysfunction in military women and men, often because of interpersonal and combat trauma. However, there are few culturally adapted treatments for intimacy issues or sexual dysfunction for military populations. The most common interventions are pharmacological treatments for erectile dysfunction and sexually transmitted infections. Most treatments for sexual concerns in the military are in the context of interventions for other clinically diagnosed disorders, particularly PTSD. The chapter concludes by enumerating priorities for further research on intimacy issues and sexual dysfunction, focusing on how efforts can be made to address and treat these significant and deleterious problems in our military service members and veterans.

Evidence-Based Practices for Psychotherapy

The next contributed chapter is on evidence-based practices for psychotherapy with active-duty service members and veterans. Active-duty service members and veterans from diverse ethnoracial backgrounds compose a large and growing military population. Chapter 5 reviews evidence-based psychotherapies for PTSD, namely, prolonged exposure and cognitive processing therapy, for this population among Black, Indigenous, and People of Color (BIPOC). The limited research examining PTSD and its treatment more broadly in BIPOC populations is presented. The empirical literature demonstrates higher rates of PTSD, as well as disparities in the quantity, quality, and efficacy of PTSD treatment for BIPOC. Culturally grounded and individualized treatment planning is recommended. Further, culturally congruent treatment modifications may be needed to promote successful engagement and retention and optimize response.

Alcohol and Substance Abuse

The next two chapters address innovations in treating alcohol and cannabis use disorders, respectively. Alcohol misuse and alcohol use disorder (AUD) are more common among veterans and ADSM than civilians. Alcohol misuse and AUD are associated with worse mental health treatment prognosis, higher healthcare utilization, more significant functional impairment, and less productivity. Accordingly, mental health professionals serving these populations should know the best practices for veterans and ADSMs impacted by alcohol misuse and AUD. Chapter 6 provides an overview of the current best practices for addressing alcohol misuse and AUD among veterans and ADSM. The chapter discusses demographic, operational stress, and cultural factors contributing to and maintaining alcohol misuse and AUD among veterans and ADSM. The chapter concludes by describing the unique challenges and future directions for addressing alcohol misuse and AUD in these populations.

Cannabis Use Disorder

Chapter 7 on cannabis use disorder (CUD) examines the prevalence, etiology, and maintenance of CUD in ADSMs and veterans. These contributors provide a historical context for cannabis use and CUD within the military, ranging from prescriptive to recreational use. They then describe the current landscape of CUD within civilians and military samples, with CUD being the most common illicit substance use disorder in the U.S. CUD is a clinical marker for long-term adverse health outcomes that can negatively impact educational and occupational functioning. It is also associated with several co-occurring mental health disorders, including anxiety and trauma-related disorders. Veterans are especially at greater risk for other forms of impairment related to CUD, given that increases in CUD diagnoses have been observed in recent years that concomitantly occur with higher rates of cannabis use among veterans. The prevalence differences of CUD observed in the civilian population and veterans are discussed. Further, legal issues related to cannabis use that are unique to military populations are reviewed. This chapter also conveys the differences in cannabis use, subsequent risk factors, and treatment approaches for ADSMs and veterans, with particular attention devoted to individual characteristics, such as ethnocultural differences and service histories.

Sleep Disorders

Chapter 8 describes treating nightmares, sleep, and insomnia disturbances. Sleep disturbances such as insomnia, nightmares, and obstructive sleep apnea are increasingly prevalent in veterans and ADSMs and result in significant impairments in physical and mental health and wellbeing. This chapter provides a comprehensive overview of these specific sleep disorders, their relations to mental and physical health, and the range of empirically supported treatments for sleep disturbances that are available to veterans and ADSMs. Within this overview, the authors highlight the racial, cultural, and socioeconomic factors associated with sleep-related health disparities across disorders, placing particular emphasis, when possible, on studies conducted on veteran and ADSM samples. The chapter concludes with a discussion of areas for future research, including the work needed to bridge the gaps in sleep-related health disparities.

Couples Therapy

The following two chapters address innovations in treating couples and families, respectively. Active-duty service members and military veterans risk encountering several unique stressors (e.g., deployments, trauma, and reintegration) that can harm intimate relationships. The Department of Defense and Veterans Health Administration has directed family involvement in ADSM and veteran care as a national priority. As such, clinicians must be attuned to the distinct context, culture, and needs of ADSM and Veteran couples. Chapter 9 provides an overview of therapeutic considerations that must be made while working with ADSM and Veteran couples. This includes exploring evidence-based couples therapy protocols that can be used with these diverse couples. The chapter concludes with a discussion of directions for future clinical practice and research that may ultimately enhance culturally responsive transitions in care for ADSM and veteran couples.

Family Therapy

The family therapy chapter is devoted to the ethnoracial and ethnocultural identities of active-duty service members, veterans, and their families (SMVF). Mainly, there is a focus on the systemic treatments indicated for ethnoracial and ethnocultural SMVF couples and families. This chapter does not review every potential diagnosis or presenting concern to be addressed, nor is it possible to represent every evidence-based treatment for SMVF. However, the aim is to attend to the treatments that have promising results for couples and families from diverse social locations. This focus emphasizes the work of interventionists who went beyond including diverse samples in their research by ensuring that their samples were representative and that they intentionally tested their design with diverse races, ethnicities, sexual orientations, or other intricacies among or between SMVF. Furthermore, Chapter 10 includes research on the role of larger systems and coordinated care regarding diversity and inclusion for SMVF and incorporates trends toward innovative ethnoracial and ethnocultural clinical research.

Depression and Persistent Depressive Disorders

Chapter 11 addresses innovations in treating depression and persistent depressive disorders in active-duty service members and veterans. Depression accounts for significant morbidity, disability, health care utilization, and attrition from military service. Depression is the most common mental health disorder associated with military personnel inpatient psychiatric hospitalizations. To no surprise, depression is also the most common mental health diagnosis after returning from an operational deployment. Between 2000 and 2021, depressive disorders were the second or third most common outpatient mental health diagnosis in the active-duty military, with adjustment disorders being the most frequent. Among veteran populations, depression is a pervasive mental illness seen within V.A. primary care settings. The chapter includes a table summarizing the methods and results of clinical trials on treating depression in military and veteran populations, including pharmacotherapy, cognitive behavioral therapy, and combination treatments. The chapter also reviews the pertinent ethnocultural issues related to treating depression in military and veteran populations. The chapter concludes with a summary of the current research gaps and the need for additional clinical trials to further advance evidence-based treatments of depression in ADSMs and veterans.

Obsessive-Compulsive Disorder and Related Disorders

Van Kirk's contribution follows, which describes obsessive-compulsive disorder and related disorders in active-duty service members and veterans. There has been growing awareness of the impact of obsessive-compulsive disorder (OCD) on active-duty military and veteran service members. More recently, the field has begun to develop a greater understanding of the relationship between trauma, stressful life events, and OCD onset/clinical presentation, noting that OCD prevalence may be higher in individuals with combat experience than in the general population. Further, it has been suggested that trauma may be associated with the development of OCD, especially in those without familial histories of OCD symptomatology. This clinical finding highlights the importance of providers having a firmer understanding of OCD and the appropriate evidence-based treatments when working with military personnel. Unfortunately, early evidence suggests that as a mental health condition, OCD is highly misdiagnosed in civilian and veteran populations, leading to higher occurrences of inappropriate/inadequate treatment. Chapter 12 overviews OCD, the common elements underlying its heterogeneous clinical presentation, and empirical-based treatment recommendations. Special considerations for clinical assessment, differential diagnosis, and treatment when working with military populations are presented.

10 Ronn Johnson

Psychotherapy Training of Predoctoral Psychology Interns, Postdocs, and Psychiatric Residents

The last chapter in the first book of this series on ADSM and veterans explores the processes for psychotherapy training of predoctoral psychology interns, postdocs, and psychiatric residents. Chapter 13 describes factors for providers to consider when supervising psychology and psychiatry trainees working with ADSMs and veterans engaged in mental health care. The authors outline service-related issues that inform the backdrop of presenting problems, shape barriers, and function as facilitators of treatment engagement. The chapter stresses the need to develop competencies in delivering evidence-based psychotherapies through didactics, clinical supervision, and experiential learning, explicitly focusing on these training populations. Several areas of special significance will be reviewed, including but not limited to military culture and related individual experiences; enhanced risk issues and the need for appropriate assessment and planning; the potential impact of disability determinations on treatment; and clinical presentations of the patients often encountered in more significant proportions within this unique population, such as traumatic brain injuries, PTSD, substance use, suicide, and homelessness. Finally, the authors note how psychotherapy practice and supervision as conducted through a lens of cultural humility impact the points of training noted above.

Conclusion

This book on assessment and health-related interventions for military personnel, veterans, and their families promotes the practice of relying on science to inform the transition of care in these diverse clinical populations. The chapters add the clinical information base for those seeking to deliver evidence-based and culturally responsive care to active-duty service members, veterans, and their families.

References

Allen, E. S., Rhoades, G. K., Stanley, S. M., & Markman, H. J. (2010). Hitting home: Relationships between recent deployment, posttraumatic stress symptoms, and marital functioning for Army couples. *Journal of Family Psychology, 24*, 280–288. https://doi.org/10.1037/a0019405

American Psychological Association [APA]. (2007). *The Psychological Needs of U.S. Military Service Members and Their Families; A Preliminary Report.* Washington, DC: American Psychological Association. Available at http://www.ptsd.ne.gov/publications/military-deployment-task-forcereport.pdf; accessed March 16, 2023.

Andrews, B., Brewin, C. R., Philpott, R., & Stewart, L. (2007). Delayed-onset posttraumatic stress disorder, systematic review of the evidence. *American Journal of Psychiatry, 164*(9), 1319–1326.

Brignone, E., Gundlapalli, A. V., Blais, R. K., Kimerling, R., Barrett, T. S., Nelson, R. E., Carter, M. E., Samore, M. H., & Fargo, J. D. (2017). Increased health care utilization and costs among veterans with a positive screen for military sexual trauma. *Medical Care, 55*(Suppl. 2), S70–S77. https://doi.org/10.1097/MLR.0000000000000767

Calhoun, P. S., Elter, J. R., Jones, E. R., Kudler, H., & Straits-Troster, K. (2008). Hazardous alcohol use and receipt of risk-reduction counseling among U.S. veterans of the wars in Iraq and Afghanistan. *Journal of Clinical Psychiatry, 69*(11), 1686–1693.

Dabovich, P. A., Eliott, J. A., & McFarlane, A. C. (2019a). The meanings soldiers attach to health and their impacts on primary health-care utilization and avoidance in an Australian high-risk combat unit. *Armed Forces & Society, 47*(2). https://doi.org/10.1177/0095327X19852652

Dabovich, P. A., Eliott, J. A., & McFarlane, A. C. (2019b). Individuate and separate: Values and identity re-development during rehabilitation and transition in the Australian Army. *Social Science & Medicine, 222,* 265–273. https://doi.org/10.1016/j.socscimed.2019.01.012

Department of Defense [DoD]. (2019). Health of the force. Retrieved from https://health.mil/Reference-Center/Reports/2020/11/24/DoDHealth-of-the-Force-2019

Ender, M. G. (2009). *American soldiers in Iraq; McSoldiers or innovative professionals?* New York: Routledge.

Finley, E. P. (2011). *Fields of Combat: Understanding PTSD among Veterans of Iraq and Afghanistan.* Ithaca: Cornell.

Goff, B. S. N., Crow, J. R., Reisbig, A. M. J., & Hamilton, S. (2007). The impact of individual trauma symptoms of deployed soldiers on relationship satisfaction. *Journal of Family Psychology, 21,* 344–353. https://doi.org/10.1037/0893-3200

Hoge, C. W., Castro, C. A., Messer, S. C., McGurk, D., Cotting, D. I., & Koffman, R. L. (2004). Combat duty in Iraq and Afghanistan, mental health problems, and barriers to care. *New England Journal Medicine, 351*(1), 13–22.

Institute of Medicine. (2010). *Returning home from Iraq and Afghanistan; Preliminary assessment of readjustment needs of Veterans, service members and their families.* Washington, DC: National Academies Press. Available at http://www.nap.edu; accessed March 16, 2012.

Kimerling, R., Gima, K., Smith, M. W., Street, A., & Frayne, S. (2007). The veterans health administration and military sexual trauma. *American Journal of Public Health, 97*(12), 2160–2166. https://doi.org/10.2105/AJPH.2006.092999

Kimerling, R., Makin-Byrd, K., Louzon, S., Ignacio, R. V., & McCarthy, J. F. (2016). Military sexual trauma and suicide mortality. *American Journal of Preventive Medicine, 50*(6), 684–691. https://doi.org/10.1016/j.amepre.2015.10.019

Miggantz, E. L. (2013). *Stigma of mental health care in the military.* San Diego: Naval Center for Combat and Operational Stress Control. Retrieved from https://ia801300.us.archive.org/7/items/StigmaWhitePaper/Stigma%20White%20Paper.pdf

Orvis, K. (2019). Department of Defense (DoD) quarterly suicide report (QSR) 4th quarter, CY 2018. Department of Defense. Available at https://www.dspo.mil/Portals/113/Documents/QSR_CY2018_Q4.pdf

Quartana, P. J., Wilk, J. E., Thomas, J. L., Bray, R. M., Olmsted, K. L. R., Brown, J. M., Williams, J., Kim, P. Y., Clarke-Walper, K., & Hoge, C. W. (2014). Trends in mental health services utilization and stigma in US soldiers from 2002–2011. *American Journal of Public Health, 104*(9), 1671–1680. https://doi.org/10.2105/AJPH.2014.301971

Sexton, M. B., Raggio, G. A., McSweeney, L. B., Authier, C. C., & Rauch, S. A. M. (2017). Contrasting gender and combat versus military sexual traumas: Psychiatric symptom severity and morbidities in treatmentseeking veterans. *Journal of Women's Health, 26*(9), 933–940. https://doi.org/10.1089/jwh.2016.6080

Surís, A., & Lind, L. (2008). Military sexual trauma: A review of prevalence and associated health consequences in veterans. *Trauma, Violence & Abuse, 9*(4), 250–269. https://doi.org/10.1177/1524838008324419

Surís, A., Lind, L., Kashner, T. M., Borman, P. D., & Petty, F. (2004). Sexual assault in women veterans: An examination of PTSD risk, health care utilization, and cost of care. *Psychosomatic Medicine, 66*(5), 749–756. https://doi.org/10.1097/01.psy.0000138117.58559.7b

Tanielian, T., & Jaycox, L. H. (2008). *Invisible wounds of war; psychological and cognitive injuries, their consequences, and services to assist recovery.* Santa Monica: RAND. Available at www.rand.org/pubs/monographs; accessed March 16, 2023.

U.S. Census Bureau, American Community Survey, Public Use Microdata Sample (PUMS). (2014)

Wang, P. S., Berglund, P. A., Olfson, M., Pincus, H. A., Wells, K. B., Kessler, R. C. (2005). Failure and delay in initial treatment contact after first onset of mental disorders in the National Comorbidity Survey Replication. *Archives of General Psychiatry, 62*, 603–613.

Watkins, K. E., Pincus, H. A., Paddock, S., et al. (2011). Care for veterans with mental and substance use disorders; good performance, but room to improve on many measures. *Health Affairs, 30*(11), 2194–2203.

Zinzow, H. M., Britt, T. W., Pury, C. L. S., Raymond, M. A., McFadden, A. C., & Burnette, C. M. (2013). Barriers and facilitators of mental health treatment seeking among active-duty Army personnel. *Military Psychology, 25*(5), 514–535. https://doi.org/10.1037/mil0000015

Culturally Responsive Psychological Treatment for Military Sexual Trauma

Kari A. Weiterschan and Vanessa Tirone

Introduction

In this chapter, we conceptualize culturally responsive care for military sexual trauma (MST) survivors through the lens of intersectional theory (Cole, 2009), which emphasizes the unique experiences and challenges of individuals identifying with more than one historically marginalized group (HMG). We begin by discussing the prevalence of MST and associated mental health consequences for service members and veterans (SM/Vs), highlighting differences among individuals from HMGs. We then review evidence-based treatments for posttraumatic stress disorder (PTSD), the most commonly diagnosed mental health condition among MST survivors. We conclude by providing case examples and recommendations for culturally responsive interventions.

Prevalence and Consequences of MST

Military sexual trauma encompasses a spectrum of sexual violations that occurred during an individual's military service, including being subject to sexual assault by physical force; non-consensual touching or groping; pressure, coercion, or threats to perform sexual acts; and sexual harassment (U.S. Department of Veterans Affairs [DVA], 2021a). Approximately 4% of male and 38% of female veterans report experiencing MST during their military service (Wilson, 2016). Service members from HMGs, including women; Black, Indigenous, and People of Color (BIPOC); and Lesbian, Gay, Bisexual, Transgender, and Queer (LGBTQ+) identifying individuals, appear to be at greater risk for experiencing MST (Haskell et al., 2010; Suris & Lind, 2008; Turchik & Wilson, 2010). The Marine Corps and Navy have the highest MST incidence rates, and enlisted personnel across all branches of service are more likely than officers to experience MST (Morral et al., 2015).

The psychological consequences of MST for SM/Vs include increased risk for posttraumatic stress disorder (PTSD), depression (Gilmore et al., 2016; Newins et al., 2020), substance abuse (Forkus et al., 2020; Goldberg et al., 2019), suicide (Kimerling et al., 2016), and self-directed violence (Gross et al., 2020b). Mental health disparities among MST survivors exist and have been associated with discrete identity-based factors, including gender. For example, female veterans are three times more likely than male veterans to be diagnosed with PTSD secondary to experiencing MST (Maguen et al., 2011), and may also be at greater risk for depression (Averill et al., 2017), particularly perinatal depression (Gross et al., 2020a). Military sexual assault has also been associated with increased risk for suicide attempts and self-directed violence among female veterans (Wilson et al., 2021).

Aspects of female veterans' MST experiences may contribute to these mental health risks. For example, encountering negative reactions, feared retaliation, or stigma in response to MST disclosures; being sexually assaulted in the presence of bystanders who did not intervene; or being made to feel sexual harassment was "normal" and "expected" have been associated with additional distress and feelings of institutional betrayal among female MST survivors (Brownstone et al., 2018; Daniel et al., 2017; Dardis et al., 2018; Holland et al., 2016). Institutional betrayal (i.e., the perception that an important institution has betrayed its members' trust; Smith & Freyd, 2013) has been associated with more severe depression and PTSD symptoms (Andresen et al., 2018). Other unique experiences of female MST survivors that may influence mental health outcomes include pregnancy that results from sexual assault and reproductive coercion (e.g., pressure to obtain an abortion because the pregnancy provides evidence of the assault or impacts readiness for duty).

Like their female counterparts, male veterans have reported confronting negative reactions to MST disclosures, which have contributed to secrecy, self-stigma, and social isolation that has implications for their mental health (Monteith et al., 2019). For example, male SM/Vs have been found to be at increased risk for experiencing suicidal ideation (Tannahill et al., 2020) and developing bipolar, psychotic, and substance-related disorders (Kimerling et al., 2007; Maguen et al., 2011) secondary to experiencing MST. Male MST survivors have also reported distress related to questioning their masculinity and sexual orientation (Monteith et al., 2019).

Increased MST–related mental health risks may also exist for individuals with historically marginalized gender and sexual orientations. For example, veterans identifying as LGBTQ+ have reported feeling stigmatized by the misuse of preferred pronouns and homophobic remarks during their military service, and consequently concealing their gender/sexual orientation as a means of self-protection, which contributed to internalized homophobia, increased substance use, and social withdrawal (Livingston et al., 2019). LGBTQ+ veterans with a history of MST have also reported greater stigma and barriers to treatment, poorer mental health outcomes, and more incidences of secondary trauma than their heterosexual counterparts (Mark et al., 2019).

SM/Vs who identify as BIPOC may also experience unique MST–related mental health concerns and barriers to treatment. For example, female SM/Vs from historically marginalized racial and ethnic groups have reported more severe depression, anxiety, and PTSD symptoms relative to non-Latinx Whites (Lehavot et al., 2019). Women of color may also experience a sense of cultural betrayal (i.e., the idea that reporting sexual violence perpetuated by men of color leaves these men vulnerable to unfair treatment by the criminal justice system and undermines the wellbeing of marginalized communities; (Gomez & Gobin, 2020) secondary to MST, which may uniquely impact their mental health. Incidences of race-related discrimination, harassment, and overtly threatening behavior within the military have also been well documented and may further contribute to the psychological sequelae of MST for BIPOC (U.S. DVA, 2020).

Taken together, it seems critical that mental health providers understand the unique MST experiences, mental health implications, and treatment needs of SM/Vs from HMGs to provide culturally responsive interventions.

Mental Health Interventions for MST Survivors

Posttraumatic stress disorder is the most prevalent mental health condition among MST survivors. In general, trauma-focused psychotherapies (e.g., cognitive processing therapy [CPT], prolonged exposure therapy [PE], eye movement desensitization and reprocessing therapy [EMDR], trauma-focused cognitive behavioral therapy [TF-CBT], brief eclectic psychotherapy [BEP], narrative exposure therapy [NET]) have been associated with greater reductions in PTSD symptoms than non-trauma focused interventions (e.g., Cusack et al., 2016; Watts et al., 2013). These therapies have also been found to reduce commonly comorbid conditions such as depression, anxiety, and sleep-wake disorders (Coventry et al., 2020). Because these treatments have the capacity to address a broad range of symptoms among MST survivors diagnosed with PTSD, they are recommended as frontline interventions (U.S. DVA, 2017).

Current VA/DOD clinical practice guidelines (U.S. DVA, 2017) recommend CPT (Resick et al., 2016), PE (Foa et al., 2007), and EMDR (Shapiro, 2018) as gold standard treatments for PTSD. CPT and PE have both been found to be effective treatments for SM/Vs with MST-related PTSD (e.g., Boehler, 2019; Suris et al., 2013), though female veterans may experience more substantial symptom reductions from CPT than male veterans (Khan et al., 2020). CPT and PE can both be effectively delivered via telehealth (Acierno et al., 2021; Maieritsch et al. 2016), which is significant given the demand for these services during the COVID-19 pandemic and the number of SM/Vs living in rural communities without accessible in-person mental healthcare (U.S. DVA, 2021b).

One advance in the delivery of trauma-focused therapies has been the implementation of massed CPT and PE, wherein patients engage in treatment 1–2 times per day over a period of 1–3 weeks (Held et al., 2019; Rauch et al., 2020; Zalta et al., 2018). Research has found moderate to large effect sizes for such massed treatments (Held et al., 2019) and symptom reductions that were maintained 6–12 months posttreatment (Held et al., 2020). Dropout rates were also significantly lower than standard formats (Beidel et al., 2017; Holder et al., 2019). Initial research on massed-CPT found significant reductions in PTSD symptoms for MST survivors, which were further improved by minor protocol modifications (i.e., offering staff sensitivity training and coping skills interventions for patients; Lofgreen et al., 2020). Thus, although trauma-focused therapies are broadly recommended for the treatment of PTSD, recent evidence has suggested there may be additional benefits of massed trauma-focused treatments with MST populations.

Unfortunately, limited research has examined differences in CPT and PE outcomes for SM/Vs from HMGs, which is a significant barrier to understanding the best practices for treating these populations and a critical area for future scholarship. However, research with civilian samples has suggested CPT is equally effective across racial and ethnic groups, though

Black-identifying individuals may be less likely to complete treatment compared with non-Latinx Whites (Lester et al., 2010). Additionally, although EMDR may be efficacious for SM/Vs with PTSD (e.g., Brickell et al., 2015; Silver et al., 2008), few studies have examined its effectiveness for MST survivors specifically and SM/Vs from HMGs.

Cultural Considerations for Working with MST Survivors

The effectiveness of trauma-focused interventions may be meaningfully enhanced when providers adopt intersectional awareness and cultural responsiveness to clients' presenting concerns. Intersectionality theory views individual strengths and vulnerabilities associated with sociocultural factors such as veteran status, military rank, gender, sexual orientation, race, ethnicity, education, partner status, income, geography, and trauma history as mutually interdependent and interactive (Crenshaw, 1989). Despite the dynamic conceptualization of identity this theory offers, mental health research often examines single identity-related variables in isolation, which makes it challenging to draw implications for best practices when working with HMGs. In the following sections, we offer several case examples of MST experiences and therapeutic interventions that address various aspects of SM/Vs identities in an attempt to bridge this knowledge gap. These examples are by no means exhaustive but are intended to illustrate intersectional case conceptualization.

Case Example 1

David identifies as a Black, gay, cisgender male and is presenting for trauma-focused treatment secondary to experiencing MST. He recalls frequent racist and homophobic remarks from his White heterosexual counterparts while serving on a combat deployment, which made him fearful they may not protect him "outside the wire." Having also encountered skepticism and accusations of complicity in response to his MST disclosure, he internalized racial and homophobic beliefs that had previously been reinforced within the civilian Black community.

Based on our clinical experience, it is not uncommon for veterans like David to experience a great deal of shame and self-blame, not only around their MST experience, but also times when they voiced their concerns about racism or homophobia and felt they were subsequently ignored or made a "target" for victimization and so they "backed down." In this case, culturally responsive interventions would include exploring experiences of racism and homophobia, which may not meet criterion A for a DSM-5 diagnosis of PTSD, but nonetheless influence the client's experiences of MST and mental health symptomology. Acknowledging, normalizing, and further examining intersections of discrimination and stigmatization within the context of providing evidence-based therapies may assist with establishing rapport and contribute to the client's growth and healing.

Case Example 2

Cherise is an MST survivor who identifies as a Latinx, heterosexual, cisgender female. She is presenting for an intake and discloses sexual abuse by an older boy in childhood, who was a friend of her family and disregarded as a perpetrator even after she confided in caregiver about his behavior. She also reported being sexually assaulted by a male officer at age 18. Cherise went on to become a high-ranking officer in the Marine Corps before retiring this past year but noted her current partner is often physically violent.

In this case, Cherise serves as an example of how many women normalize inequitable relationships and sexual violence, having been told, or internalized indiscrete messages, that it is their fault. In the military, Cherise may have had to work extra hard to prove to her male counterparts that she deserved to be a Marine. She may have viewed reporting her MST as admitting that she wasn't "tough enough." She may also worry that acknowledging the intimate partner violence within her current relationship would cause others to view her as a "victim," instead of an accomplished career Marine.

In this case, culturally responsive care would involve using behaviorally specific terms as opposed to vague, value-laden terms such as "abuse," and providing psychoeducation regarding common reactions to sexual trauma to dispel maladaptive beliefs she may have about her MST resulting from personal weakness. Exploring the responsibility that perpetrators, bystanders, and military systems play in creating vulnerability to sexual assault for certain HMGs may also help address unhelpful beliefs that if she had been stronger, or fought back harder, she could have stopped her perpetrators from committing acts of violence against her.

Taking into consideration the provided examples, we encourage clinicians to adopt an intersectional lens when delivering trauma-focused therapies to MST survivors. Foremost, it is important that clinicians recognize military affiliation as a unique aspect of identity for SM/Vs, who often espouse cultural values, norms, and customs that differ from civilians. With nearly 71% of the civilian population reporting a lack of familiarity with military culture (Pew Research Center, 2011), it should be a priority for clinicians delivering treatments to MST survivors to develop cultural competence in military culture and veterans' issues. Several online courses offered through the Center for Deployment Psychology are broadly accessible (https://deploymentpsych.org/training/training-catalog/military-cultural-competence).

From here, clinicians can begin to consider the ways in which MST experiences and other identity-based factors play a role in SM/Vs mental health and adapt screening and treatment protocols accordingly.

Regarding initial assessments, research suggests that female and sexual minority veterans may be more likely to endorse MST on a screening interview as opposed to a questionnaire, while this trend may be reversed for male veterans (Bovin et al., 2019). Female SM/Vs who previously experienced negative reactions to MST disclosures (Daniel et al., 2017) or who have internalized stigma around mental illness resulting from MST (Andresen & Blias, 2019) may also be reluctant to share information with providers that could meaningfully inform the care they receive. Providers should be mindful of the screening procedures they adopt with SM/Vs from HMGs and demonstrate sensitivity to experiences of institutional betrayal and stigmatization that may result in feelings of shame, mistrust, anger, resentment, and injustice. Validating these experiences during initial screenings and subsequent treatment interactions may engender a corrective experience and positive outcomes for MST survivors. In the context of treatment, providers should acknowledge and create space for exploring aspects of gender, racial, and sexual identity development, experiences of discrimination, and intersecting traumas to promote deeper healing for marginalized MST survivors.

Conclusion

There has been a breadth of research on the prevalence and psychological sequelae of MST among SM/Vs. Substantial support for evidence-based treatments of common mental health diagnoses among MST survivors also exists. However, less research has focused on the effectiveness of empirically supported treatments for MST survivors, specifically, beyond the scope of PTSD, and has not fully examined within-group variations based on identity-related factors exclusively. As such, we reviewed some of the existing scholarship, highlighted opportunities for future research, and offered examples and recommendations for the implementation of trauma-focused treatments from an intersectional framework to promote culturally responsive care for

MST survivors. Although there is still much to be learned, understood, and practiced, we hope this chapter contributes to advancing our knowledge of how the current best practices can be adapted to meet the needs of SM/Vs with marginalized identities who have experienced MST.

References

Acierno, R., Jaffe, A. E., Gilmore, A. K., Birks, A., Denier, C., Muzzy, W., Lopez, C. M., Tuerk, P., & Grubaugh, A. L. (2021). A randomized clinical trial of in-person vs. home-based telemedicine delivery of prolonged exposure for PTSD in military sexual trauma survivors. *Journal of Anxiety Disorders, 83.* https://doi.org/10.1016/j.janxdis.2021.102461

American Psychological Association [APA]. (2019). *Clinical practice guidelines for the treatment of depression across three age cohorts.* https://www.apa.org/depression-guideline/guideline.pdf

Andresen, F. J., & Blias, R. K. (2019). Higher self-stigma is related to lower likelihood of disclosing military sexual trauma during screening in female veterans. *Psychological Trauma, 11*(4), 372–378. https://doi.org/10.1037/tra0000406

Andresen, F. J., Monteith, L. L., Kugler, J., Cruz, R. A., & Blais, R. K. (2018). Institutional betrayal following military sexual trauma is associated with more severe depression and specific posttraumatic stress symptom clusters. *Journal of Clinical Psychology, 75*(7), 1305–1319. https://doi.org/10.1002/jclp.22773

Averill, L. A., Smith, N. B., Holens, P. L., Sippel, L. M., Bellmore, A. R., Mota, N. P., Sareen, J., Southwick, S. M., & Pietrzak, R. H. (2017). Sex differences in correlates of risk and resilience associated with military sexual trauma. *Journal of Aggression, Maltreatment, & Trauma, 28*(10), 1199–1215. https://doi.org/10.1080/10926771.2018.1522408

Beidel, D. C., Frueh, B. C., Neer, S. M., & Lejuez, C. W. (2017). The efficacy of trauma management therapy: A controlled pilot investigation of a three-week intensive outpatient program for combat-related PTSD. *Journal of Anxiety Disorders, 50,* 23–32. https://doi.org/10.1016/j.janxdis.2017.05.001

Boehler, J. (2019). The efficacy of cognitive processing therapy for PTSD related to military sexual trauma in veterans: A review. *Journal of Evidence Based Social Work, 16*(6), 595–614. https://doi.org/10.1080/26408066.2019.1666767

Bovin, M. J., Black, S. K., Kleiman, S. E., Brown, M. E., Street, A. E., Rosen, R. C., Keane, T. M., & Marx, B. P. (2019). The impact of assessment modality and demographic characteristics on endorsement of military sexual trauma. *Womens Health Issues, 29,* 67–73. https://doi.org/10.1016/j.whi.2019.03.005

Brickell, M., Russell, M. C., & Smith, R. B. (2015). The effectiveness of evidence-based treatments in treatment of active military personnel and their families. *Journal of EMDR Practice and Research, 9*(4), 198–208. https://doi.org/10.1891/1933-3196.9.4.198

Brownstone, L. M., Holliman, B. D., Gerber, H. R., & Monteith, L. L. (2018). The phenomenology of military sexual trauma among women veterans. *Psychology of Women Quarterly, 42*(4), 399–413. https://doi.org/10.1177/0361684318791154

Cole, E. (2009). Intersectionality and research in psychology. *American Psychologist, 63*(3), 170–180. https://doi.org/10.1037/a0014564

Coventry, P. A., Meader, N., Melton, H., Temple, M., Dale, H., Wright, K., Cloitre, M., Karatzias, T., Bisson, J., Roberts, N. P., Brown, J. V. E., Barbui, C., Churchill, R., Lovell, K., McMillan, D., & Gilbody, S. (2020). Psychological and pharmacological interventions for posttraumatic stress disorder and comorbid mental health problems following complex traumatic events: Systematic review and component network meta-analysis. *PLOS Medicine, 17*(8), 1–34. https://doi.org/10.1371/journal.pmed.1003262

Cusack, K., Jonas, D. E., Forneris, C. A., Wines, C., Sonis, J., Middleton, J. C., Feltner, C., Brownley, K. A., Olmsted, K. R., Greenblatt, A., Weil, A., & Gaynes, B. N. (2016). Psychological treatments for adults with posttraumatic stress disorder: A systematic review and meta-analysis. *Clinical Psychology Review, 43*, 128–141. https://doi.org/10.1016/j.cpr.2015.10.003

Daniel, S., Neria, A. N., Moore, A., & Davis, E. (2017). The impact of leadership responses to sexual harassment and gender discrimination reports on emotional distress and retention intentions in military members. *Journal of Trauma and Dissociation, 3*, 357–372. https://doi.org/10.1080/15299732.2019.1571887

Dardis, C. M., Reinhardt, K. M., Foynes, M. M., Medoff, N. E., & Street, A. E. (2018). "Who are you doing to tell? Who's going to believe you?": Women's experiences disclosing military sexual trauma. *Psychology of Women Quarterly, 42*(4), 414–429. https://doi.org/10.1177/0361684318796783

Foa, E. B., Hembree, E., & Rothbaum, B. (2007). *Prolonged exposure for PTSD: Emotional processing of traumatic experiences, therapist guide* (1st ed.). Oxford University Press. https://doi.org/10.1093/med:psych/9780195308501.001.0001

Forkus, S. R., Weiss, N. H., Goncharenko, S., Mammay, J., Church, M., & Contractor, A. A. (2020). Military sexual trauma and risky behaviors: A systematic review. *Trauma Violence Abuse*. https://doi.org/10.1177/1524838019897338

Gallegos, A. M., Cross, W., & Pigeon, W. R. (2015). Mindfulness-based stress reduction for veterans exposed to military sexual trauma: Rationale and implementation considerations. *Military Medicine, 180*(6), 684–689. https://doi.org/10.7205/MILMED-D-14-00448

Gilmore, A. K., Brignone, E., Painter, J. M., Lehavot, K., Fargo, J., Suo, Y., Simpson, T., Carter, M. E., Blais, R. K., & Gundlapalli, A. V. (2016). Military sexual trauma and co-occuring posttraumatic stress disorder, depressive disorders, and substance use disorders among returning Afghanistan and Iraq veterans. *Womens Health Issues, 26*(5), 546–554. https://doi.org/10.1016/j.whi.2016.07.001

Goldberg, S. B., Livingston, W. S., Blais, R. K., Brignone, E., Suo, Y., Lehavot, K., Simpson, T. L., Fargo, J., & Gundlapalli, A. V. (2019). A positive screen for military sexual trauma is associated with greater risk for substance use disorders in women veterans. *Psychology of Addictive Behaviors, 33*(5), 477–483. https://doi.org/10.1037/adb0000486

Gomez, J. M., & Gobin, R. L. (2020). Black women and girls & #metoo: Rape, cultural betrayal, & healing. *Sex Roles, 82*, 1–12. https://doi.org/10.1007/s11199-019-01040-0

Gross, G. M., Kroll-Desrosiers, A., & Mattocks, K. (2020a). A longitudinal investigation of military sexual trauma and perinatal depression. *Journal of Womens Health, 29*(1), 38–45. https://doi.org/10.1089/jwh.2018.7628

Gross, G. M., Ronzitti, S., Combellick, J. L., Haskell, S. G., Brandt, C. A., & Goulet, J. L. (2020b). Sex differences in military sexual trauma and severe self-directed violence. *American Journal of Preventative Medicine, 58*(5), 675–682. https://doi.org/10.1016/j.amepre.2019.12.006

Haskell, S. G., Gordon, K. S., Mattocks, K., Duggal, M., Erdos, J., Justice, A., & Brandt, C. A. (2010). Gender differences in rates of depression, PTSD, pain, obesity, and military sexual trauma among Connecticut war veterans of Iraq and Afghanistan. *Journal of Women's Health, 19*, 267–271. https://doi.org/10.1089/jwh.2008.1262

Held, P., Bagley, J. M., Klassen, B. J., & Pollack, M. H. (2019a). Intensively delivered cognitive- behavioral therapies: An overview of promising treatment delivery format for PTSD and other mental health disorders. *Psychiatric Annals, 49*(8), 339–342. https://doi.org/10.3928/00485713-20190711-01

Held, P., Klassen, B. J., Boley, R. A., Stirman, W., Smith, D. L., Brennan, M. B., Van Horn, R., Pollack, M., Karnik, N., & Zalta, A. K. (2019b). Feasibility of a 3-week intensive treatment program for service members and veterans with PTSD. *Psychological Trauma, 12*(4), 422–430. https://doi.org/10.1037/tra0000485

Held, P., Zalta, A. K., Smith, D. L., Bagley, J. M., Steigerwald, V. L., Boley, R. A., Miller, M., Brennan, M. B., Van Horn, R., & Pollack, M. H. (2020). Maintenance of treatment gains up to 12-months following a three-week cognitive processing therapy-based intensive PTSD treatment programme for veterans. *European Journal of Psychotraumatology, 11*(1), 1–10. https://doi.org/10.1080/20008198.2020.1789324

Holder, N., Holliday, R., Wilblin, J., LePage, J. P., & Suris, A. (2019). Predictors of dropout from a randomized clinical trial of cognitive processing therapy for female veterans with military sexual trauma-related PTSD. *Psychiatry Research, 274*, 87–93. https://doi.org/10.1016/j.psychres.2019.04.022

Holland, K. J., Rabelo, V. C., & Cortina, L. M. (2016). Collateral damage: Military sexual trauma and help-seeking barriers. *Psychology of Violence, 6*(2), 253–261. https://doi.org/10.1037/a0039467

Khan, A. J., Holder, N., Shiner, Y. L., Madden, E., Seal, K., Neylan, T. C., & Maguen, S. (2020). How do gender and military sexual trauma impact PTSD symptoms in cognitive processing therapy and prolonged exposure? *Journal of Psychiatric Research, 130*, 89–96. https://doi.org/10.1016/j.jpsychires.2020.06.025

Kimerling, R., Gima, K., Smith, M. W., Street, A., & Frayne, S. (2007). The Veterans Health Administration and military sexual trauma. *American Journal of Public Health, 97*(12), 2160–2166. https://doi.org/10.2105/AJPH.2006.092999

Kimerling, R., Makin-Byrd, K., Louzon, S., Ignacio, R., & McCarthy, J. (2016). Military sexual trauma and suicide mortality. *American Journal of Preventative Medicine, 50*(5), 684–691.

Lehavot, K., Beckman, K. L., Chen, J. A., Simpson, T. L., & Williams, E. C. (2019). Race/ethnicity and sexual orientation disparities in mental health, sexism, and social support among women veterans. *Psychology of Sexual Orientation and Gender Diversity, 6*(3), 347–358. https://doi.org/10.1037/sgd0000333

Lester, K., Resick, P. A., Young-Xu, Y., & Artz, C. (2010). Impact of race on early treatment termination and outcomes in posttraumatic stress disorder treatment. *Journal of Consulting and Clinical Psychology, 78*(4), 480–489. https://doi.org/10.1037/a0019551

Livingston, N. A., Berke, D. S., Ruben, M. A., Matza, A. R., & Shipherd, J. C. (2019). Experiences of trauma, discrimination, microaggressions, and minority stress among trauma-exposed LGBT veterans: Unexpected findings and unresolved service gaps. *Psychological Trauma: Theory, Research, Practice, and Policy, 11*(7), 695–703. https://doi.org/10.1037/tra0000464

Lofgreen, A. M., Tirone, V., Carroll, K. K., Rufa, A. K., Smith, D. L., Bagley, J., Zalta, A. K., Brennan, M. B., Van Horn, R., Pollack, M. H., & Held, P. (2020). Improving outcoms for a 3-week intensive treatment program for posttraumatic stress disorder in survivors of military sexual trauma. *Journal of Affective Disorders, 15*, 134–140. https://doi.org/10.1016/j.jad.2020.03.036

Maguen, S., Cohen, B., Ren, L., Bosch, J., Kimerling, R., & Seal, K. (2011). Gender differences in military sexual trauma and mental health diagnoses among Iraq and Afghanistan veterans with posttraumatic stress disorder. *Womens Health Issues, 22*(1), 61–66. https://doi.org/10.1016/j.whi.2011.07.010

Maieritsch, K. P., Smith, T. L., Hessinger, J. D., Ahearn, E. P., Eickhoff, J. C., & Zhao, Q. (2016). Randomized controlled equivalence trial comparing videoconferencing and in person delivery of cognitive processing therapy for PTSD. *Journal of Telemedicine and Telecare, 22*(4), 238–243. https://doi.org/10.1177/1357633X15596109

Mark, K. M., McNamara, K. A., Gribble, R., Rhead, R., Sharp, M-L, & Stevelink, S. A. (2019). The health and well-being of LGBTQ serving and ex-serving personnel: A narrative review. *International Review of Psychiatry, 1*, 75–94. https://doi.org/10.1080/09540261.2019.1575190

Monteith, L. L., Gerber, H. R., Brownstone, L. M., Soberay, K. A., & Bahraini, N. H. (2019). The phenomenology of military sexual trauma among male veterans. *Psychology of Men & Masculinities, 20*(1), 115–127. https://doi.org/10.1037/men0000153

Morral, A. R., Gore, K. L., & Schell, T. L. (Eds.). (2015). *Sexual assault and harassment in the U.S. military*. RAND Corporation. https://www.rand.org/pubs/research_reports/RR870z2-1.html

Najavits, L. M., & Palacholla, R. (2016). Substance abuse, military sexual trauma, and the Seeking Safety model. In L. S. Katz (Ed.), *Treating military sexual trauma*. Springer Publishing Company.

Newins, A. R., Glenn, J. J., Wilson, L. C., Wilson, S. M., Kimbrel, N. A., Beckham, J. C., & Calhoun, P. S. (2020). Psychological outcomes following sexual assault: Differences by sexual assault setting. *Psychological Services*, 1–8. https://doi.org/10.1037/ser000042

Pew Research Center. (2011). *War and sacrifice in the post-9/11 era*. http://www.pewsocialtrends.org/2011/10/05/war-and-sacrifice-in-thepost-911-era/

Rauch, S. A. M., Yasinski, C. W., Post, L. M., Jovanovic, T., Norrholm, S., Sherrill, A. M., Michopoulos, V., Maples-Keller, J. L., Black, K., Zwiebach, L., Dunlop, B. W., Loucks, L., Lannert, B., Stojek, M., Watkins, L., Burton, M., Sprang, K., McSweeney, L., Ragsdale, K., & Rothbaum, B. O. (2020). An intensive outpatient program for prolonged exposure for veterans with posttraumatic stress disorder: Retention, predictors, and patterns of change. *Psychological Services*. https://doi.org/10.1037/ser0000422

Resick, P. A., Monson, C. M., & Chard, K. M. (2016). *Cognitive processing therapy for PTSD: A comprehensive manual*. Guilford Press.

Shapiro, F. (2018). *Eye movement desensitization and reprocessing therapy* (3rd ed.). Guilford Press.

Shea, M. T., Krupnick, J. L., Belsher, B. E., & Schnurr, P. P. (2020). Non-trauma-focused psychotherapies for the treatment of PTSD: A descriptive review. *Current Treatment Options in Psychiatry, 7*, 242–257. https://doi.org/10.1007/s40501-020-00214-y

Silver, S. M., Rogers, S., & Russell, M. (2008). Eye movement desensitization and reprocessing in the treatment of war veterans. *Journal of Clinical Psychology, 64*(8), 947–957. https://doi.org/10.1002/jclp.20510

Smith, C. P., & Freyd, J. J. (2013). Dangerous safe havens: Institutional betrayal exacerbates sexual trauma. *Journal of Traumatic Stress, 26*(1), 119–124. https://doi.org/10.1002/jts.21778

Suris, A., & Lind, L. (2008). Military sexual trauma: A review of prevalence and associated health consequences in veterans. *Trauma, Violence, & Abuse, 9*(4), 250–269. https://doi.org/10.1177/1524838008324419

Suris, A., Link-Malcom, J., Chard, K., Ahn, C., & North, C. (2013). A randomized clinical trial of cognitive processing therapy for veterans with PTSD related to military sexual trauma. *Journal of Traumatic Stress, 26*(1), 28–37. https://doi.org/10.1002/jts.21765

Tannahill, H. S., Livingston, W. S., Fargo, J. D., Brignone, E., Gundlapalli, A. V., & Blais, R. K. (2020). Gender moderates the association of military sexual trauma and risk for psychological distress among VA-enrolled veterans. *Journal of Affective Disorders, 268*, 215–220. https://doi.org/10.1016/j.jad.2020.03.017

Turchik, J. A., & Wilson, S. M. (2010). Sexual assault in the U.S. military: A review of the literature and recommendations for the future. *Aggression and Violent Behavior, 15*, 267–277. https://doi.org/10.1016/j.avb.2010.01.005

United States Department of Veterans Affairs. (2017). VA/DOD clinical practice guidelines for the management of posttraumatic stress disorder and acute stress disorder. https://www.healthquality.va.gov/guidelines/MH/ptsd/VADoDPTSDCPGFinal02418.pdf

United States Department of Veterans Affairs. (2020). Survivors voices: What racial and ethnic minority military sexual trauma (MST) survivors want mental health providers to know. https://www.in.gov/dva/files/Survivors-Voices.pdf

United States Department of Veterans Affairs. (2021a). Military sexual trauma: Overview. https://www.mentalhealth.va.gov/mentalhealth/msthome/index.asp

United States Department of Veterans Affairs. (2021b). Rural veterans. https://www.ruralhealth.va.gov/aboutus/ruralvets.asp

Watts, B. V., Schnurr, P. P., Mayo, L., Young-Xu, Y., Weeks, W. B., & Friedman, M. J. (2013). Meta-analysis of the efficacy of treatments for posttraumatic stress disorder. *Journal of Clinical Psychiatry, 74*, 541–550. https://doi.org/10.4088/JCP.12r08225

Wilson, L. C. (2016). The prevalence of military sexual trauma: A meta-analysis. *Trauma, Violence, and Abuse, 19*(5), 584–597. https://doi.org/10.1177/1524838016683459

Wilson, L. C., Newins, A. R., Wilson, S. M., Elbogen, E. B., Dedert, E. A., Calhoun, P. S., Beckham, J. C., & Kimbrel, N. A. (2021). Self- and other-directed violence as outcomes of deployment-based military sexual assault in Iraq/Afghanistan-era veteran men and women. *Journal of Aggression, Maltreatment, and Trauma, 29*(6), 714–724. https://doi.org/10.1080/10926771.2020.1725213

Zalta, A. K., Held, P., Smith, D. L., Klassen, B. J., Lofgreen, A. M., Normand, P. S., Brennan, M. B., Rydberg, T. S., Boley, R. A., Pollack, M. H., & Karrnik, N. S. (2018). Evaluating patterns and predictors of symptom change during a three-week intensive outpatient treatment for veterans with PTSD. *BMC Psychiatry, 18*, 1–15. https://doi.org/10.1186/s12888-018-1816-6

Culturally Responsive Approaches for LGBT+ Active-Duty Service Members and Veterans

Natasha A. Schvey, LTJG Shannon L. Exley, and Arielle T. Pearlman

Introduction

It is estimated that there are over 1 million veterans and up to 100,000 active-duty service members (ADSM/Vs) who identify as lesbian, gay, bisexual, transgender, and/or queer (LGBTQ) (Ahlin & Douds, 2018; Department of Veteran's Affairs, 2016; Meadows et al., 2021; The Palm Center, 2018). However, these are likely underestimates given that sexual orientation and gender identity are not routinely assessed or documented within military health-care settings; potential limitations to one's willingness or ability to self-disclose, particularly among those in uniform; and the numerous additional identities that have historically been excluded from research efforts (e.g., intersex, two-spirit, gender non-binary, asexual). The latter identities, in addition to many others not listed here, comprise the plus-sign (+) often appended to the term LGBTQ. Though much of the cited research focuses on those holding LGBT identities, for the purposes of greater inclusivity, the term LGBTQ+ will be used throughout.

Given the U. S. military's historical exclusion of those with diverse sexual orientations and gender identities (McNamara et al., 2021), LGBTQ+ ADSM/Vs may be vulnerable to mental health disparities, underscoring the need for timely, supportive, and culturally responsive care. As of January 2021, LGBTQ+ persons are now eligible for military service with few exceptions, though inequities in both access to and quality of health care persist, and the need for timely and evidence-based psychological services for LGBTQ+ individuals in the military health-care system is considerable. By ensuring Department of Defense (DoD) providers are well equipped to provide skilled, affirming, and culturally responsive services, avoidable mental health disparities among LGBTQ+ ADSM/Vs may be attenuated and prevented.

The current chapter proposes a strengths-based approach, while acknowledging and attending to well-documented mental health inequities among the LGBTQ+ military community. Of critical importance, diverse sexual orientations and gender identities do not themselves confer risk for adverse mental health outcomes; rather, these disparities are primarily accounted for by stigmatization, marginalization, and individual and systemic discrimination. Conversely, social support, acceptance, identity affirmation, and both individual and community resilience—all of which may be reflected upon, channeled, and bolstered within the therapeutic milieu—have been shown to mitigate risk and improve outcomes (Meyer, 2015; Schnarrs et al., 2020; Trujillo et al., 2017).

This chapter, therefore, will provide recommendations for culturally responsive care for LGBTQ+ ADSM/Vs, with the important caveat that these individuals do not comprise a monolith, and that there is considerable heterogeneity both between and within subgroups. Considerations related to the therapeutic environment, assessment, and intervention will be discussed and limitations of existing literature and recommendations for future research to inform best practices will be noted.

LGBTQ+ Identities and Mental Health

The mental health disparities facing persons identifying as LGBTQ+ largely result from societal stigma, marginalization, and systemic inequities. Disparities are further compounded by high rates of harassment, physical assault, sexual assault, and intimate partner violence (Grant et al., 2011), as well as lack of access to timely, affirming care, and discrimination in both medical and mental health-care settings (Grant et al., 2011; Jaffee et al., 2016). In addition, military service is associated with unique stressors such as combat exposure, military sexual trauma, deployments, and permanent changes of station (Ahlin & Douds, 2018; Hall, 2011; Smith et al., 2008; Suris & Lind, 2008), as well as uniform, bathroom, and lodging requirements, all of which may confer additional risk for psychosocial distress among LGBTQ+ ADSM/Vs. In addition, stigma surrounding mental health in the military in general (Blosnich et al., 2015) and lack of adequate training in affirming care among uniformed providers (Schvey et al., 2017) may attenuate help-seeking behaviors. Furthermore, harassment, victimization, and social exclusion of LGBTQ+ ADSM/Vs may be more normative or overt in certain military settings due to a heightened emphasis on the gender binary (e.g., uniform wear, fitness requirements, and sex-segregated lodging), a culture of hypermasculinity, and the historical exclusion of many LGBTQ+ identities from open service.

The minority stress model (Meyer, 2003) provides a framework for understanding the unique risks facing those with LGBTQ+ identities. In short, one's LGBTQ+ identity contributes to both distal (i.e., prejudice, discrimination, violence) and proximal (i.e., expectations of rejection, concealment, internalized or self-stigma) minority stress processes. These processes, in turn, confer risk for adverse physical and mental health outcomes. In addition, systemic inequities, such as lack of access to appropriate services or providers adequately trained in LGBTQ+ care, and anticipated or experienced stigma and non-acceptance among providers, contribute to and exacerbate health disparities (Kcomt et al., 2020). Despite the low- or no-cost access to health care available to most ADSM/Vs, these barriers persist. For instance, over a quarter of LGBTQ+ veterans report avoiding certain health services, including mental health care and general outpatient care, due to fear of stigmatization and non-acceptance (Ahlin & Douds, 2018; Simpson et al., 2013). Holding multiple minoritized identities (i.e., race, ethnicity, disability) also influences engagement with, and quality of, mental health services. A lack of timely access to culturally responsive care may compound minority stress, thereby promoting and exacerbating risk for untoward outcomes. The resultant mental health inequities exact a significant toll on individual wellbeing as well as military readiness overall.

Working with LGBTQ+ ADSM/V Populations

Mental health professionals serve an integral role in providing culturally responsive and affirming care to LGBTQ+ ADSM/Vs. Affirming environments are safe, supportive, acknowledge an individual's full humanity, and honor patients' various and intersecting identities (Gates & Kelly, 2018). Ensuring affirming care necessitates that providers interrogate their own beliefs and biases well before entering the therapeutic space and consciously commit to self-evolution and reflective practices. Providers must also educate themselves and seek consultation from colleagues and supervisors with experience and training in providing care to LGBTQ+ clients. Vitally, it is not a client's responsibility to educate the provider, as this emotional labor may impede trust and rapport, thereby harming the therapeutic alliance. Additionally, recognition of how cultural and contextual factors intersect with sexual orientation and gender identity is critical to culturally responsive and affirmative care (American Psychological Association, 2015).

Providers should familiarize themselves with available resources for LGBTQ+ inclusive services and supports both within their local military installations as well as nationally (Hinrichs & Donaldson, 2017). Given that ADSM/Vs may only have access to a particular set of providers, it is of heightened importance that they are equipped to provide affirming and responsive care. Particularly relevant for LGBTQ+ ADSM/Vs, available social supports should be assessed and engaged when appropriate. Identification of affirming sources of social support is imperative to wellbeing and mitigating adverse outcomes; however, providers are advised not to assume that a client's family or unit is a viable or safe source of social support. In addition, the client's resilience, strength, and identity pride should be acknowledged, and when appropriate, employed to empower the patient and bolster self-efficacy (Perrin et al., 2020).

Additional considerations are warranted depending on whether the provider is uniformed or civilian, and whether the client is on active duty or veteran status. For instance, when providing care for transgender ADSMs, providers should familiarize themselves with the Department of Defense Instruction 1300.28 "In-Service Transition for Transgender Service Members" (DoDi 1300.28, Section 3.3.b) (e.g., establishing a diagnosis of gender dysphoria, developing a treatment plan, and ensuring ongoing communication with the client's command). As eligibility for the coverage of affirming care is currently contingent upon a diagnosis of gender dysphoria, clinicians must familiarize themselves with relevant institutional policies and procedures, while also remaining sensitive to the fact that transgender patients have diverse care needs and that not all transgender patients have gender dysphoria (in which clinically significant distress or impairment is a key criterion) (Ashley, 2021). In supportive and affirming environments, gender incongruence may not be accompanied by distress nor impairment, thus affirming care should focus upon bolstering self-acceptance and identity exploration, rather than the amelioration of dysphoria. As transition is a highly individualized and personal process that may evolve over the course of months or years, providers should refrain from presupposing a particular desired outcome or therapeutic goal, and instead, work collaboratively with the patient to foster exploration of gender identity, expression, and whether steps towards social and/or medical transition are desired. In consultation with the patient, and when appropriate, providers may formally advise a change in gender marker in the Defense Enrollment Eligibility Reporting System (DEERS). Transparency with regard to the provider's role, the restraints of institutional policy, and any limits to confidentiality is imperative to a successful and supportive therapeutic experience, and particularly salient for LGBTQ+ ADSM/Vs.

Gender expression, gender identity, and sexuality are all highly individual; clinicians are encouraged to listen to and trust their clients' subjective experiences and empower their clients to explore and develop these identities as indicated. Importantly, providers should also refrain from assuming that LGBTQ+ clients want or need to engage in an exploration of identity. Patients may not yet be ready, may have already completed this self-exploration, and/or may wish to focus therapeutic attention on topics entirely separate from gender or sexuality. Providers and clients are encouraged to discuss treatment goals collaboratively and revisit them frequently to ensure potentially changing needs are adequately met.

Multidisciplinary teams may be indicated for the delivery of comprehensive, affirming care. Clinicians serve an important role in coordinating this care and are encouraged to liaise with other medical providers (e.g., endocrinology, reproductive health) to ensure holistic care when indicated. To facilitate this, many medical treatment facilities now offer Transgender Care Teams that provide multidisciplinary treatment planning and oversight of all aspects of affirming care for ADSM/Vs, including behavioral health, urology, gynecology, and endocrinology. However, Transgender Care Teams are not available across all branches nor medical treatment facilities, and thus significant inequities in access to comprehensive affirming care persist. Worth noting is that "gatekeeping" and "wait-and-see" approaches to gender exploration are non-neutral and adversely impact quality of care as well as threaten client health and safety. Providers must problem solve if these care teams are unavailable and cultivate a safe and collaborative environment in which clients can explore their identities free from preconceived expectations, arbitrary waiting periods, or unnecessary hurdles that may be iatrogenic.

Assessment/Therapeutic Environment

Providers and staff are integral to creating safe, accepting, and affirming therapeutic environments where clients may discuss sexual orientation, sexual practices, and gender identity without fear of judgment or derision (Jost & Janicka, 2020). To accomplish this, providers and staff must practice cultural humility and responsivity, engage in reflective practices, and continually self-educate. This is especially important as appropriate terminology evolves rapidly (for a comprehensive list of terms, see: https://pflag.org/glossary). In addition, acknowledgement that sexuality and gender exist on a spectrum, are non-binary constructs, and are highly subjective and best understood by the clients themselves, is imperative to fostering rapport, trust, and effective communication (American Psychological Association, 2015).

Ensuring authentic affirming care also demands significant internal reflection. Providers should spend time outside of sessions to reflect on their own biases such as heteronormative assumptions, internalized heterosexism, homophobia, and cisgenderism while taking action to mitigate these biases (Chang & Cohen, 2021; Domínguez et al., 2015). These efforts are critical given that therapist attitudes toward those with LGBTQ+ identities are linked to the quality of care provided, the strength of the therapeutic alliance, and patients' health-care–seeking behaviors (American Psychological Association, 2015). For example, 13% of respondents from the 2015 National Transgender Discrimination Survey reported that one or more professionals, such as a psychologist, counselor, or religious advisor, had tried to stop them from being transgender. Further, nearly one-quarter (23%) of respondents reported avoiding health care they needed due to fears of discrimination (James et al., 2016). The 2011 National Transgender Discrimination Survey additionally found that 19% of respondents reported being refused medical care because they were transgender or gender nonconforming (Grant et al., 2011).

Cultivating and promoting a warm, welcoming environment for all clients begins prior to the first session. This includes the use of intake forms and queries that do not presuppose heterosexuality or a gender binary, refraining from gendered salutations when greeting a client, ensuring visible statements on nondiscrimination, and use of various indicators of acceptance in the waiting room or office (i.e. rainbow flags, promotional materials displaying a range of diverse sexual orientations and genders, and pronoun pins worn by staff) (Hinrichs & Donaldson, 2017). Vitally, providers are encouraged to seek credentialing and up-to-date trainings relevant to the provision of LGBTQ+ care and ensure that these credentials are visible in informational materials.

Sexual orientation and gender identity are independent from one another and must be assessed and addressed separately. During intake, clinicians can normalize stating their pronouns when introducing themselves. Clients should then be asked to share their name and pronouns, should they feel comfortable. Intake forms should include one item that assesses sex assigned at birth and a separate item that assesses gender identity, the latter of which should include several options including: "Not listed (please specify)" as well as "I prefer not to say." In addition, sexual orientation may be included in intake forms, though clinicians should be mindful that for some, disclosing sexual orientation and/or sexual practices may require trust and assurances of confidentiality, and may be better suited for the therapeutic setting. Gender neutral facilities should also be widely available and accessible; this is critical given that 59% of transgender or gender diverse adults report avoiding using public restrooms due to discomfort or fear of confrontation (James et al., 2016). Ample opportunities for anonymous feedback should also be provided such that patients may rate their satisfaction with the care provided and offer suggestions or input for continued improvement. Providers and staff play integral roles in mitigating negative experiences and providing a safe, welcoming, and affirming environment for LGBTQ+ ADSM/Vs.

Specific Approaches for LGBTQ+ Clients

Providers must not assume that one's sexuality or gender identity are directly or even tangentially related to their presenting complaints, and instead must work collaboratively with clients to identify proximal and distal treatment goals. Areas of focus may or may not include distress related to stigma, marginalization, rejection, internalized homophobia/transphobia, identity concealment and/or disclosure, oppression, and victimization. However, these experiences are not typically included in standard intake interviews or questionnaires, particularly within behavioral health settings. Providers should sensitively assess and attend to these experiences over the course of therapy, as determined by the provider's clinical judgment and the client's comfort level. In addition, safety in the home, intimate partner violence, and other concurrent risk factors that may not routinely be assessed should be sensitively attended to in intakes and interviews.

There are several approaches providers should consider when caring for LGBTQ+ clients. Specifically, the LGBTQ relationally based positive psychology framework has shown promise and emphasizes a strengths-based approach, drawing on tenets from positive psychology (Domínguez et al.,

2015). Relational-cultural theory (RCT) similarly posits that clinicians should seek to empower clients and empathize with their experiences (Flores & Sheely-Moore, 2020). Overall, affirmative, strengths-based frameworks have empirical support in civilian samples (Boroughs et al., 2015; Chesworth et al., 2017; Hinrichs & Donaldson, 2017; Johnson, 2012; Pepping, Lyons, & Morris, 2018; Ramirez et al., 2013) and may be applicable and well suited for ADSM/Vs.

Other widely accepted and empirically supported therapies for LGBTQ+ clients include dialectical behavioral therapy (DBT) (Chang & Cohen, 2021; Cohen et al., 2021) and cognitive behavioral therapy (CBT)-based interventions (W. Hall et al., 2019). In a study of LGB veterans, a DBT skills-training approach that emphasized minority stress, emotion regulation, and mindfulness reduced depressive symptoms and internalized stigma (Cohen et al., 2021). Health education programs may also be effective either on their own or adjunctive to psychotherapy, depending on patient need. One such program for LGBT veterans targeting identity exploration, military culture, and self-advocacy within health-care settings resulted in reduced mental health symptoms, greater resilience, and greater intention to access care (Lange et al., 2020).

Beyond these studies, data on treatments specifically for LGBTQ+ ADSM/Vs are sparse. Though many therapeutic modalities are generally applicable across civilian and military settings, ADSM/Vs may present with stressors and mental health concerns specific to their service and subsequently may benefit from a tailored and specialized approach. The historical marginalization and exclusion of LGBTQ+ service members warrants specific attention within the therapeutic context as it may impact trust and rapport, particularly within military health-care settings (Lange et al., 2020; McNamara et al., 2021).

In addition to providing clinical care, mental health professionals must also serve as allies and advocates, working to combat oppression, marginalization, misinformation, and systemic barriers to care. This may include advocating for equitable and timely access to affirming care and helping to identify and mitigate barriers to care (Hinrichs & Donaldson, 2017). This is critical given well-documented inequities in access to and quality of care across geographic settings, including both homestead and deployment locales. Within military settings, mental health providers should liaise with leadership and command when indicated, provide relevant resources, and facilitate training to ensure a safe, inclusive environment. Psychologists and mental health providers have an important responsibility to promote social justice, for instance, by taking action against and reporting discriminatory practices, ensuring access to high quality affirming health care or providing relevant referrals, advocating for gender affirmation when indicated, combating health inequities, and educating others about the importance of affirming care (American Psychological Association, 2015; Pachankis, 2018).

Gaps and Future Directions

There is a paucity of data on psychotherapeutic approaches specifically for LGBTQ+ ADSM/Vs. Given the robust links between mental health and military readiness, research is needed to develop, assess, and ultimately disseminate affirming frameworks for evidence-based care for this understudied population. Existing evidence-based therapeutic approaches may require adaptation to account for unique military cultural considerations including deployments, particularly to locations intolerant of LGBTQ+ identities or practices, or where access to affirming care may be limited. Changes of station may also disrupt continuity of care, and the historical exclusion of LGBTQ+ service members may promote distrust of military health care and concerns about confidentiality. Some barriers may be mitigated, for instance, through expanded use of telehealth and embedded behavioral health clinics within primary care. Working with LGBTQ+ veteran care coordinators may help to ensure a smoother transition from active duty to veteran status.

Future work should assess to what extent the therapeutic needs of ADSMs and veterans differ. For instance, among ADSMs, medical readiness requirements for deployability and retention may be most salient, whereas for veterans, reintegration to the civilian sector and exploration of their new identity as a veteran may be of primary concern. Further, as much of the cited research has focused primarily on LGBT individuals, oftentimes as a monolith, further attention to the mental health needs of specific subgroups of sexual and gender minorities is warranted. Similarly, research examining treatment effectiveness for individuals with intersecting marginalized identities is required. Research indicates that mental health outcomes may indeed be worse among those with more minoritized identities due to multiple marginalization experiences (Cyrus, 2017); thus, providers should ensure they attend to and honor all facets of a client's identity.

Lastly, improving education and training in the care of LGBTQ+ clients, particularly within the military milieu, is critical. Training for clinicians emphasizes the importance of self-monitoring, continuing education, consultation, supervision, and staying abreast with current research. These efforts may be even more critical for military providers who are often encouraged to be "generalists" given the high volume of clients they see, as opposed to civilian providers who might instead specialize in select client groups. It is incumbent upon clinicians to engage in reflective practices and undergo self-assessment to determine whether they are adequately trained in the provision of LGBTQ+–related care. Of note, nearly half of TGD individuals who completed a national survey reported needing to educate their providers on their care needs (Grant et al., 2011) and in a survey of over 200 military family physicians, the majority reported no clinical education or training in transgender-related care (Schvey et al., 2017). For those who lack the competency, additional specialized training and consultation is warranted. In some cases, it may be necessary to refer out to specialists; however, this should be carefully considered given that culturally responsive care in certain geographic locations, military installations, or deployment settings may be scant or unavailable, which may create delays in access to potentially life-saving care.

Conclusion

Mental health providers can play a critical role in mitigating the effects of oppression and marginalization, providing affirming care, and empowering clients to explore their sexuality and gender within the context of a safe and supportive therapeutic relationship. Mental health providers, particularly those in uniform, have a responsibility to raise the standard of care and ensure timely access to potentially life-saving mental health services. By providing warm, affirming, and evidence-based care, mental health providers are uniquely poised to support LGBTQ+ ADSM/Vs and optimize the mental health and psychosocial functioning of this important and underserved group.

Acknowledgement

The authors would like to acknowledge LT Nicholas E. Grant, Ph.D., ABPP (he/him) for his contributions to this chapter.

References

Ahlin, E. M., & Douds, A. S. (2018). Many shades of green: Assessing awareness of differences in mental health care needs among subpopulations of military veterans. *International Journal of Offender Therapy and Comparative Criminology*, 62(10), 3168–3184.

American Psychological Association [APA]. (2015). Guidelines for psychological practice with transgender and gender nonconforming people. *American Psychologist*, 70(9), 832–864.

Ashley, F. (2021). The misuse of gender dysphoria: Toward greater conceptual clarity in transgender health. *Perspectives on Psychological Science, 16*(6), 1159–1164.

Blosnich, J. R., Gordon, A. J., & Fine, M. J. (2015). Associations of sexual and gender minority status with health indicators, health risk factors, and social stressors in a national sample of young adults with military experience. *Annals of Epidemiology, 25*(9), 661–667.

Boroughs, M. S., Bedoya, C. A., O'Cleirigh, C., & Safren, S. A. (2015). Toward defining, measuring, and evaluating LGBT cultural competence for psychologists. *Clinical Psychology: Science and Practice, 22*(2), 151–171.

Center, T. P. (2018). *Department of Defense Issues First-Ever Official Count of Active Duty Transgender Service Members.*

Chang, C. J., & Cohen, J. M. (2021). *Doing affirmative dialectical behavior therapy with LGBTQ+ People: Clinical recommendations.* DBT Bulletin, 6, 11–15. American Psychological Association. https://doi.org/10.1037/0000039-013

Chesworth, B., Filippelli, A., Nylund, D., Tilsen, J., Minami, T., & Barranti, C. (2017). *Feedback-informed treatment with LGBTQ clients: Social justice and evidence-based practice.* American Psychological Association. https://doi.org/10.1037/0000039-013

Cohen, J. M., Norona, J. C., Yadavia, J. E., & Borsari, B. (2021). Affirmative dialectical behavior therapy skills training with sexual minority veterans. *Cognitive and Behavioral Practice, 28*(1), 77–91.

Cyrus, K. (2017). Multiple minorities as multiply marginalized: Applying the minority stress theory to LGBTQ people of color. *Journal of Gay & Lesbian Mental Health, 21*(3), 194–202.

Domínguez, D. G., Bobele, M., Coppock, J., & Peña, E. (2015). LGBTQ relationally based positive psychology: An inclusive and systemic framework. *Psychological Services, 12*(2), 177.

Flores, C. A., & Sheely-Moore, A. I. (2020). Relational-cultural theory–based interventions with LGBTQ college students. *Journal of College Counseling, 23*(1), 71–84.

Gates, T. G., & Kelly, B. (2018). Affirming and strengths-based models of practice. In M. Dentato (Ed.), *Social work practice with the LGBTQ community: The intersection of history, health, mental health, and policy factors.* New York: Oxford University Press.

Grant, J., Mottet, L., & Tanis, J. (2011). *Injustice at Every Turn: A Report of the National Transgender Discrimination Survey 2011.* Washington, DC: National Center for Transgender Equality and National Gay and Lesbian Task Force.

Hall, L. (2011). The importance of understanding military culture. *Social Work in Health Care, 50*(1), 4–18.

Hall, W., Ruiz Rosado, B., & Chapman, M. V. (2019). Findings from a feasibility study of an adapted cognitive behavioral therapy group intervention to reduce depression among LGBTQ (lesbian, gay, bisexual, transgender, or queer) young people. *Journal of Clinical Medicine, 8*(7), 949.

Hinrichs, K. L., & Donaldson, W. (2017). Recommendations for use of affirmative psychotherapy with LGBT older adults. *Journal of Clinical Psychology, 73*(8), 945–953.

Jaffee, K. D., Shires, D. A., & Stroumsa, D. (2016). Discrimination and delayed health care among transgender women and men. *Medical Care, 54*(11), 1010–1016.

James, S. E., Herman, J. L., Rankin, S., Keisling, M., Mottet, L., & Anafi, M. (2016). *The Report of the 2015 U.S. Transgender Survey.* Retrieved from Washington, DC.

Johnson, S. D. (2012). Gay affirmative psychotherapy with lesbian, gay, and bisexual individuals: Implications for contemporary psychotherapy research. *American Journal of Orthopsychiatry, 82*(4), 516.

Jost, A. M., & Janicka, A. (2020). Patient-centered care: Providing safe spaces in behavioral health settings. In M. Forcier, G. Van Schalkwyk, & J. Turban (Eds.), *Pediatric Gender Identity*. Springer, Cham. Retrieved from: https://doi.org/10.1007/978-3-030-38909-3_7

Kcomt, L., Gorey, K. M., Barrett, B. J., & McCabe, S. E. (2020). Healthcare avoidance due to anticipated discrimination among transgender people: A call to create trans-affirmative environments. *SSM-Population Health, 11*, 100608.

Lange, T. M., Hilgeman, M. M., Portz, K. J., Intoccia, V. A., & Cramer, R. J. (2020). Pride in all who served: Development, feasibility, and initial efficacy of a health education group for LGBT veterans. *Journal of Trauma & Dissociation, 21*(4), 484–504.

McNamara, K. A., Lucas, C. L., Goldbach, J. T., Holloway, I. W., & Castro, C. A. (2021). You don't want to be a candidate for punishment: A qualitative analysis of LGBT service member outness. *Sexuality Research and Social Policy, 18*, 144–159.

Meadows, S. O., Engel, C. C., Collins, R. L., Beckman, R. L., Breslau, J., Bloom, E. L., & Hawes-Dawson, J. (2021). 2018 Department of defense health related behaviors survey (HRBS). In *Rand Health Quarterly*. Santa Monica.

Meyer, I. H. (2003). Prejudice, social stress, and mental health in lesbian, gay, and bisexual populations: Conceptual issues and research evidence. *Psychological Bulletin, 129*(5), 674.

Meyer, I. H. (2015). Resilience in the study of minority stress and health of sexual and gender minorities. *Psychology of Sexual Orientation and Gender Diversity, 2*(3), 209.

Pachankis, J. E. (2018). The scientific pursuit of sexual and gender minority mental health treatments: Toward evidence-based affirmative practice. *American Psychologist, 73*(9), 1207.

Pepping, C. A., Lyons, A., & Morris, E. M. (2018). Affirmative LGBT psychotherapy: Outcomes of a therapist training protocol. *Psychotherapy, 55*(1), 52.

Perrin, P. B., Sutter, M. E., Trujillo, M. A., Henry, R. S., & Pugh Jr, M. (2020). The minority strengths model: Development and initial path analytic validation in racially/ethnically diverse LGBTQ individuals. *Journal of Clinical Psychology, 76*(1), 118–136.

Ramirez, M. H., Rogers, S. J., Johnson, H. L., Banks, J., Seay, W. P., Tinsley, B. L., & Grant, A. W. (2013). If we ask, what they might tell: Clinical assessment lessons from LGBT military personnel post-DADT. *Journal of Homosexuality, 60*(2–3), 401–418. Retrieved from https://doi.org/10.1080/00918369.2013.744931

Schnarrs, P. W., Stone, A. L., Salcido, R., Georgiou, C., Zhou, X., & Nemeroff, C. B. (2020). The moderating effect of resilience on the relationship between adverse childhood experiences (ACEs) and quality of physical and mental health among adult sexual and gender minorities. *Behavioral Medicine, 46*(3–4), 366–374.

Schvey, N. A., Blubaugh, I., Morettini, A., & Klein, D. A. (2017). Military family physicians' readiness for treating patients with gender dysphoria. *JAMA Internal Medicine, 177*(5), 727–729.

Simpson, T. L., Balsam, K. F., Cochran, B. N., Lehavot, K., & Gold, S. D. (2013). Veterans administration health care utilization among sexual minority veterans. *Psychological Services, 10*(2), 223.

Smith, T. C., Ryan, M. A., Wingard, D. L., Slymen, D. J., Sallis, J. F., & Kritz-Silverstein, D. (2008). New onset and persistent symptoms of post-traumatic stress disorder self reported after deployment and combat exposures: Prospective population based US military cohort study. *BMJ, 336*(7640), 366–371.

Suris, A., & Lind, L. (2008). Military sexual trauma: A review of prevalence and associated health consequences in veterans. *Trauma, Violence, & Abuse, 9*(4), 250–269.

Trujillo, M. A., Perrin, P. B., Sutter, M., Tabaac, A., & Benotsch, E. G. (2017). The buffering role of social support on the associations among discrimination, mental health, and suicidality in a transgender sample. *International Journal of Transgenderism, 18*(1), 39–52.

U.S. Department of Veterans Affairs. (2016). LGBT veteran health care—male veterans: Gay and bisexual health care [PDF]. Retrieved from https://www.patientcare.va.gov/LGBT/docs/va-pcs-lgbt-factsheet-gay-bisexual.pdf

4 Assessment and Treatment of Intimacy Issues and Sexual Disorders in Active-Duty Service Members and Veterans

Chandra E. Khalifian, Katerine T. Rashkovsky, and Kayla Knopp

Introduction

Sexual functioning is an essential, though often overlooked, component of comprehensive health care for military and veteran populations. This chapter reviews the assessment and treatment of sexual health in military service members and veterans. Current research suggests high rates of sexual dysfunction in all military service members and veterans, often because of interpersonal and combat trauma. We describe the prevalence of different types of sexual concerns, as well as the risk and protective factors for developing sexual dysfunction, among military women, men, and LGBTQ+ individuals. We also

DOI: 10.4324/9781003185949-4

evaluate the current psychological, medical, and interdisciplinary approaches to treating sexual symptoms and disorders in military and veteran groups.

Women in the Military and Sexual Health

Prevalence

Most research suggests sexual dysfunction is a prevalent issue for women military service members and veterans, with prevalence rates as high as 62% (Shepardson et al., 2021). Women with military sexual trauma (MST) have even greater rates of sexual concerns: they are about 1.5 times more likely to report a sexual pain, desire, or arousal disorder than women without MST (Turchik et al., 2012). In a 2018 study, Garneau-Fournier et al. reported that 74.4% of women veterans with MST ($N = 1,339$) endorsed symptoms of sexual dysfunction. Women veterans with posttraumatic stress disorder (PTSD) also have elevated risk, with one study showing almost 41% of 284 female veterans reporting elevated sexual concern scores and almost 13% reporting elevated dysfunctional sexual behavior (i.e., using sex to deal with distress; Schnurr et al., 2009). Among types of sexual dysfunction, sexual pain has been found to be one of the most common concerns reported (Pulverman & Creech, 2019; Sadler et al., 2012). Women veterans also report low levels of sexual satisfaction in general, regardless of whether they have a sexual dysfunction diagnosis or are engaged in treatment for sexual concerns (Breyer et al., 2016).

Despite their prevalence, other research suggests these sexual problems may be underdiagnosed in military and veteran women. When examining VHA medical charts, only 1% to 2.4% of female veterans have a sexual dysfunction diagnosis recorded (Cohen et al., 2012; Turchik et al., 2012). This suggests that female veterans may be underreporting during medical visits or VHA clinicians are not assessing and tracking women's sexual concerns in their medical charts.

Risk and Protective Factors

Research has identified some demographic risk factors for problems with sexual functioning, particularly age and relationship status. Among women veterans with MST, Garneau-Fournier et al. (2018) found that unmarried women were more likely to have any type of sexual dysfunction, and younger women reported more sexual pain and lower orgasmic functioning on average. However, married veterans are more likely to have symptoms of sexual dysfunction than divorced veterans. Another study by Breyer et al. (2016) showed that being married or living with a partner was associated with higher rates of sexual activity and satisfaction in women veterans.

Research suggests that physical health plays a major role in sexual functioning of women veterans. Gynecological injuries from sexual assault are related to increased sexual concerns (Sadler et al., 2012). Poor physical health-related quality of life has been shown to be associated with more sexual problems in women veterans (Garneau-Fournier et al., 2018; Mccall-Hosenfeld et al., 2009; Sadler et al., 2012), even across an 11-year time period (Suvak et al., 2012).

A history of traumatic experiences places women veterans at particular risk for developing issues with sexual functioning. Intimate partner violence (IPV) and history of sexual trauma, including childhood sexual assault (CSA), have been found to be associated with dysfunctional sexual behaviors in women veterans (Combellick et al., 2019; Pulverman & Creech, 2019; Sadler et al., 2012; Suvak et al., 2012). Additionally, sexual trauma in the military is connected to higher rates of sexually transmitted infections (STIs) and sexual dysfunction diagnoses and symptoms in women veterans, including low sexual satisfaction and dysfunctional sexual behaviors, such as indiscriminate sexual contact and using sex to deal with distress (Pulverman et al., 2019; Suvak et al., 2012; Turchik et al., 2012). Some research suggests that the link between MST and sexual dysfunction is largely mediated by negative emotional processes, physical health-related quality of life, lack of a close partner, and gynecological illness (Blais et al., 2018; Mccall-Hosenfeld et al., 2009).

Further, having a PTSD diagnosis is connected to lower sexual satisfaction and desire and worse overall sexual functioning in women military service members and veterans, regardless of the type of trauma (Bird et al., 2021; Breyer et al., 2016; Garneau-Fournier et al., 2018; Pulverman & Creech, 2019; Sadler et al., 2012; Wells et al., 2019). Women veterans with PTSD are less likely to be sexually active and find sex less important on average than women veterans without PTSD (Breyer et al., 2012). PTSD symptoms, particularly anhedonia and dysphoric arousal, have also been linked to worse sexual functioning (Blais et al., 2018, 2020a, 2020b). Overall, despite there being little research on sexual dysfunction in women veterans with PTSD, the studies that do exist show a connection between various aspects of sexual functioning and PTSD symptoms.

Sexual dysfunction is also associated with other mental health diagnoses and symptoms. Women veterans with any mental health diagnoses were more likely to report vaginal pain and other sexual problems (Cohen et al., 2012). In particular, research has shown a consistent association between depression and sexual dysfunction in women veterans, including low desire and sexual pain (Garneau-Fournier et al., 2018; Pulverman & Creech, 2019; Sadler et al., 2012; Turchik et al., 2012), although one study found that a connection between depression and sexual health concerns was present only in African American women veterans (Gobin & Allard, 2016). Another study found positive associations between sexual problems and symptoms of depression, anxiety, and alcohol problems among women veterans, but not men (Suvak et al., 2012). This study found that depressive symptoms were the most robust predictor of sexual functioning, with negative affectivity being most strongly associated with worse sexual satisfaction for female (but not male) veterans. Medication treatments for depression, including selective serotonin reuptake inhibitors (SSRIs) and venlafaxine (Effexor), are both significantly associated with low sexual desire and sexual dysfunction symptoms in women veterans (Garneau-Fournier et al., 2018). Substance use disorders have also been linked to problems with sexual functioning and increased chances of having a sexually transmitted infection or sexual dysfunction diagnosis (Sadler et al., 2012; Turchik et al., 2012). Overall, mental health problems, substance use, and related medications appear to negatively impact female sexual functioning in military women.

Treatment

Given these robust links between sexual trauma, PTSD, and sexual dysfunction, much of the research on treating sexual dysfunction in women military service members and veterans is through the lens of treating PTSD; however, findings from this research have been mixed. In a study of prolonged exposure (PE) and present-centered therapy (PCT) to treat PTSD, Schnurr et al. (2009) found that sexual concerns improved in both treatment conditions when PTSD symptoms improved, and that these gains were maintained for six months following treatment. Additionally, a study of cognitive processing therapy (CPT) found that sexual satisfaction, arousal, and desire improved in proportion to improvements in PTSD for women trauma survivors, including women veterans, irrespective of trauma type (Wells et al., 2019). In contrast, a PE treatment study examining both men and women found that sexual desire did not change over the course of treatment (Badour et al., 2020), although this study did not analyze data from women in isolation. These studies suggest that treating PTSD may be an important component of improving sexual functioning among military and veteran women with PTSD symptoms, but more research in this area is needed.

Men in the Military and Sexual Health

Prevalence

Studies conducted on male military service members and veterans indicate a high rate of sexual dysfunction in this population, with prevalence rates ranging from 25% to 32% (Breyer et al., 2016; Shepardson et al., 2021). Erectile dysfunction (ED) is particularly prevalent (Shepardson et al., 2021).

Prevalence of sexual dysfunction among male veterans appears highly related to trauma and PTSD. In a survey of male Canadian Armed Forces personnel and veterans, most (69.8%) of whom met screening criteria for probable PTSD, 71% of study participants endorsed a lack of sexual desire/pleasure and 40% reported sexual pain and problems during intercourse (Richardson et al., 2020). Another study found that 63% of PTSD–diagnosed combat veterans reported low sexual desire and 62% reported problems with arousal (Badour et al., 2015). Other studies found that more than 80% of male veterans with PTSD reported one or several kinds of sexual dysfunction (Ahmadi et al., 2007; Cosgrove et al., 2002; Letourneau et al., 1997; Prisant et al., 1994). Sexual disinterest (37–44%) and avoidance of sex (48%) are also prominent concerns in male veterans with PTSD (Letourneau et al., 1997; Litz et al., 1992). Regarding ED, studies have reported that between 40% and 69% of combat veterans with PTSD experienced erectile problems, such as premature ejaculation, erectile disorders, or other ejaculation problems (Ahmadi et al., 2007; Letourneau et al., 1997; Prisant et al., 1994). All individuals in a group of 37 male veterans with spinal cord injury reported ED (Khak et al., 2016). In a sample of 663 male veterans who reported experiencing military sexual trauma (MST), 81.5% endorsed ED symptoms (Garneau-Fournier et al., 2018). Sexual dysfunction is a common concern among male military veterans, particularly those who are struggling with traumatic injury or PTSD.

Risk/Protective Factors

Regarding demographic risk factors for sexual dysfunction, some research has linked race, relationship status, and age to male military service members' and veterans' and sexual functioning. Regarding race, findings have been mixed, with some research reporting higher rates of sexual problems in veterans of color (Hosain et al., 2013; Wilcox et al., 2014), but others finding that White veterans reported more problems with desire and arousal (Badour et al., 2015). In terms of relationship status, a study found that sexual problems and

ED were higher in non-married veterans (Wilcox et al., 2014). Badour et al. (2015) also found that older age predicted ED and medication use, as well as arousal problems.

Physical health problems also put male veterans at greater risk of sexual dysfunction (Ahmadi et al., 2007). In a study of Canadian Forces active-duty service members and veterans, McIntyre-Smith et al. (2015) found that the relationship between PTSD symptom severity and sexual functioning was mediated by bodily pain. Higher limitations in usual role activities due to physical problems (i.e., not being able to wash dishes due to hand injury) showed a weak association with lower erectile functioning, while lower vitality (i.e., strength and energy) predicted worse orgasmic functioning and high bodily pain predicted lower sexual satisfaction. Conversely, scoring higher on perceived masculinity was associated with greater sexual desire (McIntyre-Smith et al., 2015). Therefore, physical limitations and how men perceive their physical functioning seem to be related to sexual functioning.

Mental health problems appear to be even more central to the sexual functioning of male veterans. Depression symptoms and problematic substance use are risk factors for arousal problems, sexual dysfunction disorders, risky sexual behavior, and increased odds of having a sexually transmitted infection (STI); Badour et al., 2015; Combellick et al., 2019; Turchik et al., 2012). Sexual functioning may be related to suicidal ideation in male veterans, with a recent study reporting that decreased sexual pleasure and frequency was associated with more recent suicidal ideation (Khalifian et al., 2020). Trauma exposure is also related to sexual dysfunction in male veterans, with combat exposure predicting problems with sexual desire and compulsive sexual behavior (Badour et al., 2015; Smith et al., 2014). Traumatic events associated with moral injury (i.e., events that transgress deep moral convictions or values) were uniquely associated with sexual anxiety beyond just general combat exposure (Bhalla et al., 2018). Male veterans who have experienced military sexual trauma are more likely to have an STI or sexual dysfunction disorder (most typically a form of ED) than peers who have not experienced MST (Turchik et al., 2012). Sexual dysfunction symptoms also tend to be more persistent in men with MST than in women with MST (O'Brien et al., 2008).

Most sexual dysfunction studies in male veterans have been conducted in the context of PTSD. PTSD has been linked to sexual disinterest (Litz et al., 1992), lower overall sexual satisfaction (Bird et al., 2021; Cosgrove et al., 2002; McIntyre-Smith et al., 2015; Zerach et al., 2010), arousal problems (Badour et al., 2015), decreased sexual frequency, pain, and ED (Antičević & Britvić, 2008). Some research has failed to find these associations (e.g.,

Beaulieu et al., 2015; Richardson et al., 2020; Suvak et al., 2012). Interestingly, PTSD appears to have a distinct impact on types of sexual behavior that may be more emotionally intimate or vulnerable; for example, those with PTSD engaged in the same frequency of masturbation as those without PTSD but had fewer sexual fantasies (Antičević & Britvić, 2008). In qualitative interviews conducted by Decker et al. (2020), veterans also reported engaging in sexual risks that made them feel alive, while avoiding the risk of entering an intimate relationship. Specific clusters of PTSD symptoms may have a stronger impact on sexual functioning than others. Multiple studies emphasize the connection between avoidance and numbing symptoms of PTSD and sexual dysfunction, particularly fears of intimacy, sexual anxiety, and low sexual desire and pleasure (Badour et al., 2015; Bhalla et al., 2018; Nunnink et al., 2010; Richardson et al., 2020; Riggs, 2014). Research has also found links between negative alterations in cognition and mood and sexual desire (Letica-Crepulja et al., 2019).

Treatment

Research regarding treatment of sexual dysfunction in male military service members and veterans has focused almost exclusively on erectile dysfunction. Within the U.S. Department of Veterans Affairs (VA) medical centers, where roughly half of U.S. military veterans receive care, sildenafil (Viagra) and other phosphodiesterase type 5 inhibitor (PDE5) medications are commonly used to treat erectile dysfunction, with prescriptions limited to four doses per month per veteran (Department of Veterans Affairs, 2020). However, a study looking at the efficacy of sildenafil in a group of 266 combat-exposed war veterans who met criteria for PTSD found that sildenafil did not have better results than placebo, and those in the sildenafil arm of the trial experienced a greater number of treatment-emergent adverse events (Safarinejad et al., 2009). Sussman et al. (2016) also found that veterans in their sample were mostly neutral to dissatisfied with their current erectile dysfunction treatment, 89% of which was PED5 medication, largely due to the limited access to ED medication (i.e., only 4 doses per month), the ineffectiveness of treatment (i.e., poor quality and length of sexual encounters), the lack of information about ED, physical adverse events (e.g., headaches), and psychological and relational concerns. Nonetheless, the majority (80%) of participants were planning to continue their current treatments. The authors identified a lack of knowledge regarding ED as a major barrier to care, as their research also suggested discussing ED with one's primary care provider did not necessarily lead to increased knowledge of ED.

Sussman et al. (2016) also identified other interventions that are being used to treat ED in the VA. About 70% of their sample engaged in one or more behavioral changes to reduce ED, such as taking medications at different times and decreasing the use of tobacco and alcohol. A small percentage (2.5%) of their sample also reported some other kind of treatment for ED, such as using vacuum pumps, suppositories, over-the-counter medications, injections, and non-PDE5 medications. A recent study evaluating the use of vacuum constriction devices accompanied by psychological intervention in veterans with ED found that 53 out of 56 participants became able to maintain erections with the device and that all participants would recommend the device to others (Beaudreau et al., 2021).

Although behavioral interventions for men's sexual problems are well supported by research evidence (see Krzastek et al., 2019 for a review), limited research has been conducted evaluating these treatments in military or veteran populations. One older study evaluated interdisciplinary sex therapy (i.e., involving both physical and mental health-care professionals) for veteran men as treatment for erectile dysfunction, premature ejaculation, and delayed ejaculation (David & Blight, 1978). Therapists used in vivo desensitization tasks and assigned between-session activities with veterans' spouses to communicate affection and reduce pressure to perform sexually. Twenty-four out of 36 participants in this trial completely resolved their sexual concerns, with the authors underscoring that having a willing and supportive spouse was essential to succeeding in treatment. Multiple case studies looking at interdisciplinary sexual health interventions for veterans with paraplegia and spinal cord injury/dysfunction found that patients were using skills that they learned in treatment and benefited by having their functional and emotional needs addressed (Hess et al., 2007); however, although all participants were using the skills taught, they were having various degrees of success with establishing and maintaining intimate relationships (Hough et al., 2013). These researchers identified several barriers to providing efficacious care: institutional limitations in prescribing ED medications, difficulties collaborating with pharmaceutical teams at the VA, VA staff avoidance of discussing sexual health, and patients lacking a formal means of readiness for sexual health intervention (Brundage et al., 2020). Further, when behavioral interventions target mental health issues and do not address sexual functioning directly, sexual problems do not seem to improve (Badour et al., 2020), and those with greater sexual problems at baseline reported less improvement of both PTSD and depression symptoms after treatment (Badour et al., 2016). These findings emphasize the need to target sexual problems directly.

LGBTQ+ People in the Military and Sexual Health

Lesbian, gay, bisexual, transgender, and queer/questioning (LGBTQ+) military service members and veterans are a severely understudied population. As such, there has been very little research focusing on the sexual health and functioning of this military subgroup. The existing studies evaluating LGBTQ+ military members' sexual health are in the context of larger studies that include mostly heterosexual participants. DiMauro et al. (2018) examined sexual vs. non-sexual trauma in female veterans and the impact that these different trauma types had on sexual functioning. The study sample was 6.7% LGBTQ+. Results from the full sample showed that sexual trauma was associated with lower sexual satisfaction, PTSD and depressive symptoms, and higher suicidal ideation, but was not associated with differences in sexual functioning, and that trauma type moderated the relationship between sexual functioning and suicidality only in those with sexual trauma; however, it is unclear to what extent these results apply specifically to the small number of LGBTQ+ participants. Another study conducted by Garneau-Fournier et al. (2018) examined sexual dysfunction in a sample of 2,002 veterans who experienced military sexual trauma. Although most of the sample was heterosexual, 9.9% ($n = 198$) identified as gay, lesbian, bisexual, or other. The only finding concerning LGBTQ+ status was that identifying as a sexual minority was associated with a decreased likelihood of sexual pain among women. These are the only studies currently available to our knowledge regarding sexual health in LGBTQ+ military service members and veterans, highlighting a massive gap in the literature.

Future Directions

The sexual functioning of many military subgroups, such as LGBTQ+ veterans and those in committed relationships, are vastly understudied. Furthermore, most treatments for sexual concerns outside of erectile dysfunction have not been evaluated in military service members and veterans, who are a unique population with different characteristics from the civilian community. We conclude by enumerating priorities for further research on intimacy issues and sexual dysfunction, focusing on how we can begin to address and treat these prominent and deleterious problems in our military service members and veterans.

Risk and Protective Factors

More research is needed to explicate links between military-specific experiences and sexual functioning in both women and men. Although the existing literature emphasizes associations between PTSD and sexual functioning, many of the findings are mixed or contradictory, and studies are limited that examine specific aspects of sexuality—such as arousal, sexual pain, and orgasm—as well as specific aspects of PTSD, such as trauma type. Research on sexual functioning in other military populations is even more limited, including women and men with other or no impairing physical or mental health conditions. Further, nearly all existing studies are observational, leaving important open questions regarding causality and direction of associations. More research is needed on how sexuality impacts and is impacted by physical and mental health among military service members and veterans. Finally, the existing literature has a notable focus on risk factors for poor sexual functioning; future research would benefit from extending focus to protective factors and predictors of healthy sexuality as well.

Understudied Populations

Like the broader literature on sexual functioning, the existing research on sexual functioning within military populations focuses overwhelmingly on those presumed to be cisgender and heterosexual. Additional research is needed on military populations identifying as sexual or gender minorities, with particular focus on how the unique history of sexual and gender minority status in the military (e.g., "Don't Ask, Don't Tell") shapes experiences of sexuality. Importantly, widely used sexual functioning assessments may not be valid among LGBTQ+ individuals (Schardein & Nikolavsky, 2021), which could lead to under- or misdiagnosis; validating clinical assessments is likely an important first step toward understanding and treating sexual problems among sexual and gender minority service members and veterans.

Ethnic and racial differences in military service member and veteran experiences of sexuality and intimacy are also significantly understudied. One study looking at male White, African American, and Hispanic OIF/OEF veterans found that prevalence of sexual dysfunction was significantly higher among African Americans than Whites (Hosain et al., 2013). Age was a risk factor for sexual dysfunction across all three groups. Marital status and hypertension were only significant risk factors for Whites and African Americans, while PTSD was a significant risk factor only for Hispanics and African Americans. Another study supports this finding, reporting that Black, Hispanic, and other non-White male military service members were significantly more at risk for sexual functioning problems than their White counterparts (Wilcox et al., 2014). This is consistent with similar studies on male civilians (Laumann et al., 1999). To our knowledge, there are no further studies examining sexual functioning, intimacy, and ethnoracial differences among veteran samples. However, varying cultures often speak about and have history with sex and intimacy in unique ways that impact sexual functioning. For example, studies on civilian college students show that Asian Americans are significantly more conservative in attitudes toward casual sex than Hispanic and Euro-Americans (Ahrold & Meston, 2010), which may lead to reduced sexual engagement outside of committed relationships and possible stigma associated with more casual encounters. Some cultures also have a history of practicing genital mutilation to ensure virginity until marriage, take away sexual desire, and remove sexual pleasure (Monagan, 2009), which, though it may no longer be practiced, may impact the way that descendants of these cultures view sex and intimacy. The cultural norms and histories influence how these constructs are experienced, particularly at the intersection of military service member and ethnoracial identities. Research must be conducted with these considerations in mind.

Additionally, existing research has focused predominantly on individual sexual functioning without considering the relational context, leaving important future questions regarding the role and characteristics of intimate partners. This is particularly important in military populations given the strains military service can exert on interpersonal relationships (e.g., disruptions from deployment and relocation, incentives related to marriage and monogamy, and experiences of traumatic stress and sequelae). A growing body of research supports the importance of relationship functioning among military populations for multiple physical and mental health outcomes (e.g., Riviere et al., 2017). Incorporating this focus into sexuality research and interventions is likely to be beneficial.

Treatment

Amidst the research on sexual dysfunction in military populations, there is a noticeable dearth of studies of interventions and treatments. Among civilian women, effective treatments include hormone therapy, pharmacotherapy, and psychological or behavioral interventions (Weinberger et al., 2019). For civilian men, many treatment studies have focused on medical interventions for erectile dysfunction (Krzastek et al., 2019), with some additional focus on hormone therapy (Corona et al., 2017) and behavioral treatments (Bilal et al., 2020; Bossio et al., 2018) for more general sexual functioning. Research is needed to confirm the effectiveness of these interventions in military populations, particularly regarding psychological and behavioral interventions, which are underutilized and understudied.

Treating sexual dysfunction effectively among military populations may require some adaptation to established interventions to accommodate unique risk and protective factors faced by service members and veterans. A history of trauma and presence of PTSD symptoms may make interventions that emphasize physical touch, emotional intimacy, interpersonal trust, or feelings of vulnerability more challenging, particularly for those who experienced sexual or other interpersonal trauma. Trauma-informed treatment may necessitate more psychoeducation about the impact of trauma and PTSD on sexual functioning, as well as a slower pace or graduated hierarchy through interventions that expose individuals to feared stimuli. Culturally responsive care may also include gently challenging unhelpful beliefs about sexuality learned through military experiences. Providers should also be aware of other mental and physical health comorbidities common among military service members that may impact sexuality, such as increased sexual risk-taking due to substance use or limited physical mobility due to traumatic injury. If mental health symptoms are present along with sexual dysfunction, the research reviewed here suggests evidence-based treatment for a psychological disorder such as PTSD is likely to be a useful part of a sexual dysfunction treatment plan. This may be particularly true for men, as civilian research focuses heavily on pharmacological treatments for sexual problems, which may not sufficiently address psychological factors common in military populations.

Conclusions

Although more attention to sexual functioning among military populations is needed, the existing research demonstrates that military experiences, particularly those that lead to mental and physical health problems, may put service members at increased risk of sexual dysfunction. As sexual functioning is an important part of whole health and overall wellbeing for many individuals, clinicians working with military service members should be sure to assess sexual functioning and incorporate sexual health into patients' treatment plans. Further, for individuals with mental health symptoms, treating mental health disorders—as well as addressing any sexual side effects of medications used to treat these disorders—is also important for improving sexual functioning.

A holistic approach to treatment that incorporates sexual and interpersonal functioning as well as physical and mental health is an important part of caring for military service members and veterans.

References

Ahmadi, K., Ranjebar-Shayan, H., & Raiisi, F. (2007). Sexual dysfunction and marital satisfaction among the chemically injured veterans. *Indian Journal of Urology, 23*(4), 377–382. https://doi.org/10.4103/0970-1591.36710

Ahrold, T. K., & Meston, C. M. (2010). Ethnic differences in sexual attitudes of U.S. college students: Gender, acculturation, and religiosity factors. *Archives of Sexual Behaviors, 39*, 190–202. https://doi.org/10.1007/s10508-008-9406-1

Antičević, V., & Britvić, D. (2008). Sexual functioning in war veterans with posttraumatic stress disorder. *Croatian Medical Journal, 49*(4), 499–505. https://doi.org/10.3325/cmj.2008.4.499

Badour, C. L., Gros, D. F., Szafranski, D. D., & Acierno, R. (2015). Problems in sexual functioning among male OEF/OIF veterans seeking treatment for posttraumatic stress. *Comprehensive Psychiatry, 58*(2015), 74–81. https://doi.org/10.1016/j.comppsych.2014.12.012

Badour, C. L., Gros, D. F., Szafranski, D. D., & Acierno, R. (2016). Sexual problems predict PTSD and depression symptom change among male OEF/OIF veterans completing exposure therapy. *Psychiatry, 176*(4), 403–417. https://doi.org/10.1080/00332747.2016.1142774

Badour, C. L., Cox, K. S., Goodnight, J. R. M., Flores, J., Tuerk, P. W., & Rauch, S. A. M. (2020). Sexual desire among veterans receiving prolonged exposure therapy for PTSD: Does successful PTSD treatment also yield improvements in sexual desire? *Psychiatry (New York), 83*(1), 70–83. https://doi.org/10.1080/00332747.2019.1672439

Beaudreau, S. A., Van Moorleghem, K., Dodd, S. M., Liou-Johnson, V., Suresh, M., & Gould, C. E. (2021). Satisfaction with a vacuum constriction device for erectile dysfunction among middle-aged and older veterans. *Clinical Gerontologist, 44*(3), 307–315. https://doi.org/10.1080/07317115.2020.1823922

Beaulieu, G. R., Latini, D. M., Helmer, D. A., Powers-James, C., Houlette, C., & Kauth, M. R. (2015). An exploration of returning veterans' sexual health issues using a brief self-report measure. *Sexual Medicine, 3*(4), 287–294. https://doi.org/10.1002/sm2.92

Bhalla, A., Allen, E., Renshaw, K., Kenny, J., & Litz, B. (2018). Emotional numbing symptoms partially mediate the association between exposure to potentially morally injurious experiences and sexual anxiety for male service members. *Journal of Trauma and Dissociation, 19*(4), 417–430. https://doi.org/10.1080/15299732.2018.1451976

Bilal, A., & Abbasi, N. Ul, H. (2020). Cognitive behavioral sex therapy: An emerging treatment option for nonorganic erectile dysfunction in young men: A feasibility pilot study. *Sexual Medicine, 8*(3), 396–407. https://doi.org/10.1016/j.esxm.2020.05.005

Bird, E. R., Piccirillo, M., Garcia, N., Blais, R., & Campbell, S. (2021). Relationship between post-traumatic stress disorder and sexual difficulties: A systematic review of veterans and military personnel. *AJO-DO Clinical Companion*. https://doi.org/10.1016/j.jsxm.2021.05.011

Blais, R. K., Monteith, L. L., & Kugler, J. (2018). Sexual dysfunction is associated with suicidal ideation in female service members and veterans. *Journal of Affective Disorders*, 226(August 2017), 52–57. https://doi.org/10.1016/j.jad.2017.08.079

Blais, R. K., Livingston, W. S., & Fargo, J. D. (2020a). Higher depression severity mediates the association of assault military sexual trauma and sexual function in partnered female service members/veterans. *Journal of Affective Disorders*, 261(April 2019), 238–244. https://doi.org/10.1016/j.jad.2019.09.072

Blais, R. K., Zalta, A. K., & Livingston, W. S. (2020b). Interpersonal trauma and sexual function and satisfaction: The mediating role of negative affect among survivors of military sexual trauma. *Journal of Interpersonal Violence*. https://doi.org/10.1177/0886260520957693

Bossio, J. A., Basson, R., Driscoll, M., Correia, S., & Brotto, L. A. (2018). Mindfulness-based group therapy for men with situational erectile dysfunction: A mixed-methods feasibility analysis and pilot study. *Journal of Sexual Medicine*, 15(10), 1478–1490. https://doi.org/10.1016/j.jsxm.2018.08.013

Breyer, B., Cohen, B., Berterthal, D., Rosen, R., Neylan, T., & Seal, K. (2012). The association of posttraumatic stress disorder with sexual dysfunction in male Iraq and Afghanistan veterans. *Journal of Urology*, 187(4S), e559. https://doi.org/10.1016/j.juro.2012.02.1803

Breyer, B. N., Fang, S. C., Seal, K. H., Ranganathan, G., Marx, B. P., Keane, T. M., & Rosen, R. C. (2016). Sexual health in male and female Iraq and Afghanistan U.S. war veterans with and without PTSD: Findings from the VALOR cohort. *Journal of Traumatic Stress*, 29(3), 229–236. https://doi.org/10.1002/jts.22097

Brundage, J. A., Williams, R. D., Powell, K., Raab, J., Engler, C., Rosin, N., & Sepahpanah, F. (2020). An interdisciplinary sexual health rehabilitation program for veterans with spinal cord injury: Case reports. *Sexuality and Disability*, 38(2), 343–353. https://doi.org/10.1007/s11195-020-09629-0

Cohen, B. E., Maguen, S., Bertenthal, D., Shi, Y., Jacoby, V., & Seal, K. H. (2012). Reproductive and other health outcomes in Iraq and Afghanistan women veterans using VA health care: Association with mental health diagnoses. *Physiology & Behavior*, 176(1), 139–148. https://doi.org/10.1016/j.whi.2012.06.005.Reproductive

Combellick, J. L., Dziura, J., Portnoy, G. A., Mattocks, K. M., Brandt, C. A., & Haskell, S. G. (2019). Trauma and sexual risk: Do men and women veterans differ? *Women's Health Issues*, 29, S74–S82. https://doi.org/10.1016/j.whi.2019.04.014

Corona, G., Rastrelli, G., Morgentaler, A., Sforza, A., Mannucci, E., & Maggi, M. (2017). Meta-analysis of results of testosterone therapy on sexual function based on international index of erectile function scores. *European Urology*, 72(6), 1000–1011. https://doi.org/10.1016/j.eururo.2017.03.032

Cosgrove, D., Gordon, Z., Bernie, J. E., Ham, S., Montoya, D., Stein, M. B., & Monga, M. (2002). Sexual dysfunction in combat veterans with post-traumatic stress disorder. *Urology*, 60(5), 881–884. www.theijoem.com

David, J. R., & Blight, E. M. (1978). Interdisciplinary treatment of male sexual dysfunction in a military health care setting. *Journal of Sex and Marital Therapy*, 4(1), 29–34. https://doi.org/10.1080/00926237808403002

Decker, S. E., Pavlo, A., Harper, A., Herring, Y., & Black, A. C. (2020). Themes in experiences of PTSD symptoms and relationships among male veterans with risky sexual behavior. *Psychological Trauma: Theory, Research, Practice, and Policy*, 12(7), 678–686. https://doi.org/10.1037/tra0000569

Department of Veterans Affairs, Veterans Health Administration, VHA Directive 1340(2). July 6, 2017. Updated June 26, 2020.

DiMauro, J., Renshaw, K. D., & Blais, R. K. (2018). Sexual vs. non-sexual trauma, sexual satisfaction and function, and mental health in female veterans. *Journal of Trauma and Dissociation*, 19(4), 403–416. https://doi.org/10.1080/15299732.2018.1451975

Garneau-Fournier, J., Habarth, J., & Turchik, J. A. (2018). Factors associated with sexual dysfunction symptoms among veterans who have experienced military sexual trauma. *International Journal of Sexual Health*, 30(1), 28–41. https://doi.org/10.1080/19317611.2017.1404541

Gobin, R. L., & Allard, C. B. (2016). Associations between sexual health concerns and mental health symptoms among African American and European American women veterans who have experienced interpersonal trauma. *Personality and Individual Differences*, 100, 37–42. https://doi.org/10.1016/j.paid.2016.02.007

Hess, M. J., Hough, S., & Tammaro, E. (2007). The experience of four individuals with paraplegia enrolled in an outpatient interdisciplinary sexuality program. *Sexuality and Disability*, 25(4), 189–195. https://doi.org/10.1007/s11195-007-9055-7

Hosain, G. M. M., Latini, D. M., Kauth, M. R., Goltz, H. H., & Helmer, D. A. (2013). Racial differences in sexual dysfunction among postdeployed Iraq and Afghanistan veterans. *American Journal of Men's Health*, 7(5), 374–381. https://doi.org/10.1177/1557988312471842

Hough, S., Stone, M. T., & Buse, D. C. (2013). Dating and relationship psychoeducational group for veterans with spinal cord injury/dysfunction: A historical account of an initial clinical course. *Sexuality and Disability*, 31(4), 337–359. https://doi.org/10.1007/s11195-013-9330-8

Khak, M., Hassanijirdehi, M., Afshari-Mirak, S., Holakouie-Naieni, K., Saadat, S., Taheri, T., & Rahimi-Movaghar, V. (2016). Evaluation of sexual function and its contributing factors in men with spinal cord injury using a self-administered questionnaire. *American Journal of Men's Health*, 10(1), 24–31. https://doi.org/10.1177/1557988314555122

Khalifian, C. E., Knopp, K., Wilks, C. R., Wooldridge, J., Sohn, M. J., Thomas, D., & Morland, L. A. (2020). The association between sexual functioning and suicide risk in U.S. military veteran couples seeking treatment for post-traumatic stress disorder. *Archives of Sexual Behavior*, 49(5), 1601–1613. https://doi.org/10.1007/s10508-019-01577-x

Krzastek, S. C., Justin, B., Smith, R. P., & Kovac, J. R. (2019). Recent advances in the understanding and management of erectile dysfunction. *Journal of Clinical Endocrinology and Metabolism*, 80(7), 1985–1988. https://doi.org/10.1210/jcem.80.7.7608245

Laumann, E. O., Paik, A., & Rosen, R. C. (1999). Sexual dysfunction in the United States: Prevalence and predictors. *JAMA*, 281(6), 537–544. https://doi.org/10.1001/jama.281.6.537

Letica-Crepulja, M., Stevanović, A., Protućer, M., Popović, B., Salopek-Žiha, D., & Vondraček, S. (2019). Predictors of sexual dysfunction in veterans with post-traumatic stress disorder. *Journal of Clinical Medicine*, 8(4), 432. https://doi.org/10.3390/jcm8040432

Letourneau, E. J., Schewe, P. A., & Frueh, B. C. (1997). Preliminary evaluation of sexual problems in combat veterans with PTSD. *Journal of Traumatic Stress*, 10(1), 125–132. https://doi.org/10.1023/A:1024868632543

Litz, B. T., Keane, T. M., Fisher, L., Marx, B., & Monaco, V. (1992). Physical health complaints in combat-related post-traumatic stress disorder: A preliminary report. *Journal of Traumatic Stress*, 5(1), 131–141. https://doi.org/10.1007/BF00976818

McCall-Hosenfeld, J. S., Liebschutz, J. M., Spiro III, A., & Seaver, M. R. (2009). Sexual assault in the military and its impact on sexual satisfaction in women veterans: A proposed model. *Journal of Women's Health, 18*(6), 901–909.

McIntyre-Smith, A., Cyr, K. S., & King, L. (2015). Sexual functioning among a cohort of treatment-seeking canadian military personnel and veterans with psychiatric conditions. *Military Medicine, 180*(7), 817–824. https://doi.org/10.7205/MILMED-D-14-00125

Monagan, S. L. (2009). Patriarchy: Perpetuating the practice of female genital mutilation. *International Research Journal of Arts & Humanities, 37*(37), 83–101.

Nunnink, S. E., Goldwaser, G., Afari, N., Nievergelt, C. M., & Baker, D. G. (2010). The role of emotional numbing in sexual functioning among veterans of the Iraq and Afghanistan wars. *Military Medicine, 175*(6), 424–428. https://doi.org/10.7205/MILMED-D-09-00085

O'Brien, C., Gaher, R. M., Pope, C., & Smiley, P. (2008). Difficulty identifying feelings predicts the persistence of trauma symptoms in a sample of veterans who experienced military sexual trauma. *Journal of Nervous and Mental Disease, 196*(3), 252–255. https://doi.org/10.1097/NMD.0b013e318166397d

Prisant, M. L., Carr, A. A., Bottini, P. B., Solursh, D. S., & Solursh, L. P. (1994). Sexual dysfunction with antihypertensive drugs. *Archives of Internal Medicine, 154*(7), 730–736.

Pulverman, C. S., & Creech, S. K. (2019). The impact of sexual trauma on the sexual health of women veterans: A comprehensive review. *Trauma, Violence, and Abuse*, 1–16. https://doi.org/10.1177/1524838019870912

Pulverman, C. S., Creech, S. K., Mengeling, M. A., Torner, J. C., Syrop, C. H., & Sadler, A. G. (2019). Sexual assault in the military and increased odds of sexual pain among female veterans. *Obstetrics and Gynecology, 134*(1), 63–71. https://doi.org/10.1097/AOG.0000000000003273

Richardson, J., Ketcheson, F., King, L., Forchuk, C. A., Hunt, R., St. Cyr, K., Nazarov, A., Shnaider, P., McIntyre-Smith, A., & Elhai, J. D. (2020). Sexual dysfunction in male Canadian Armed Forces members and veterans seeking mental health treatment. *Military Medicine, 185*(1–2), 68–74. https://doi.org/10.1093/milmed/usz163

Riggs, D. S. (2014). Traumatized relationships: Symptoms of posttraumatic stress disorder, fear of intimacy, and marital adjustment in dual trauma couples. *Psychological Trauma: Theory, Research, Practice, and Policy, 6*(3), 201–206. https://doi.org/10.1037/a0036405

Riviere, L. A., Merrill, J. C., & Clarke-Walper, K. (2017). Marital status and marital quality differences in the postdeployment mental and physical health of service members. *Military Behavioral Health, 5*(3), 254–264. https://doi.org/10.1080/21635781.2017.1316803

Sadler, A. G., Mengeling, M. A., Fraley, S. S., Torner, J. C., & Booth, B. M. (2012). Correlates of sexual functioning in women veterans: Mental health, gynecologic health, health status, and sexual assault history. *International Journal of Sexual Health, 24*(1), 60–77. https://doi.org/10.1080/19317611.2011.640388

Safarinejad, M. R., Kolahi, A. A., & Ghaedi, G. (2009). Safety and efficacy of sildenafil citrate in treating erectile dysfunction in patients with combat-related post-traumatic stress disorder: A double-blind, randomized and placebo-controlled study. *BJU International, 104*(3), 376–383. https://doi.org/10.1111/j.1464-410X.2009.08560.x

Schardein, J. N., & Nikolavsky, D. (2021). Sexual functioning of transgender females post-vaginoplasty: Evaluation, outcomes and treatment strategies for sexual dysfunction. *Sexual Medicine Reviews*. https://doi.org/10.1016/j.sxmr.2021.04.001

Schnurr, P. P., Lunney, C. A., Forshay, E., Thurston, V. L., Chow, B. K., Resick, P. A., & Foa, E. B. (2009). Sexual function outcomes in women treated for posttraumatic stress disorder. *Journal of Women's Health*, *18*(10), 1549–1557. https://doi.org/10.1089/jwh.2008.1165

Shepardson, R. L., Mitzel, L. D., Trabold, N., Crane, C. A., Crasta, D., & Funderburk, J. S. (2021). Sexual dysfunction and preferences for discussing sexual health concerns among veteran primary care patients. *Journal of the American Board of Family Medicine*, *34*(2), 357–367. https://doi.org/10.3122/JABFM.2021.02.200326

Smith, P. H., Potenza, M. N., Mazure, C. M., Mckee, S. A., Park, C. L., & Hoff, R. A. (2014). Compulsive sexual behavior among male military veterans: Prevalence and associated clinical factors. *Journal of Behavioral Addictions*, *3*(4), 214–222. https://doi.org/10.1556/JBA.3.2014.4.2

Sussman, J. C., Smith, H. M., Larsen, S. E., & Reiter, K. E. (2016). Veterans' satisfaction with erectile dysfunction treatment. *Federal Practitioner*, *33*(5), 33–37.

Suvak, M. K., Brogan, L. A., & Shipherd, J. C. (2012). Predictors of sexual functioning in a sample of U.S. Marines: An 11-year follow-up study. *International Journal of Sexual Health*, *24*(1), 26–44. https://doi.org/10.1080/19317611.2011.640387

Turchik, J. A., Pavao, J., Nazarian, D., Iqbal, S., McLean, C., & Kimerling, R. (2012). Sexually transmitted infections and sexual dysfunctions among newly returned veterans with and without military sexual trauma. *International Journal of Sexual Health*, *24*(1), 45–59. https://doi.org/10.1080/19317611.2011.639592

Weinberger, J. M., Houman, J., Caron, A. T., & Anger, J. (2019). Female sexual dysfunction: A systematic review of outcomes across various treatment modalities. *Sexual Medicine Reviews*, *7*(2), 223–250. https://doi.org/10.1016/j.sxmr.2017.12.004

Wells, S. Y., Glassman, L. H., Talkovsky, A. M., Chatfield, M. A., Sohn, M. J., Morland, L. A., & Mackintosh, M. A. (2019). Examining changes in sexual functioning after cognitive processing therapy in a sample of women trauma survivors. *Women's Health Issues*, *29*(1), 72–79. https://doi.org/10.1016/j.whi.2018.10.003

Wilcox, S. L., Redmond, S., & Hassan, A. M. (2014). Sexual functioning in military personnel: Preliminary estimates and predictors. *Journal of Sexual Medicine*, *11*(10), 2537–2545. https://doi.org/10.1111/jsm.12643

Zerach, G., Anat, B. D., Solomon, Z., & Heruti, R. (2010). Posttraumatic symptoms, marital intimacy, dyadic adjustment, and sexual satisfaction among ex-prisoners of war. *Journal of Sexual Medicine*, *7*(8), 2739–2749. https://doi.org/10.1111/j.1743-6109.2010.01784.x

Evidence-Based Practices for Psychotherapy with Active-Duty Service Members and Veterans

Maria C. Crouch, Jennifer M. Loya, and Joan M. Cook

Number and Proportion of Diverse Active-Duty Service Members and Veterans

Racial and ethnic minorities compose approximately 31% of the 1.3 million active-duty service members (ADSM), 26% of the 0.8 million selected reserve personnel (Department of Defense, 2019) and 25% of the over 20 million total veteran population (National Center for Veterans Analysis and Statistics, 2018). Of ADSMs, 17% are Black ($n = 227{,}736$), 5% are Asian ($n = 62{,}110$), 3% are multiracial ($n = 39{,}596$), 1% are Native Hawaiian or Pacific Islander ($n = 15{,}319$), 1% are American Indian and Alaska Native ($n = 14{,}627$), and 4% identify as "other" ($n = 54{,}376$). Almost 53% of those who listed race as "other" reported being Hispanic, and overall, almost 17% of ADSMs reported being Hispanic, with 18% of White ADSMs reporting Hispanic heritage ($n = 167{,}666$). Reserve member representation by race is comparable.

DOI: 10.4324/9781003185949-5

The proportion of racial and ethnic minorities are expected to increase to approximately 35% of ADSM and veterans by 2040 (National Center for Veterans Analysis and Statistics, 2018). When comparing the percentage of ADSMs to the civilian population, racially and ethnically diverse ADSMs are slightly more represented than among civilians, whereas White ADSMs representation is proportional to the general population, and Asian ADSMs are slightly less represented compared to civilians. However, Department of Defense (2020) data indicated that both active and reserve Black, Asian, and Hispanic officers are unrepresented in contrast to White members. When comparisons were made among enlisted members and across paygrades, it was found that Black, Indigenous, and People of Color (BIPOC) representation decreased as leadership roles/pay grades increased.

Of the veteran population, 15% are Black ($n = 2.5$ million), 10% are Hispanic ($n = 1.6$ million), 3% are multiracial ($n = 457,555$), 2% are Asian ($n = 360,479$), 2% identify as "other" ($n = 297,514$), 1% are American Indian/Alaska Native ($n = 166,263$), and less than 1% are Native Hawaiian or Pacific Islander ($n = 47,099$). Notably, American Indian/Alaska Native ADSMs and veterans have the highest rates of service per capita than any other racial group (Goss et al., 2017).

Rates of Trauma, PTSD, and Mental Health Service Utilization in BIPOC

The research on trauma, posttraumatic stress disorder (PTSD), and mental health service utilization and outcome in ADSMs and veterans from BIPOC populations have several limitations that should be noted upfront. Most relied on retrospective reports of traumatic stress and PTSD. While some research comes from large-scale representative samples, the majority rely on convenience or clinical samples from single site specialty clinics, or the use of Department of Veterans Affairs (VA) health-care records. In addition, this research largely compares either Black individuals to White individuals or places all BIPOC individuals in a non-White category. These caveats are important to interpreting the current literature, as well as highlighting areas and subpopulations in need of further investigation, and what is needed to improve clinical practice for all ADSMs and veteran members of BIPOC populations. For example, American Indian/Alaska Native veterans have high rates of PTSD, lower quality of life and more health disparities than non-Native veterans, and notable historical and contemporary traumas in addition to combat and combat exposure (Goss et al., 2017, 2019; Hansford & Jobson,

2022). Moreover, American Indian/Alaska Native members are rarely examined as a distinct group when examining PTSD treatment outcome in ASMD and veterans.

In general, there have been reports of elevated prevalence rates of trauma, PTSD, and other mental health issues (e.g., major depressive disorder) for some BIPOC veteran and service member populations compared to White counterparts (Chen et al., 2015; Loo, n.d.; Nichter et al., 2020). Such factors that have been found to contribute to the development of PTSD among ADSMs and veterans include (1) the extent to which they were exposed to combat, (2) firing a weapon during war-zone exposure, (3) witnessing injuries that threaten life or the death of another person, and (4) the degree to which one receives social support after traumatic exposure (Chen et al., 2015). However, in addition to service-related PTSD risk factors, BIPOC ADSMs and veterans are also exposed to other forms of trauma that contribute to PTSD prevalence and severity, particularly race-related stressors. While beyond the scope of this chapter, it is important to note that extrapolating broader understandings of the research examining PTSD among BIPOC individuals can be difficult, given the varied approach to ethnoracial differences, such as the way data is collected and interpreted (e.g., grouping BIPOC individuals in a non-White category), ethnic variations and power differentials in the researcher-participant dynamic (e.g., BIPOC participants might be less likely to engage with White researchers/providers), measurement equivalence (e.g., tests are often not normed on racial groups outside of the dominant group), and an emphasis on combat-related predictors of trauma and a de-emphasis on race-related stressors.

Data on the impact of ethnoracial differences in treatment of PTSD is mixed. For example, in a subsample of male theater veterans ($N = 248$) from the National Vietnam Veterans Readjustment Study, Black ($n = 70$) and Hispanic ($n = 84$) veterans report greater exposure to war-related traumatic stress and were more likely to develop incident PTSD compared to White counterparts ($n = 94$; Dohrenwend et al., 2008). In a large population-based cohort of 20,563 veterans who served during the Operation Enduring Freedom and Operation Iraqi Freedom (OEF/OIF) era (13,162 OEF/OIF veterans and 7,401 veterans who served during the OEF/OIF era but were not deployed to those conflicts), there was increased risk of a positive screen for PTSD among Black veterans compared to other racial groups (Dursa et al., 2014). Relatedly, in a sample of active-duty male military personnel seeking treatment for PTSD, Hispanic/Latino/x and Black ADSMs reported greater PTSD symptoms compared to non-Hispanic White ADSMs (Kaczkurkin et al., 2016).

In a sample of 9,420 veterans recently separated from the military (White $n = 6,222$; Black $n = 1,027$; Hispanic/Latinx $n = 1,313$; Asian, Native Hawaiian, or Pacific Islander $n = 420$; multiracial $n = 438$), McClendon et al. (2019) examined patterns and correlates of PTSD screening across race/ethnicity and gender. Rates of positive PTSD screens were highest among Black veterans (36.3%), followed by multiracial (35.7%), Hispanic/Latino (30.6%), and White (22.5%) veterans. While not included in the analyses due to low sample size, American Indian/Alaska Native (43.3%) veterans did screen positive for PTSD at a higher rate than other groups. Regarding the intersectionality of race/ethnicity and gender, multiracial female (48.1%) and Black male (37.9%) veterans had the highest rates of positive PTSD screens. Additionally, Asian, Native Hawaiian, or Pacific Islander male veterans (19.8%) had the lowest rates of positive PTSD screens. Furthermore, Black, Hispanic/Latina/x, and multiracial female veterans had significantly higher odds of positive PTSD screens than White female veterans. However, gender differences did emerge for multiracial women veterans. While controlling for other variables (e.g., trauma exposure, social support) impacting positive PTSD screens partially or fully accounted for the elevation among Black and Hispanic/Latina/x veterans but remained the same for multiracial veterans.

The empirical literature on PTSD treatment outcomes (not solely focused on evidence-based psychotherapies or predating their wide dissemination and implementation) for veterans from racial minority backgrounds has been limited, and the findings are somewhat varied. Many studies have found that, generally, race and ethnicity were not related to changes in PTSD symptoms or to treatment response. In a study of VA residential PTSD programming among 65 Vietnam veterans (85% White; other races were not reported), race was not a significant predictor of treatment response (Johnson & Lubin, 1997). However, in a more recent, national sample of over 2,000 veterans undergoing PTSD residential treatment, Sripada et al. (2020a) found four latent classes of PTSD symptoms: a low-symptom class, a moderate-symptom class with high reexperiencing, a moderate-symptom class with high emotional numbing, and a high-symptom class. Symptom classes differed by race/ethnicity, with non-White veterans more likely to be in the moderate class with high reexperiencing symptoms.

Mental health treatment initiation and response are varied for BIPOC veterans. In one study among veterans who served in Iraq and Afghanistan (Koo et al., 2016), Asian/Pacific Islander women and Black men were more likely to screen positive for PTSD at treatment initiation compared to other racial groups. Hispanic men were also more likely to screen for PTSD. In addition, symptom cluster differences were significant among racial/ethnic groupings by gender, which have important implications for screening and treatment and the salience of incorporating culture and gender. For example, Hispanic women were more likely to report emotional numbing, which has been salient in prior research but has not been examined by gender.

Maguen et al. (2014) conducted a large retrospective analysis of VA health care records of nearly 40,000 Iraq and Afghanistan veterans who initiated mental health treatment within one year of post-deployment PTSD diagnosis. Women had significantly more PTSD symptoms improve posttreatment compared to men, which is important given that women—in general, among the civilian population—are at a greater risk of PTSD. Black veterans were also less likely to have symptoms improve compared to White counterparts, regardless of time-to-treat. Also, those who had a negative screen at treatment follow-up were more likely to be White. Moreover, ethnoracial and/or gender differences in treatment initiation and response could also be explained by social norms (e.g., acceptability of emotional expression for women) and cultural norms (e.g., disclosure of trauma histories and associated symptoms, help-seeking behaviors).

Using national VA health care records, Hebenstreit et al. (2015) found that race/ethnicity were significantly associated with female Iraq and Afghanistan veterans' completion of minimally adequate care (i.e., at least nine mental health outpatient visits within a 15-week period or at least 12 consecutive weeks of medication use) for PTSD. Namely, Black and Hispanic women were less likely to engage with and complete care. In addition, in a sample of veterans who were receiving VA outpatient PTSD services, those from non-White populations were less likely to achieve improved PTSD symptoms; perhaps due to higher rates of attrition, lower levels of ethnic matching of patients and providers, and no adaptation in the interventions (e.g., change in intervention intensity, change in modality; Sripada et al., 2017). These findings suggest a need to reduce delays in initiating mental health care as well as targeted efforts to improve PTSD treatment outcomes among BIPOC populations.

Using national cohort data of VA patients who were recently diagnosed with PTSD, Black and Latina/o/x veterans were less likely to receive an adequate trial of pharmacotherapy, and Black veterans were less likely to receive a minimal trial of any treatment in the six months after diagnosis (Spoont et al., 2015). Importantly, these differences were not due to differences by group, cultural variables, or their access to care, thus indicating that there is a treatment disparity for these groups (Spoont et al., 2009). Further, research (Spoont et al., 2009, 2015, 2017) has demonstrated that Black veterans with PTSD are less likely to receive any therapy overall, individual therapy (as opposed to group treatment), minimally adequate dose of treatment, or medication trial, as well as have significantly longer wait times for treatment and are less likely to complete PTSD treatment (Castro et al., 2015; Eliacin et al., 2018; Rosenheck et al., 1995; Saha et al., 2008; Spoont et al., 2017).

In a study of 232 veterans from Iraq and Afghanistan who were receiving treatment at a VA PTSD clinic within the first year of return from deployment, engagement in psychotherapy, pharmacotherapy, or both was not associated with differences in race/ethnicity (Haller et al., 2016). However, it has been demonstrated that Black and Hispanic veterans experienced increased discrimination and trauma exposure while deployed in Iraq and Afghanistan, which likely contributes to increased negative mental health outcomes (Muralidharan et al., 2016). This was particularly salient for women of color in contrast to White women. Considerations of gender differences in addition to racial differences is integral to culturally relevant PTSD treatment for ADSMs and veterans.

Evidence-Based Psychotherapies (EBPs) for PTSD

There are numerous guidelines for the treatment of PTSD (Hamblen et al., 2019). The majority converge to designate several psychotherapies as evidence based (EBPs). For example, the Guideline Development Panel for the Treatment of PTSD in Adults, American Psychological Association (2019) strongly recommended prolonged exposure (PE; Foa et al., 2019) and cognitive processing therapy (CPT; Resick et al., 2016), as well as conditionally recommended brief eclectic psychotherapy for PTSD (BEPP; Gersons et al., 2015), eye movement desensitization and reprocessing (EMDR; Shapiro, 2017) and narrative exposure therapy (NET; Schauer et al., 2011). All these treatments are trauma-focused, meaning they involve the processing of traumatic material.

Over the past two decades, the VA has invested significant resources to provide their mental health workforce with training, supervision, staffing, and implementation support in sixteen EBPs (Karlin & Cross, 2014). Beginning in 2006 and 2007, this unprecedented national training initiative included two EBPs for PTSD: PE and CPT. Numerous efforts were made to assist in the training and implementation of these two EBPs (Karlin et al., 2010), including policy changes mandating their availability at all VA facilities (Department of Veterans Affairs, 2008), designation of local EBP coordinators (or champions) at each medical center, and a PTSD mentor program to help PTSD clinic managers make organizational changes to increase the likelihood that the EBPs would be implemented (Bernardy et al., 2011). For the purpose of this chapter, we primarily focus on PE and CPT. In addition to the numerous randomized controlled trials (RCTs) examining PE and CPT among civilians, RCTs examining PE and CPT have been conducted with veteran samples (for review, see Schnurr et al., 2022; Steenkamp & Litz, 2013).

Prolonged Exposure (PE)

In brief, PE is an eight- to 15-session manualized individual therapy with four primary components: (1) psychoeducation about trauma, (2) breathing training, (3) in vivo exposure (hierarchy of avoided trauma-related situations and stimuli and then hierarchical exposure to these safe but avoided situations and stimuli), and (4) imaginal exposure (verbal retelling of the most distressing trauma). In a review of 38 RCTs of PE, inclusion of ethnoracial minorities, other than Black participants, was low (Benuto et al., 2020). In an examination of the influence of ethnicity on the effectiveness of cognitive behavioral treatment for PTSD, particularly PE, in 95 female civilians of sexual and non-sexual assault, there were no differences in treatment efficacy or dropout between Black ($n = 35$) and White participants ($n = 60$; Zoellner et al., 1999). Additionally, in a RCT with 173 civilians, there were clinically equivalent PTSD outcomes for Black ($n = 43$) and White participants ($n = 130$) in both PE and the pharmacotherapy (sertraline) conditions. However, Black participants attended fewer sessions in PE and sertraline than White participants (Kline et al., 2020).

One study (Ghafoori & Khoo, 2020) conducted among a community-based sample of low-income, diverse patients seeking mental health treatment for traumatic stress found ethnoracial differences in probable PTSD and related symptomology after treatment (e.g., the sixth week of PE). The White group had a higher likelihood of probable PTSD compared to the Latinx group at six weeks into treatment. The White group also had a higher likelihood of probable anxiety compared to the Black, Hispanic/Latina/o/x, and "Other" groupings, and probable depression in contrast to the "Other" grouping. It is critical to observe that this research (as does a vast majority) uses White participants as the reference group. While this is a common practice, it is, arguably at best, reifying the normalcy of whiteness and, at worst, perpetuating racism (Johfre & Freese, 2021). Additionally, due to small sample sizes, many researchers often organize racial/ethnic groups into an "other" category.

Namely, the aforementioned study (Ghafoori & Khoo, 2020) grouped American Indian/Alaska Native, "mixed race ethnicity," Asian, and "other" into an overarching "Other" racial category. In contrast, a growing number of studies exclude racial/ethnic groups from analyses when participant numbers are too small for meaningful group comparisons. For example, several strategies include counting American Indian/Alaska Native peoples as an analytic group regardless of other races reported; collecting data about Tribal affiliation and disaggregate data based on Tribe; and considering effect sizes or at a minimum descriptive reporting what is known about the sample (Crouch & Andrew, 2022). Nevertheless, understanding racial and ethnic differences and responses in the early stages of treatment are integral to tailoring trauma treatment for BIPOC ADSMs and veterans.

Cognitive Processing Therapy (CPT)

CPT is a 12-session manualized treatment focusing on the relationship between unhealthy and distorted thinking patterns related to trauma by teaching new and adaptive ways of thinking. CPT can be delivered in group, individual, or combined formats. In a meta-analysis of the effectiveness of CPT for treating PTSD (Asmundson et al., 2019), the number of studies conducted among ethnoracial minorities, other than the Black population, was low. In an examination of the influence of race on CPT treatment in 308 female civilians with interpersonal violence-related PTSD, there were no differences in treatment outcomes between Black and White participants. However, Black participants were significantly less likely to complete treatment compared to White participants (Lester et al., 2010).

A study by Schulz et al. (2006) demonstrated the effectiveness of CPT in a population of individuals of foreign-born refugees (i.e., Afghanistan, Yugoslavia, Bosnia- Herzegovina) who resettled in the U.S. Most treatments were done at the participants' homes due to poverty and lack of resources or the nature of the trauma (e.g., fears related to being in public). CPT adapted for a naturalistic setting with the use of an interpreter within a refugee population was found to be equally effective as the results from RCTs. Also, length of sessions was not as important as alleviation of symptoms and the educational and skill building processes of CPT. In other words, some participants needed more than 12, and some needed less than 12 sessions. CPT has been found to be an adaptable and efficacious method for PTSD treatment with the general population, veterans, refugees, and other groups.

Effect of Race, Ethnicity, and Culture on EBP Treatment Outcomes in ADSMs and Veterans

Research on race, ethnicity, and culture is integral to understanding and improving EBP treatment outcomes for underserved groups; however, this type of research is limited in ADSMs and veterans. Among 134 service members who completed PE or CPT at a military outpatient clinic (reportedly, 55.7% White, 20.9% Black, 19.0% Hispanic, and 3.8% Asian), ethnicity was not related to symptom change in PTSD (Aronson et al., 2018). In a sample of 259 veterans who received CPT in an outpatient clinic (reportedly, 87.6% White, 6.5% Hispanic, and 3.5% Black), there were no demographics, including race, that were associated with change in PTSD symptoms or explained variance in treatment response (Roberge et al., 2019). Similarly, in a retrospective chart review evaluating the effectiveness of PE and CPT in one VA specialty clinic, there were no significant differences in outcome between Hispanic and White veterans (Jeffreys et al., 2014).

Additionally, in an evaluation of a manualized group therapy in a 10-week, VA combat-related program conducted with 450 veterans (61.8% non-Hispanic Black; the rest were non-Hispanic White), PTSD symptom reduction occurred irrespective of race (Coleman et al., 2018). Using the same sample of veterans, another paper reported that racial and ethnic make-up of groups was also not related to outcomes (Cusack et al., 2019). Importantly, however, improvement was a function of educational attainment, emphasizing that socioeconomic factors can contribute to social equity, quality of life, and treatment effectiveness.

In a small RCT for military sexual trauma-related PTSD among female veterans, there were no differences between Black and White veterans in change in PTSD symptoms over the course of CPT (Holliday et al., 2017). In addition, there were no differences based on race in the number of sessions attended and rates of early termination. However, in a clinical sample of veterans with PTSD who received CPT through an outpatient VA program, ethnicity was one of the variables that influenced the trajectory of PTSD symptom reductions during treatment (Schumm et al., 2013). Across three latent symptom classes, with class one being the most severe PTSD and depression symptoms and class three being the least severe, it was found that the largest proportion of minority individuals (36%) comprised class one. Class one had the most severe self-reported symptoms pre- and posttreatment and exhibited the least improvement. It has been posited that PTSD symptoms are exacerbated by racism and discrimination, and treatment and therapeutic alliance is impacted by limited availability of ethnic matching of provider and patient among ethnoracial minority groups.

Other treatment outcomes, such as suicidal ideation, have also been examined. For example, in a study of 303 veterans (64.4% White, 26.1% Black, 0.3% Asian, 3.0% Hispanic/Latina/o/x, 1.0% American Indian/Alaska Native, and 2.3% "other") who received CPT in a VA residential PTSD treatment program, suicidal ideation significantly decreased over the course of treatment, and this change did not differ based on race/ethnicity (Stayton et al., 2019). It is important to note, though, that for the purpose of multilevel modeling, race/ethnicity were condensed to White and non-White.

Comparatively, other studies have found differences in treatment outcomes between racial/ethnic groups. For example, Maguen et al. (2019) conducted an examination of factors related to initiation and completion of EBPs for PTSD, namely PE and CPT, over a 15-year period in over 260,000 Iraq and Afghanistan War veterans. Whereas 22.8% of the veterans with PTSD receiving mental health care initiated an EBP, less than 10% completed treatment; specifically, 1.9% completed PE, and 7.4% completed CPT. In examining race/ethnicity, veterans who completed PE were more likely to be Black than any other race (e.g., White, American Indian/Alaska Native, Asian, Native Hawaiian/Other Pacific Islander). It was also found that Black veterans were also more likely to receive PE sooner. While more research is needed to understand this finding, other research (Jeffreys et al., 2014) has found that Black veterans receiving PE had significant improvement in PTSD symptoms in contrast to other racial groups.

Additionally, in a national sample of 2,715 veterans (66.1% White, 25.9% Black, 2.1% American Indian/Alaskan, 2.2% Asian/Pacific Islander, and 3.7% "other"/of an unknown race; furthermore, 8.9% identified as Hispanic) engaged in VA residential PTSD treatment across the U.S., identifying as Black was one of the predictors of poor treatment response (Sripada et al., 2019). Also, using national data from VA PTSD residential treatment programs, Gross et al. (2021) examined symptom outcome differences between Black ($n = 834$) and White ($n = 2,036$) veterans. Black veterans experienced less PTSD symptom reduction during treatment and increased depressive symptom recurrence following discharge. In a large sample of VA patients across treatment setting (e.g., specialty clinics, outpatient) diagnosed with PTSD who were undergoing PE or CPT, White veterans were more likely to experience meaningful change (i.e., at least 50% reduction in PTSD symptoms) within the first eight sessions and subsequently (Sripada et al., 2020b). This suggests that BIPOC populations may need to have treatment enhanced or adapted to achieve meaningful change.

Treatment-Seeking, Access, Barriers, Preferences, Engagement, and Retention

While most of the research indicates that treatment outcomes for a range of mental health conditions do not differ by race or ethnicity, there are important mental health treatment disparities in racial and ethnic minority military service members and veterans (Goetter & Blackburn, 2019; Gross et al., 2021). This is consistent with research conducted on civilians, indicating that racial and ethnic minorities have lower rates of access and perceive more barriers to mental health treatment than non-minorities (Goetter & Blackburn, 2019).

Koo et al. (2015) examined the health-care utilization rates (i.e., primary care, mental health outpatient, emergency services) of 309,050 Afghanistan and Iraq veterans who had a least one psychiatric diagnosis and received care between 2001 and 2012. When looking at minority groupings collapsed and in comparison to White veterans, there were no significant differences. However, when the minority groupings were categorized separately (i.e., Black, Hispanic/Latinx, Asian/Pacific Islander, American Indian, multiracial), differences emerged. It was found that minority groups were admitted to inpatient care significantly less, with Black and Hispanic men the most affected. Notably, Asian/Pacific Islander veterans utilize emergency services less frequently. Additionally, whereas women utilized mental health outpatient services more than men, American Indian and Hispanic women underutilized this service. Furthermore, understanding access, utilization, and barriers at the intersection of diverse ethnoracial ADSMs and veteran groups is salient to creating culturally relevant care, mitigating barriers, and increasing engagement and retention. Moreover, the study methods highlight the importance of viewing ethnoracial groups as distinct cultural communities, avoiding overgeneralizing and perpetuating biases, and acquiring a nuanced and accurate understanding of treatment utilization of ethnoracial groups.

One way to increase engagement and outcomes might be to address racism. Racism is built on beliefs that one group of people is superior to another group (or groups) based on biological characteristics (e.g., color of skin, hair texture, and facial features). Due to White supremacy—the core of racism that indicates that White people are better than BIPOC people—White, as well as light-skinned people who may "pass" (or appear) as White, are given unearned privileges solely due to their race (Singh, 2019). To target racism, treatment providers should take an equitable approach to provide treatment for BIPOC populations. In other words, treatment should be provided for, as well as offered to, people who identify as Black, Hispanic, Asian/Pacific Islander, American Indian/Alaska Native, or multiracial when needed.

Moreover, treatment needs reciprocity, whereby relationships are forged by acknowledging power dynamics, understanding and discussing sociopolitical oppressions, giving attention to culture as a key aspect of treatment, and prioritizing the cultural/ethnoracial matching of provider and patient (see Goodman & Gorski, 2014).

Ways to Engage BIPOC ADSMs and Veterans in Mental Health Treatment

One of the most important and yet widely overlooked aspects of EBPs for treating PTSD among BIPOC is the role of the therapist. In an examination of the effect of clinician-veteran pairing in the treatment of PTSD, Black veterans had higher rates of early termination and received fewer psychotherapy sessions when treated by White providers (Rosenheck et al., 1995). This could be due to several variables, including social attitudes, racial discrimination, and internalized oppression. For example, one study (Eliacin et al., 2018) observed that Black veterans attune to cues in the treatment setting (e.g., culturally competent care, diversity, and inclusivity) with the lack thereof signaling the presence of racial biases. Black veterans reported perceiving more racial bias in treatment settings when there was little to no Black representation in visual arts displayed in clinical settings and fewer BIPOC providers. These perceptions are compounded by societal discriminatory views and assumptions based on race and personal moralized attributes (e.g., higher frequency of incarceration) that were upheld by health-care providers. Furthermore, discriminatory provider views are associated with poor treatment engagement and retention. However, there is a noteworthy disconnect between BIPOC patient perceptions and those of health care providers.

Recent survey research (Eliacin et al., 2019) with providers across three VA medical centers found that workforce diversity was viewed as not important to health-care equity within the treatment setting. Despite this belief, a systematic review (Hall et al., 2015) of 15 studies indicated that almost all providers given implicit association tests for implicit biases rated White patients more positively than people of color. However, even though there is a BIPOC preference for same-race providers, the broad mental health workforce in the VA and the Department of Defense and civilian sectors (e.g., psychologists, psychiatrists, social workers, marriage and family counselors) are predominately White.

In one study (Laska et al., 2013) concerning the evaluation of therapeutic skills, it was found that expert-level supervisor therapists were able to accurately identify successful therapists through interpersonal and supervisory interactions outside of the therapy room. Supervisors, without watching therapist sessions, were able to accurately rate therapist effectiveness as it correlated to therapeutic outcomes. Supervisors' ratings of successful therapists were deduced to the following four themes: (1) *reducing avoidance*: therapists were able to address client avoidance and be directive while also considering contextual client factors, (2) *language used in supervision*: therapists were able to receive feedback, be honest about their mistakes, and had high levels of self-awareness, (3) *flexible interpersonal style*: therapists were able to be open to flexing schedules and accommodate clients where they are and within their culture, and (4) *strong therapeutic alliance*: therapists were able to go beyond being supportive and were able to be a balanced mix of genuine, firm, and warm. The clients in the study were veterans from diverse wars, of different ages, and came from different backgrounds; however, salient therapist factors coupled with the use of EBP for PTSD were the keys to positive client outcomes.

Another way to expand care broadly, quickly, and effectively to underserved, underrepresented, and hard to access groups, such as individuals who are BIPOC, is through telehealth. Telehealth delivery is a feasible option to traditional office-based treatment overcoming several barriers and expanding access to care. An ethnically diverse sample of veterans with PTSD were asked to identify their modality preference for receiving PE (Ridings et al., 2019). There was no clear preference for one modality (i.e., home-based telehealth, office-based telehealth, or in-home-in-person), and each modality was preferred by at least a quarter of all veterans. In response to the COVID-19 pandemic, the VA rapidly implemented teletherapy for mental health services due to prior efforts and rollouts of this modality (Zhang et al., 2022). Teletherapy provided for continuity of care for severely mentally ill veterans and mitigated suicide attempt, overdose, and PTSD symptomology. A systematic review (Turgoose et al., 2018) of teletherapy for PTSD treatment (predominantly PE) among veterans observed that telehealth delivery was effective in decreasing PTSD symptomology, the therapeutic process was equal to in-person services or enhanced (e.g., satisfaction ratings), was cost-effective, and inevitably increased access.

Some BIPOC populations may prefer telehealth. For example, American Indian/Alaska Native veterans live in rural areas at a higher rate than all other veteran groups. In order to meet this gap, American Indian Telemental Health Clinics were developed over a 14-year period to facilitate accessible, person-centered, culturally congruent care for this population. Technology is used for mental and physical health care, cultural facilitation (including Native values, family, Indigenous healers, and related spiritual concepts), and care and benefit coordination to increase engagement and retention. The cornerstone of respect is used to build and increase provider-patient alliances, attend to past hurts and distrust with the Western medical system and U.S. government, and increase culture within treatments to address the whole person (mind, body, spirit) within the sociopolitical and historical context. Furthermore, successfully identifying relevant benefits/services and feeling more connected with one's provider and peers within the VA system are associated with a decrease in PTSD symptoms.

Future Directions for Research and Practice

There are several major limitations that need to be addressed to improve the research base as well as clinical practice, including inclusion and attention to psychiatric comorbidities, more nuanced breakdown of BIPOC populations, and the importance of intersectionality. Most research on ethnoracial differences among ADSMs and veterans, as well as civilians with PTSD, does not address comorbid psychiatric disorders, including substance use disorders (SUD). In a small RCT for 79 treatment-seeking veterans with SUDs and co-occurring PTSD, Black participants reported greater decreases in substance use during treatment, but greater increases during follow-up (Brown et al., 2020). Regarding PTSD symptoms, Black veterans reported higher PTSD severity than White counterparts at baseline; however, there were no significant differences in diagnostic remission for PTSD at the end of treatment. This study highlights the nuanced and potentially interactive nature of trauma and co-occurring issues that, when considered together, could lead to fuller case conceptualizations. A systematic approach and understanding of contextual factors contributing to symptoms, and targeted treatment that considers the interconnectivity in comorbid symptom changes, could contribute to more positive outcomes.

As stated earlier, most of the empirical literature focuses on treatment utilization and outcome differences between Black versus White participants, or by placing all individuals from BIPOC populations in one comparison condition. Doing this obfuscates any potential differences that may be there. With many racial and ethnic minorities in the military and veteran population, their unique trauma histories, additional stressors associated with racism and discrimination, clinical presentations, health concomitants and treatment needs, and preferences are imperative to document and address. Moreover, it is equally important that research includes BIPOC voices in the development, design, and interpretation of results as much as BIPOC communities need to be represented within treatment groups (Bharat et al., 2021).

Taken further, most of the studies that examine predictors or moderators of treatment outcome seem to examine the individual effects of sociodemographic categories (e.g., race/ethnicity, age, disability status, socioeconomic status, sexual orientation, and gender) as opposed to their intersectionality. An intersectional lens might yield more nuanced understanding and substantive findings. To provide quality mental health care to military and veteran populations, there should be a competent incorporation of culture. This might include religious and spiritual beliefs, acculturation, ethnic identity, cultural attitudes, and folk healing (Goss et al., 2017; Tseng & Streltzer, 2001) as well as competence in military or warrior culture (Zwiebach et al., 2019). Thus, cultural adaptations and treatment that considers the whole person within their context and culture are necessary for adequate and relevant PTSD treatment among BIPOC ADSMs and veterans.

References

Aronson, K. R., Welsh, J. A., Fedotova, A., Morgan, N. R., Perkins, D. F., & Travis, W. (2018). Treating PTSD in active-duty service members using cognitive processing therapy or prolonged exposure therapy: Examining everyday practice at a military outpatient clinic. *Military Psychology*, *30*(6), 465–475. https://doi.org/10.1080/08995605.2018.1478550

Asmundson, G. J. G., Thorisdottir, A. S., Roden-Foreman, J. W., Baird, S. O., Witcraft, S. M., Stein, A. T., Smits, J. A. J., & Powers, M. B. (2019). A meta-analytic review of cognitive processing therapy for adults with posttraumatic stress disorder. *Cognitive Behaviour Therapy*, *48*(1), 1–14. https://doi.org/10.1080/16506073.2018.1522371

Benuto, L. T., Bennett, N. M., & Casas, J. B. (2020). Minority participation in randomized controlled trials for prolonged exposure therapy: A systematic review of the literature. *Journal of Traumatic Stress*, *33*(4), 420–431. https://doi.org/10.1002/jts.22539

Bernardy, N. C., Hamblen, J. L., Friedman, M. J., Ruzek, J. I., & McFall, M. E. (2011). Implementation of a posttraumatic stress disorder mentoring program to improve treatment services. *Psychological Trauma: Theory, Research, Practice, and Policy*, *3*(3), 292–299. https://doi.org/10.1037/a0024847

Bharat, B., Chenneville, T., Gabbidon, K., & Foust, C. (2021). Considerations for psychological research with and for People of Color and oppressed intersecting identities in the United States. *Translational Issues in Psychological Science*. Advance online publication. https://doi.org/10.1037/tps0000285

Brown, D. G., Flanagan, J. C., Jarnecke, A., Killeen, T. K., & Back, S. E. (2020). Ethnoracial differences in treatment-seeking veterans with substance use disorders and co-occurring PTSD: Presenting characteristics and response to integrated exposure-based treatment. *Journal of Ethnicity in Substance Abuse*, *21*, 1141–1164. https://doi.org/10.1080/15332640.2020.1836699

Castro, F., AhnAllen, C. G., Wiltsey-Stirman, S., Lester-Williams, K., Klunk-Gillis, J., Dick, A. M., & Resick, P. A. (2015). African American and European American veterans' perspectives on receiving mental health treatment. *Psychological Services*, *12*(3), 330–338. https://doi.org/10.1037/a0038702

Chen, X., Yang, G., Tang, B., Liu, Y., Kang, P., Wang, M., & Zhang, L. (2015). A meta-analysis of risk factors for combat-related PTSD among military personnel and veterans. *PLoS One, 10*(3), e0120270. https://doi.org/10.1371/journal.pone.0120270

Coleman, J. A., Lynch, J. R., Ingram, K. M., Sheerin, C. M., Rappaport, L. M., & Trapp, S. K. (2018). Examination of racial differences in a posttraumatic stress disorder group therapy program for veterans. *Group Dynamics: Theory, Research, and Practice, 22*(3), 129–142. https://doi.org/10.1037/gdn0000086

Crouch, M. C., & Andrew, N. T. (2022). Strategies for inclusivity of American Indian and Alaska Native peoples in behavior therapy research: Within-group diversity, data, and ethical recommendations. *The Behavior Therapist, 45*(5), 168–174. https://www.abct.org/journals/the-behavior-therapist-journal/

Cusack, S. E., Coleman, J. A., Rappaport, L. M., & Sheerin, C. (2019). Moderation of improvement in self-efficacy following group psychotherapy for PTSD. *Psychological Services, 6*(4), 657–663. https://doi.org/10.1037/ser0000260

Department of Defense. (2019). *2019 Demographics profile of the military community.* https://download.militaryonesource.mil/12038/MOS/Reports/2019-demographics-report.pdf

Department of Defense. (2020). *Department of Defense board on diversity and inclusion report.* https://media.defense.gov/2020/Dec/18/2002554852/-1/-1/0/DOD-DIVERSITY-AND-INCLUSION-FINAL-BOARD-REPORT.PDF

Department of Veterans Affairs. (2008). *Uniform mental health services in VA medical centers and clinics (VHA handbook 1160.01).* Veterans Health Administration.

Dohrenwend, B. P., Turner, J. B., Turse, N. A., Lewis-Fernandez, R., & Yager, T. J. (2008). War-related posttraumatic stress disorder in Black, Hispanic, and majority White Vietnam veterans: The roles of exposure and vulnerability. *Journal of Traumatic Stress, 21*(2), 133–141. https://doi.org/10.1002/jts.20327

Dursa, E. K., Reinhard, M. J., Barth, S. K., & Schneiderman, A. I. (2014). Prevalence of a positive screen for PTSD among OEF/OIF and OEF/OIF-era veterans in a large population-based cohort. *Journal of Traumatic Stress, 27*(5), 542–549. https://doi.org/10.1002/jts.21956

Eliacin, J., Coffing, J. M., Matthias, M. S., Burgess, D. J., Bair, M. J., & Rollins, A. L. (2018). The relationship between race, patient activation, and working alliance: Implications for patient engagement in mental health care. *Administration and Policy in Mental Health and Mental Health Services Research, 45*(1), 186–192. https://doi.org/10.1007/s10488-016-0779-5

Eliacin, J., Cunningham, B., Partin, M. R., Gravely, A., Taylor, B. C., Gordon, H. S., Saha, S., & Burgess, D. J. (2019). Veterans Affairs providers' beliefs about the contributors to and responsibility for reducing racial and ethnic health care disparities. *Health Equity, 3*(1), 436–448. https://doi.org/10.1089/heq.2019.0018

Foa, E., Hembree, E., Rothbaum, B. O., & Rauch, S. (2019). *Prolonged exposure therapy for PTSD: Emotional processing of traumatic experiences therapist guide.* Oxford University Press.

Gersons, P. R. B., Meewisse, M., & Nijdam, M. J. (2015). Brief eclectic psychotherapy for PTSD. In Schnyder, U. & Cloitre, M. (Eds.), *Evidence-based treatments for trauma-related psychological disorders.* Springer International Publishing.

Ghafoori, B., & Khoo, S. F. (2020). A pilot study of racial and ethnic differences in mental health outcomes during the first 6 weeks of trauma-focused treatment. *Community Mental Health Journal, 56*(8), 1592–1602. https://doi.org/10.1007/s10597-020-00620-9

Goetter, E. M., & Blackburn, A. M. (2019). Mental health treatment disparities in racial and ethnic minority military service members and veterans. In Williams, M. T., Rosen, D. C., & Kanter, J. W. (Eds.), *Eliminating race-based mental health disparities: Promoting equity and culturally responsive care across settings* (pp. 307–325). Context Press/New Harbinger Publications.

Goodman, R. D., & Gorski, P. C. (2014). *Decolonizing multicultural counseling through social justice*. Springer.

Goss, C. W., Richardson, W. J., Dailey, N., Bair, B., Nagamoto, H., Manson, S. M., & Shore, J. H. (2017). Rural American Indian and Alaska Native veterans' telemental health: A model of culturally centered care. *Psychological Services, 14*(3), 270–278. https://doi.org/10.1037/ser0000149

Goss, C., Richardson, W., & Shore, J. (2019). Outcomes and lessons learned from the Tribal Veterans Representative Program: A model for system engagement. *Journal of Community Health, 44*, 1076–1085. https://doi.org/10.1007/s10900-019-00683-0

Gross, G., Smith, N., Holliday, R., Rozek, D., Hoff, R., & Harpaz-Rotem, I. (2021). Racial disparities in clinical outcomes of veterans affairs residential PTSD treatment between black and white veterans. *Psychiatric Services*. Advance online publication. https://doi.org/10.1176/appi.ps.202000783

Guideline Development Panel for the Treatment of PTSD in Adults, American Psychological Association. (2019). Summary of the clinical practice guideline for the treatment of posttraumatic stress disorder (PTSD) in adults. *The American Psychologist, 74*(5), 596–607. https://doi.org/10.1037/amp0000473596

Hall, W. J., Chapman, M. V., Lee, K. M., Merino, Y. M., Thomas, T. W., Payne, B. K., Eng, E., Day, S. H., & Coyne-Beasley, T. (2015). Implicit racial/ethnic bias among health care professionals and its influence on health care outcomes: A systematic review. *American Journal of Public Health, 105*(12), e60–e76. https://doi.org/10.2105/AJPH.2015.302903

Haller, M., Myers, U. S., McKnight, A., Angkaw, A. C., & Norman, S. B. (2016). Predicting engagement in psychotherapy, pharmacotherapy, or both psychotherapy and pharmacotherapy among returning veterans seeking PTSD treatment. *Psychological Services, 13*(4), 341–348. https://doi.org/10.1037/ser0000093

Hamblen, J. L., Norman, S. B., Sonis, J. H., Phelps, A. J., Bisson, J. I., Nunes, V. D., Megnin-Viggars, O., Forbes, D., Riggs, D. S., & Schnurr, P. P. (2019). A guide to guidelines for the treatment of posttraumatic stress disorder in adults: An update. *Psychotherapy, 56*(3), 359–373. https://doi.org/10.1037/pst0000231

Hansford, M., & Jobson, L. (2022). Sociocultural context and the posttraumatic psychological response: Considering culture, social support, and posttraumatic stress disorder. *Psychological Trauma, 14*(4), 669–679. https://doi.org/10.1037/tra0001009

Hebenstreit, C. L., Madden, E., Koo, K. H., & Maguen, S. (2015). Minimally adequate mental health care and latent classes of PTSD symptoms in female Iraq and Afghanistan veterans. *Psychiatry Research, 230*, 90–95. https://doi.org/10.1016/j.psychres.2015.08.028

Holliday, R. P., Holder, N. D., Williamson, M. L. C., & Suris, A. (2017). Therapeutic response to cognitive processing therapy in White and Black female veterans with military sexual trauma-related PTSD. *Cognitive Behaviour Therapy, 46*(5), 432–446. https://doi.org/10.1080/16506073.2017.1312511

Jeffreys, M. D., Reinfeld, C., Nair, P. V., Garcia, H. A., Mata-Galan, E., & Rentz, T. O. (2014). Evaluating treatment of posttraumatic stress disorder with cognitive processing therapy and prolonged exposure therapy in a VHA specialty clinic. *Journal of Anxiety Disorders, 28*(1), 108–114. https://doi.org/10.1016/j.janxdis.2013.04.010

Johfre, S. S., & Freese, J. (2021). Reconsidering the reference category. *Sociological Methodology, 51*(2), 253–269. https://doi.org/10.1177/0081175020982632

Johnson, D. R., & Lubin, H. (1997). Treatment preferences of Vietnam veterans with posttraumatic stress disorder. *Journal of Traumatic Stress, 10*(3), 391–405. https://doi.org/10.1023/A:1024885103409

Kaczkurkin, A. N., Asnaani, A., Hall-Clark, B., Peterson, A. L., Yarvis, J. S., Foa, E. B., & STRONG STAR Consortium. (2016). Ethnic and racial differences in clinically relevant symptoms in active duty military personnel with posttraumatic stress disorder. *Journal of Anxiety Disorders, 43*, 90–98. https://doi.org/10.1016/j.janxdis.2016.09.004

Karlin, B. E., Ruzek, J. I., Chark, K. M., Eftekhari, A., Monson, C. M., Hembree, E. A., Resick, P. A., & Foa, E. B. (2010). Dissemination of evidence-based psychological treatment for posttraumatic disorder in the Veterans Health Administration. *Journal of Traumatic Stress, 23*(6), 663–673. https://doi.org/10.1002/jts.20588

Karlin, B. E., & Cross, G. (2014). From the laboratory to the therapy room: National dissemination and implementation of evidence-based psychotherapies in the U.S. Department of Veterans Affairs Health Care System. *American Psychologist, 69*(1), 19–33. https://doi.org/10.1037/a0033888

Kline, A. C., Feeny, N. C., & Zoellner, L. A. (2020). Race and cultural factors in an RCT of exposure and sertraline for PTSD. *Behaviour Research and Therapy, 132*, 103690. https://doi.org/10.1016/j.brat.2020.103690

Koo, K. H., Madden, E., & Maguen, S. (2015). Race-ethnicity and gender differences in VA health care service utilization among U.S. veterans of recent conflicts. *Psychiatric Services, 66*(5), 507–513. https://doi.org/10.1176/appi.ps.201300498

Koo, K. H., Hebenstreit, C. L., Madden, E., & Maguen, S. (2016). PTSD detection and symptom presentation: Racial/ethnic differences by gender among veterans with PTSD returning from Iraq and Afghanistan. *Journal of Affective Disorders, 189*, 10–16. https://doi.org/10.1016/j.jad.2015.08.038

Laska, K. M., Smith, T. L., Wislocki, A. P., Minami, T., & Wampold, B. E. (2013). Uniformity of evidence-based treatments in practice? Therapist effects in the delivery of cognitive processing therapy for PTSD. *Journal of Counseling Psychology, 60*(1), 31–41. https://doi.org/10.1037/a0031294

Lester, K., Artz, C., Resick, P. A., & Young-Xu, Y. (2010). Impact of race on early treatment termination and outcomes in posttraumatic stress disorder treatment. *Journal of Consulting and Clinical Psychology, 78*(4), 480–489. https://doi.org/10.1037/a0019551

Loo, C. M. (n.d.). *PTSD among ethnic minority veterans*. US Department of Veteran Affairs. https://www.ptsd.va.gov/professional/treat/type/ethnic_minority_vets.asp

Maguen, S., Madden, E., Neylan, T. C., Cohen, B. E., Bertenthal, D., & Seal, K. H. (2014). Timing of mental health treatment and PTSD symptom improvement among Iraq and Afghanistan veterans. *Psychiatric Services, 65*(12), 1414–1419. https://doi.org/10.1176/appi.ps.201300453

Maguen, S., Li, Y., Madden, E., Seal, K. H., Neylan, T. C., Patterson, O. V., DuVall, S. L., Lujan, C., & Shiner, B. (2019). Factors associated with completing evidence-based psychotherapy for PTSD among veterans in a national healthcare system. *Psychiatry Research, 274*, 112–128. https://doi.org/10.1016/j.psychres.2019.02.027

McClendon, J., Perkins, D., Copeland, L. A., Finley, E. P., & Vogt, D. (2019). Patterns and correlates of racial/ethnic disparities in posttraumatic stress disorder screening among recently separated veterans. *Journal of Anxiety Disorders, 68*, 102145. https://doi.org/10.1016/j.janxdis.2019.102145

Muralidharan, A., Austern, D., Hack, S., & Vogt, D. (2016). Deployment experiences, social support, and mental health: Comparison of Black, White, and Hispanic U.S. veterans deployed to Afghanistan and Iraq. *Journal of Traumatic Stress, 29*(3), 273–278. https://doi.org/10.1002/jts.22104

National Center for Veterans Analysis and Statistics. (2018). *Veteran population projections 2020-2040.* https://www.va.gov/vetdata/docs/Demographics/New_Vetpop_Model/Vetpop_Infographic2020.pdf

Nichter, B., Haller, M., Norman, S., & Pietrzak, R. H. (2020). Risk and protective factors associated with comorbid PTSD and depression in U.S. military veterans: Results from the national health and resilience in veterans' study. *Journal of Psychiatric Research, 121,* 56–61. https://doi.org/10.1016/j.jpsychires.2019.11.008

Resick, P. A., Monson, M. C., & Chard, C. M. (2016). *Cognitive processing therapy for PTSD: A comprehensive manual.* Guilford Press.

Ridings, L. E., Moreland, A. D., Petty, K. H. (2019). Implementing trauma-focused CBT for children of veterans in the VA: Providing comprehensive services to veterans and their families. *Psychological Services, 16*(1), 75–84.

Roberge, E. M., Weinstein, H. R., & Bryan, C. J. (2019). Predicting response to cognitive processing therapy: Does trauma history matter? *Psychological Trauma: Theory, Research, Practice, and Policy.* Advance online publication. https://doi.org/10.1037/tra0000530

Rosenheck, R., Fontana, A., & Cottrol, C. (1995). Effect of clinician-veteran racial pairing in the treatment of posttraumatic stress disorder. *American Journal of Psychiatry, 152*(4), 555–563. https://doi.org/10.1176/ajp.152.4.555

Saha, S., Freeman, M., Toure, J., Tippens, K. M., Weeks, C., & Ibrahim, S. (2008). Racial and ethnic disparities in the VA health care system: A systematic review. *Journal of General Internal Medicine, 23*(5), 654–671. https://doi.org/10.1007/s11606-008-0521-4

Schauer, M., Neuner, F., & Elbert, T. (2011). *Narrative exposure therapy* (2nd ed.). Hogrefe.

Schnurr, P. P., Chard, K. M., Ruzek, J. I., Chow, B. K., Resick, P. A., Foa, E. B., Marx, B. P., Friedman, M. J., Bovin, M. J., Caudle, K. L., Castillo, D., Curry, K. T., Hollifield, M., Huang, G. D., Chee, C. L., Astin, M. C., Dickstein, B., Renner, K., Clancy, C. P., & Shih, M. (2022). Comparison of prolonged exposure vs cognitive processing therapy for treatment of posttraumatic stress disorder among US veterans: A randomized clinical trial. *JAMA Network Open, 5*(1), e2136921. https://doi.org/10.1001/jamanetworkopen.2021.36921

Schulz, P. M., Resick, P. A., Huber, L. C., & Griffin, M. G. (2006). The effectiveness of cognitive processing therapy for PTSD with refugees in a community setting. *Cognitive and Behavioral Practice, 13*(4), 322–331. https://doi.org/10.1016/j.cbpra.2006.04.011

Schumm, J. A., Walter, K. H., & Chard, K. M. (2013). Latent class differences explain variability in PTSD symptom changes during cognitive processing therapy for veterans. *Psychological Trauma: Theory, Research, Practice, and Policy, 5*(6), 536–544. https://doi.org/10.1037/a0030359

Shapiro, F. (2017). *Eye movement desensitization and reprocessing (EMDR) therapy: Basic principles, protocols and procedures.* (3rd ed.). The Guilford Press.

Singh, A. A. (2019). *The racial healing handbook: Practical activities to help you challenge privilege, confront systemic racism & engage in collective healing.* New Harbinger Publications.

Spoont, M. R., Hodges, J., Murdoch, M., & Nugent, S. (2009). Race and ethnicity as factors in mental health service use among veterans with PTSD. *Journal of Traumatic Stress, 22*(6), 648–653. https://doi.org/10.1002/jts.20470

Spoont, M. R., Nelson, D. B., Murdoch, M., Sayer, N. A., Nugent, S., Rector, T., & Westermeyer, J. (2015). Are there racial/ethnic disparities in VA PTSD treatment retention? *Depression and Anxiety, 32*(6), 415–425. https://doi.org/10.1002/da.22295

Spoont, M. R., Sayer, N. A., Kehle-Forbes, S. M., Meis, L. A., & Nelson, D. B. (2017). A prospective study of racial and ethnic variation in VA psychotherapy services for PTSD. *Psychiatric Services, 68*(3), 231–237. https://doi.org/10.1176/appi.ps.201600086

Sripada, R. K., Blow, F. C., Rauch, S. A. M., Ganoczy, D., Hoff, R., Harpaz-Rotem, I., & Bohnert, K. M. (2019). Examining the nonresponse phenomenon: Factors associated with treatment response in a national sample of veterans undergoing residential PTSD treatment. *Journal of Anxiety Disorders, 63*, 18–25. https://doi.org/10.1016/j.janxdis.2019.02.001

Sripada, R. K., Pfeiffer, P. N., Rampton, J., Ganoczy, D., Rauch, S. A., Polusny, M. A., & Bohnert, K. M. (2017). Predictors of PTSD symptom change among outpatients in the U.S. Department of Veterans Affairs Health Care *System, 30*(1), 45–53.

Sripada, R. K., Hoff, R., Pfeiffer, P. N., Ganoczy, D., Blow, F. C., & Bohnert, K. M. (2020a). Latent classes of PTSD symptoms in veterans undergoing residential PTSD treatment. *Psychological Services, 17*(1), 84–92. https://doi.org/10.1037/ser0000284

Sripada, R. K., Ready, D. J., Ganoczy, D., Astin, M. C., & Rauch, S. (2020b). When to change the treatment plan: An analysis of diminishing returns in VA patients undergoing prolonged exposure and cognitive processing therapy. *Behavior Therapy, 51*(1), 85–98. https://doi.org/10.1016/j.beth.2019.05.003

Stayton, L. E., Martin, C. E., Pease, J. L., & Chard, K. M. (2019). Changes in suicidal ideation following cognitive processing therapy in a VA residential treatment program. *Military Psychology, 31*(4), 326–334. https://doi.org/10.1080/08995605.2019.1630230

Steenkamp, M. M., & Litz, B. T. (2013). Psychotherapy for military-related posttraumatic stress disorder: Review of the evidence. *Clinical Psychology Review, 33*, 45–53. https://doi.org/10.1016/j.cpr.2012.10.002

Tseng, W. S., & Streltzer, J. (2001). *Culture and psychotherapy: A guide to clinical practice.* American Psychiatric Publishing.

Turgoose, D., Ashwick, R., & Murphy, D. (2018). Systematic review of lessons learned from delivering tele-therapy to veterans with post-traumatic stress disorder. *Journal of Telemedicine and Telecare, 24*(9), 575–585. https://doi.org/10.1177/1357633X17730443

Zhang, J., Boden, M., & Trafton, J. (2022). Mental health treatment and the role of telemental health at the veterans health administration during the COVID-19 pandemic. *Psychological Services, 19*(2), 375–385. https://doi.org/10.1037/ser0000530

Zoellner, L. A., Feeny, N. C., Fitzgibbons, L. A., & Foa, E. B. (1999). Response of African American and Caucasian women to cognitive behavioral therapy for PTSD. *Behavior Therapy, 30*(4), 581–595. https://doi.org/10.1016/S0005-7894(99)80026-4

Zwiebach, L., Lannert, B. K., Sherrill, A. M., McSweeney, L. B., Sprang, K., Goodnight, J. R., Lewis, S. C., & Rauch, S. A. M. (2019). Military cultural competence in the context of Cognitive Behavioural Therapy. *The Cognitive Behaviour Therapist, 12*(e5), 1–13. https://doi.org/10.1017/S1754470X18000132

Alcohol and Substance Abuse Services for Active-Duty Service Members and Veterans

Jeremiah A. Schumm, Anthony R. Kelemen, and Lily K. Taplin

Introduction

Substance use disorders (SUDs) are characterized by continued use of alcohol or other drugs, despite experiencing repeated, detrimental consequences related to the substance use (American Psychiatric Association, 2013). Data from the 2019 National Survey of Drug Use and Health (Substance Abuse and Mental Health Services Administration, 2020) found that 1.3 million veterans (6.2%) had SUDs. Among those with SUDs, alcohol use disorder (AUD) was more prevalent (80.8%) versus other drug use disorder (26.9%). Between 2016 and 2019, past year rates of AUD were higher for veterans age 25 or younger (9.1–14.8%) versus those who were age 26 or older (3.9–5.0%; Substance Abuse and Mental Health Services Administration, 2020). During this same time period, those 25 or younger had higher rates of opioid medication

DOI: 10.4324/9781003185949-6

misuse (6.0–10.1%) and cannabis use disorder (1.2–4.3%) versus those who were 26 or older (opioid pain misuse = 2.3–3.3%; cannabis use disorder = 0.5–0.9%). In summary, these prevalence data show that SUDs, particular alcohol use disorder, are prevalent among veterans and active duty service members (ADSMs) Therefore, it is important that clinicians are familiar with first-line psychological approaches for addressing these conditions.

Prior to turning our attention to first-line psychological treatments for SUDs, it is important to acknowledge the role of medication-based treatments for SUDs. Department of Veterans Affairs/Department of Defense (2021) guidelines strongly recommend naltrexone and topiramate for the treatment of moderate to severe AUD. These medications help to reduce cravings for alcohol, thereby leading to reductions in heavy drinking among those with moderate to severe AUD. In addition, opioid agonists including buprenorphine/naloxone and methadone are shown to be effective for treating opioid use disorder (OUD) by blocking the opioid neuroreceptors, and these medications are strongly recommended for the treatment of OUD. The guidelines found that there was not enough evidence to recommend for or against medications for the treatment of other SUDs. In summary, medications are strongly recommended for veterans and ADSMs who exhibit moderate to severe AUD or opioid use disorder, and they can be delivered alongside of psychological treatments for SUDs.

First-Line Psychological Treatments

There are various first-line psychological treatments that have been suggested and recommended for veterans/ADSMs with SUDs (Department of Veterans Affairs/Department of Defense, 2021). These approaches are diverse in their theoretical and conceptual underpinnings, thereby providing a range of options that can be matched to patients' needs and preferences.

Motivational Enhancement Therapy

Motivational enhancement therapy (MET) was developed by William Miller and colleagues and is a four-session treatment largely based on motivational interviewing (MI). The principles of MI have been rigorously studied and have been shown to be efficacious in brief interventions for alcohol misuse (Vasilaki et al., 2006). Although MI is broader, MET was specifically developed to "produce rapid, internally motivated change" in those who struggle with alcohol addiction (Miller et al., 1995). The MET therapist is supportive and nonconfrontational, and assumes the client has their own capacity for change. The therapist's role is to use MI skills to help the client realize their own motivation and commitment.

MET is divided into three phases: building motivation for change, strengthening the commitment to change, and follow-through strategies (Miller et al., 1995). Additionally, MET is generally intended to take place over four structured sessions with some assessment measures administered before the initial session as outlined in the manual. The initial session preferably involves the client's significant other or dedicated support person, and it is spent reviewing the results of any assessment measures given and providing education on therapist and client roles and responsibilities. Additionally, the initial session generally aims to begin eliciting motivation for change, or phase 1, using motivational interviewing skills. After motivation for change is elicited, the goal then shifts toward commitment to change, or phase 2. Session 2 generally begins with a review of session 1, and then the client and therapist pick up where they left off to continue moving through the phases of treatment. Once commitment to change is established, therapy then focuses on follow-through, which involves reviewing the client's progress and revisiting phase 1 and phase 2 if needed to discuss the client's motivation, commitment, and plans to reach their goals. Sessions 3 and 4 are booster sessions ideally focused on follow-though. Session 3 is typically scheduled for week 6, and session 4 is typically scheduled for week 12. Overall, MET is a manualized but flexible treatment that is designed to bring about change in individuals with alcohol addiction in only four sessions.

MET is suggested for veterans/ADSMs with alcohol use disorder and cannabis use disorder (Department of Veterans Affairs/Department of Defense, 2021). With MET being both brief and effective for these disorders, it can be especially useful when longer-term or frequent sessions are not feasible. This approach may also be preferred for individuals who are have lower motivation for changing their alcohol use (Witkiewitz et al., 2010) and for those who exhibit higher levels of anger (Project MATCH Research Group, 1998). Regarding best practices for implementing MET with marginalized groups of veterans and ADSMs, research is very limited and greatly needed. However, decades of research suggest MI can be used and culturally adapted to meet the needs of a wide range of individuals with different diversity variables. A meta-analysis by Lundahl et al. (2010) included 119 studies and concluded that "MI may be particularly attractive to groups who have experienced social rejection and societal pressure" (p. 153). A more recent systematic review has also found that cultural adaptations have been successful in enhancing MI for marginalized racial/ethnic groups (Self et al., 2023. Overall, being grounded in MI principles, MET is inherently person-centered and can be tailored to meet the needs of individuals from many different backgrounds.

Cognitive-Behavioral Therapy

Cognitive-behavioral therapy (CBT) focuses on helping individuals to identify and change ways of thinking and behavioral patterns that increase risk for substance use problems, while developing skills that promote abstinence and reduce problematic substance use. CBT is based upon social learning theory models and assumes that cognitive and behavioral patterns relevant to substance use are derived from modeling as well as operant and classical conditions principles. Although there are multiple CBT protocols for targeting various SUDs (cf., Carroll, 1998; Kadden et al., 2003), they share many common elements. They are skills-oriented and teach clients ways of addressing psychological and emotional barriers to sobriety (e.g., coping with difficult emotions that trigger urges to use, managing cravings). CBT protocols use behavioral rehearsal or worksheets to help individuals to gain these skills. They also teach skills to help individuals navigate interpersonal challenges relevant to recovery (e.g., assertiveness and refusal of others' offers for alcohol or drugs). A common strategy is to engage patients in role play as a strategy for developing these skills. In addition, CBT protocols help clients engage in a functional analysis to understand environmental triggers, cognitive-emotional states, and behavioral responses that result in substance use. Individuals learn skills for coping with relapses and teach ways for them to move forward in their recovery following relapses. CBT protocols vary in length and typically involve at least 12 sessions.

CBT is well-researched for multiple SUDs. It is suggested for veterans/ADSMs who exhibit alcohol use disorder (Department of Veterans Affairs/Department of Defense, 2021). The Project MATCH study found that it worked better for those with less severe alcohol use disorder and lower levels of anger (Project MATCH Research Group, 1998). CBT is also suggested for veterans/ADSMs with cannabis use disorder, and it is recommended for those with cocaine use disorder (Department of Veterans Affairs/Department of Defense, 2021). In non-veteran samples, there is promising evidence for the efficacy of culturally adapted CBT (Paris et al., 2018) and CBT that incorporates mindfulness-based practices for people of color (Dela Cruz et al., 2022); however, more research is needed on these CBT–based therapies for veterans and ADSMs with SUDs.

Community Reinforcement Approach

The community reinforcement approach (CRA) was developed in the 1970s and is based on concepts of operant conditioning (Meyers et al., 2011). This multidimensional, comprehensive treatment was originally developed to target alcohol misuse utilizing what is known about behavior modification through reinforcement. Around the time of its creation, both behaviorist B. F. Skinner and the creator of CRA, Nate Azrin, saw reinforcement (as opposed to punishment) as a preferred and powerful approach to increasing desirable behaviors and eliminating undesirable behaviors. Accordingly, CRA aims to help individuals develop a fulfilling lifestyle and environment that reinforces sobriety more than it reinforces drug and alcohol use. Clinicians utilizing CRA ultimately work toward the "elimination of positive reinforcement for drinking" and the "enhancement of positive reinforcement for sobriety" (Miller et al., 1999, p. 117).

CRA is quite flexible and can be modified to fit the needs of the individual. However, CRA involves several components: CRA functional analysis, sobriety sampling, CRA treatment planning, behavior skills training, job skills, social/recreational counseling, relapse prevention, and relationship counseling (Meyers et al., 2005). Initially, a functional analysis is used to clarify what triggers substance use (antecedents), what substance is used, how much is used, and when it is used, as well as the short-term positive and long-term negative consequences (Meyers et al., 2011). Sobriety sampling involves a client-clinician agreement in which the client will abstain from substance use for a specific amount of time so the client can experience it as a trial with the goal of learning skills and working toward longer periods of abstinence. The CRA treatment plan traditionally involves the happiness scale and goals of counseling forms that give the client a way to assess their life satisfaction in different areas and then come up with measurable goals and ways to achieve those goals (Meyers et al., 2005). Behavior skills training includes problem-solving skills, communication skills, and drink/drug refusal training. Jobs skills training involves helping the client obtain and maintain employment, which reinforces a sober lifestyle. Social and recreational counseling involves helping the client build an enjoyable social life that is highly reinforcing yet free of harmful substance misuse. Relapse prevention helps clients to gain the skills they need in order to navigate through situations that might lead to relapse. Finally, relationship counseling aims to help the client improve their relationship with their significant other if they have one. Overall, CRA is an effective evidence-based treatment that is flexible and comprehensive, helping individuals improve general problem areas, relationships, and social and occupational aspects of their lives, and work toward building skills that will allow them to create a life that reinforces long-term sobriety.

CRA is suggested for veterans/ADSMs with alcohol use disorder (Department of Veterans Affairs/Department of Defense, 2021). Given the attention to social and environmental influence CRA has, this approach may be favorable when working with veterans/ADSMs considering the military's strong cultural influence on alcohol misuse (Meadows et al., 2022). Additionally, CRA may be a good choice for clinicians and clients who prefer a nonconfrontational style as the client is encouraged to make the argument for change and small changes and efforts are highly praised (Miller et al., 1999). An internet-based version of CRA was found to have higher acceptability and to promote more improved comping among racial and ethnic minority individuals versus White individuals (Campbell et al., 2017). CRA appears to work best in conjunction with contingency management (Department of Veterans Affairs/Department of Defense, 2021), which is described next.

Contingency Management

Contingency management (CM) is a treatment that, like CRA, is based on operant conditioning and is a highly effective treatment for alcohol and substance use disorders (Higgins and Petry, 1999). Additionally, it is cost effective and is strongly supported by an abundance of research (McPherson et al., 2018). What is unique about CM is that it typically involves some sort of tangible reinforcement, such as money, vouchers, or something else that is valuable or meaningful. Those receiving treatment for alcohol or substance use disorders would be rewarded for their abstinence, medication compliance, and attendance. However, the rewards would be withheld whenever the person does not stick to their target behaviors. In other words, their receiving rewards is contingent on them successfully sticking to their treatment goals. It is common and, in many cases, preferred to combine CM with CRA as research has shown that both can be highly effective when used together (Meyers et al., 2011; Higgins and Petry, 1999).

CM is suggested for veterans/ADSMs with alcohol use disorder (Department of Veterans Affairs/Department of Defense, 2021). In 2011, the VA health-care system took steps to implement CM training practice among its providers on a nationwide level (Petry et al., 2014). Regarding the implementation of CRA with or without CM specifically with marginalized groups of veterans and ADSMs, research is extremely limited. However, a large study that examined gender and racial differences among adolescents found that the CRA treatment process and outcomes were similar across gender and racial groups (Godley et al., 2011). Overall, clinicians are encouraged to be flexible and collaborative so that elements of CRA/CM are adapted to be most relevant and effective for the individual.

Behavioral Couple Therapy

Behavioral couple therapy (BCT) uses intimate partner relationships to build and sustain support for sobriety while simultaneously working to improve intimate partner relationship functioning. BCT assumes a bidirectional association between substance use problems and relationship functioning, such that substance use problems can worsen relationship functioning while relationship problems can worsen substance use. Consistent with these assumptions, research has shown that substance use problems are associated with worse relationship functioning (Marshal, 2003) and greater likelihood of dissolution (Cranford, 2014). Furthermore, relationship hostility and aggression predict worse substance use problems and relapse (Fairbairn & Cranford, 2016).

BCT protocols were developed by Barbara McCrady (McCrady et al., 2016) and Timothy O'Farrell (O'Farrell, 1993). The protocol by McCrady initially focuses on sobriety-focused skills building for the individual with the SUD. The protocol by O'Farrell initially focuses on a couple recovery contract for helping the partner with the SUD to achieve sobriety. Both protocols utilize reinforcement-based principles to promote sobriety and improve relationship functioning. For example, BCT therapists help couples to plan and follow through with non-substance-related, shared rewarding activities that are enjoyable to both partners (e.g., planning a date to go to the movies). Couples also learn the strategy "catch your partner doing something nice" as a way of noticing and reinforcing the opposite partner's pleasing behaviors. Both protocols also teach communication skills training and problem solving. A relapse prevention plan and plan for responding to relapse if it occurs is developed as the couple ends BCT.

Typically, BCT includes 12–24 sessions using a one-couple-at-a-time delivery format. However, the protocol can be delivered in group format. BCT is compatible with other SUD treatments, including being delivered as part of a multicomponent treatment composed of BCT plus individual or group therapy and recovery medication. Schumm and Renno (2021) describe practical guidance and considerations in delivering BCT in everyday clinical settings and considerations when delivering BCT through telehealth.

BCT is recommended for veterans/ADSMs with alcohol use disorder (Department of Veterans Affairs/Department of Defense, 2021). BCT is well established as part of a multicomponent treatment package, and has evidence for its efficacy as a standalone intervention (Hogue et al., 2021). Some of the earliest research on BCT was conducted in VA clinics (cf., O'Farrell & Cutter, 1984). Subsequent randomized controlled trials have shown that BCT produces superior substance use and relationship outcomes over other bone fide psychotherapies for alcohol use disorder (Hogue et al., 2021).

Twelve-Step-Oriented Therapy

Twelve-step-oriented therapy is a widely practiced form of SUD psychotherapy that has been manualized and described in protocols used in the Project MATCH study for individuals with alcohol use disorder (Nowinski et al., 1999) and the NIDA collaborative cocaine study (Mercer & Woody, 1999). The term "12-step" is derived from the traditional 12 steps to recovery that were originally described by the founders of Alcoholics Anonymous (AA). This approach conceptualizes SUDs as diseases and teaches clients to think about SUDs as having an allergy to the addictive substance or a chronic medical condition that causes severe negative reactions to these substances. Therefore, 12-step therapies promote abstinence from substances. They strongly encourage clients to engage in mutual help groups such as AA and Narcotics Anonymous (NA) and to find an AA or NA sponsor to help them in working through the 12 steps of recovery. The sponsors are themselves in recovery and thus provide a peer-based source of recovery support. The AA and NA groups provide additional sources of sober support. The therapy is skills focused and has some overlap with CBT in its teaching behavioral strategies that promote recovery (e.g., coping with cravings, structuring one's time with activities that are incompatible with substance use). However, 12-step therapy is unique in that therapists are familiar with the 12 steps and can help clients in working through these. The traditions of AA and NA are based in a religious, Christian-oriented approach to acknowledging God as a higher power and religious and spiritual practice is emphasized as an important element to recovery. A study by Timko et al. (2006) found that veterans who were engaged in religious practice were more likely to attend AA and endorse acceptance of AA philosophy. Therefore, 12-step may be a good fit for veterans/ADSMs for whom being a Christian is an important identity variable, and it may not be a good fit for individuals who are non-Christian or otherwise not religious. AA and NA are grassroots organizations and more recently groups have formed in AA and NA traditions that do not emphasize Christianity or spirituality and instead encourage individuals to define their own "higher power" as something that is personally meaningful to them when working through the 12 steps.

Research on 12-step–oriented approaches supports their efficacy in treating SUDs. The Department of Veterans Affairs/Department of Defense (2021) suggests that 12-step facilitation should be considered for veterans/ADSMs with alcohol use disorder. A Cochrane Review of AA and 12-step facilitation concluded with a high certainty of evidence that this approach produces more continuous days of abstinence than MET or CBT (Kelly et al., 2020). The Project MATCH study (Project MATCH Research Group, 1998) found that 12-step facilitation was superior to MET and CBT for individuals who exhibit more severe alcohol problems and had support systems that exhibited more support for drinking. This suggests that AA and 12-step facilitation may be preferred for veterans/ADSMs who have worse alcohol problems and who are involved in social systems that exhibit high support for drinking. In addition, the Department of Veterans Affairs/Department of Defense (2021) recommends individual drug counseling, which is the 12-step–oriented manualized approach from the NIDA collaborative cocaine study (Mercer & Woody, 1999), for veterans/ADSMs with cocaine use disorder. Finally, 12-step facilitation is recommended for veterans/ADSMs following relapse or who are in early recovery as a way to encourage mutual help group involvement (Department of Veterans Affairs/Department of Defense, 2021).

Unique Challenges

It is important to consider ways in which military culture and demographics impact substance misuse and SUDs among veterans and ADSMs. Approximately half (53.8%) of younger military personnel have reported binge drinking at least one time (i.e., having at least five drinks on one occasion; Ames & Cunradi, 2004). In general, younger male veterans tend to experience more alcohol misuse and abuse compared to older veterans and female veterans (Jakupcak et al., 2010). Compared to younger female military personnel (8.1%), younger male military personnel report significantly higher rates of heavy alcohol use (32.2%) across all service branches (Ames & Cunradi, 2004).

There are also differences in alcohol misuse present between service branches of the military. AUD diagnoses and alcohol misuse are most common in the Marines and least common in the air force (Schuler et al., 2022). Furthermore, military personnel in the Marines, Army, and Navy are two to three times more likely to experience multiple mental health conditions and substance use issues compared to the Air Force (Schuler et al., 2022).

Research shows that across the military branches male ADSMs exhibit higher rates of heavy drinking than female ADSMs. Within the Marines, younger men have higher rates of heavy alcohol use (38.6%), reporting heavy alcohol use versus women (12.9%; Ames & Cunradi, 2004). Following this trend, men in the Army exhibit higher rates of heavy alcohol use (32.8%) versus their female counterparts (6.3%; Ames & Cunradi, 2004). Approximately 31.8% of young male military personnel in the Navy report heavy alcohol use, while 11.5% of young female military personnel report heavy alcohol use (Ames & Cunradi, 2004). Finally, in the Air Force, 24.5% of young male military personnel report heavy alcohol use, while 6.3% of young female military personnel report heavy alcohol use (Ames & Cunradi, 2004).

Compared to the civilian population, veterans have several unique factors that may contribute to substance misuse and mental health issues in general. For example, characteristics of military deployment or service can act as significant predictors of alcohol misuse or alcohol use disorders (Jakupcak et al., 2010). Military personnel who were regularly in combat roles during deployment were more likely to have symptoms related to PTSD (Fear et al., 2010). Further, veterans who experienced more exposure to injuries, threats of death, and violent situations during their deployment period were more likely to experience and report alcohol misuse (Wilk et al., 2010). When veterans PTSD symptoms present themselves during the post-deployment period, emotional numbing and avoidance are significantly associated with alcohol misuse (Jakupcak et al., 2010). Direct and indirect killing during deployment is also a significant predictor for mental health conditions including PTSD, interpersonal relationship issues, problems with anger management, and alcohol misuse (Maguen et al., 2010).

In addition, military sexual trauma (MST) is associated with more negative mental health symptoms for male and female veterans (Gradus et al., 2008). MST is significantly associated with increased rates of depression, alcohol misuse, PTSD, impaired physical health, and chronic physical health issues (Suris & Lind, 2008). Depressive symptoms related to MST, have been found to mediate the relation between MST and alcohol misuse among female veterans (Gradus et al., 2008).

Disparities and Barriers to SUD Treatment

Mental health conditions can also contribute to barriers to treatment in the veteran population. Common diagnoses among veterans, including traumatic brain injury (TBI) and PTSD can co-occur with substance use disorders and impact treatment (Corrigan & Cole, 2008). Alcohol misuse can cause or exacerbate symptoms of TBI and PTSD, or alcohol misuse can be a result of symptoms related to TBI and PTSD (Corrigan & Cole, 2008). These conditions all can have significant neuropsychological effects on the individual, including emotional functioning, social behavior, planning, setting goals, utilizing cognitive skills, and correcting errors (Corrigan & Cole, 2008). Symptoms related to the interaction of these conditions can result in the individual experiencing significantly more difficulty when performing cognitive tasks, regulating their mood, and completing daily responsibilities (Corrigan & Cole, 2008). This could cause the treatment prognosis and adherence to suffer when working with these veterans. Other military-specific and systemic barriers (e.g., policies requiring records of treatment participation in military personnel member's record) may prevent service members from voluntarily participating in certain treatments and interventions (Dworkin et al., 2018). Access to military-specific barriers and factors can assist mental health providers in utilizing preventative and intervention techniques during treatment with military personnel and veterans.

Disparities and barriers to receiving SUD care are also observed for veterans and ADSMs based upon race, gender, and sexual orientation. Black veterans are less likely than non-Black veterans to be started and retained on first-line medications for treating opioid use disorder (Manharpra et al., 2017, 2020). Therefore, initiatives are needed to improve the understanding of preferences and barriers related to these treatments for black veterans. Although gender differences were not found for receipt of treatments for opioid use disorders, Peltier et al. (2021) found that female veterans with opioid use disorders had a higher number of psychiatric diagnoses than their male counterparts. In addition, Ayers et al. (2022) found that non-cisgender and non-heterosexual service members had higher rates of co-occurring AUD and other mental health disorders than cisgender, heterosexual service members. These findings suggest that the need for specialty care to address co-occurring mental health disorders and SUD may differ based upon veterans' and ADSMs' gender identity and sexual orientation.

Conclusions

Substance misuse and SUDs, particularly AUD, are prevalent among military members and ADSMs. Therefore, it is imperative that clinicians who are working with these populations are familiar with the first-line psychological treatments that are available for treating SUDs and reducing substance misuse. First-line psychological approaches for SUDs are diverse in their theoretical orientations for addressing SUDs and include protocols that range in their length and intensity toward addressing these conditions. Fortunately, this provides veterans and ADSMs and the clinicians that serve them with a range of psychological treatment options that can be used to match the type of SUD and characteristics and preferences of the veteran/ADSM. At this time, the available research on how these treatment processes and outcomes may vary across gender and racial groups in military and ADSM populations is limited. Additionally, there is limited research on how these treatments can be better adapted to enhance treatment initiation, retention, and outcomes for these specific groups. Accordingly, more research in these areas is greatly needed and encouraged. Clinicians are encouraged to be flexible and collaborative in choosing and implementing appropriate SUD treatments in a culturally sensitive manner. The integration of empirically based preventative and intervention psychological techniques for clients with SUDs has the potential to significantly reduce the prevalence of SUDs and increase the positive outcomes of treatment of SUDs in the ADSM and veteran populations.

References

American Psychiatric Association [APA] (2013). *Diagnostic and statistical manual of mental disorders* (5th ed.). Author.

Ames, G., & Cunradi, C. (2004). Alcohol use and preventing alcohol-related problems among young adults in the military. *Alcohol Research & Health, 28*, 252–257.

Ayer, L., Ramchand, R., Karimi, G., & Wong, E. C. (2022). Co-occurring alcohol and mental health problems in the military: Prevalence, disparities, and service utilization. *Psychology of Addictive Behaviors, 36*(4), 419–427. https://doi.org/10.1037/adb0000804

Campbell, A. N. C., Montgomery, L., Sanchez, K., Pavlicova, M., Hu, M., Newville, H., Weaver, L., & Nunes, E. V. (2017). Racial/ethnic subgroup differences in outcomes and acceptability of an internet-delivered intervention for Substance Use Disorders. *Journal of Ethnicity in Substance Abuse, 16*(4), 460–478. https://doi.org/10.1080/15332640.2017.1300550

Carroll, K. M. (1998). *A cognitive-behavioral approach: Treating cocaine addiction.* National Institute of Drug Abuse.

Corrigan, J. D., & Cole, T. B. (2008). Substance Use Disorders and clinical management of traumatic brain injury and posttraumatic stress disorder. *JAMA, 300*, 720–721. https://doi.org/10.1001/jama.300.6.720

Cranford, J. A. (2014). DSM-IV alcohol dependence and marital dissolution: Evidence from the national epidemiologic survey on alcohol and related conditions. *Journal of Studies on Alcohol and Drugs, 75*, 520–529. https://doi.org/10.15288/jsad.2014.75.520

Dela Cruz, G. A., Johnstone, S., Kim, H. S., & Castle, D. J. (2022). Review of third-wave therapies for substance use disorders in people of color and collectivist cultures: Current evidence and future directions. *Psychology of Addictive Behaviors.* https://doi.org/10.1037/adb0000883

Department of Veterans Affairs/Department of Defense (2021). *VA/DoD clinical practice guidelines for the management of substance use disorder.* Author.

Dworkin, E. R., Bergman, H. E., Walton, T. O., Walker, D. D., & Keysen, D. L. (2018). Co-occurring post-traumatic stress disorder and alcohol use disorder in U.S. military and veteran populations. *Alcohol Research: Current Reviews, 39,* 161–169.

Fairbairn, C. E., & Cranford, J. A. (2016). A multimethod examination of negative behaviors during couples interactions and problem drinking trajectories. *Journal of Abnormal Psychology, 125,* 805–810. https://doi.org/10.1037/abn0000186.supp

Fear, N. T., Jones, M., Murphy, D., Hull, L., Clversen, A., Coker, B., Machell, L., Sundin, J., Woodhead, C., Jones, N., Greenberg, N., Landau, S., Dandeker, C., Rona, R. J., Hotopf, M., & Wessely, S. (2010). What are the consequences of deployment to Iraq and Afghanistan on the mental health of the UK armed forces? A cohort study. *Lancet, 375,* 1783–1797. https://doi.org/10.1016/S0140-6736(10)60672-1

Godley, S. H., Hedges, K., & Hunter, B. (2011). Gender and racial differences in treatment process and outcome among participants in the adolescent community reinforcement approach. Psychology of addictive behaviors. *Journal of the Society of Psychologists in Addictive Behaviors, 25*(1), 143–154. https://doi.org/10.1037/a0022179

Gradus, J. L., Street, A. E., Kelly, K., & Stafford, J. (2008). Sexual harassment experiences and harmful alcohol use in a military sample: Differences in gender and the mediating role of depression. *Journal of Studies on Alcohol and Drugs, 69,* 348–351. https://doi.org/10.15288/jsad.2008.69.348

Higgins, S. T., & Petry, N. M. (1999). Contingency management. Incentives for sobriety. *Alcohol Research & Health, 23*(2), 122–127.

Hogue, A., Schumm, J. A., MacClean, A., & Bobek, M. (2021). Couple and family therapy for substance use disorders: Evidence base update 2010-2019. *Journal of Marital and Family Therapy, 48,* 178–203. https://doi.org/10.1111/jmft.12546

Jakupcak, M., Tull, M. T., McDermott, M. J., Kaysen, D., Hunt, S., & Simpson, T. (2010). PTSD symptom clusters in relationship to alcohol misuse among Iraq and Afghanistan war veterans seeking post-deployment VA health care. *Addictive Behaviors, 35,* 840–843. https://doi.org/10.1016/j.addbeh.2010.03.023

Kadden, R., Carroll, K. M., Donovan, D., Cooney, N., Monti, P., Adams, D., et al. (2003). *Cognitive-behavioral coping skills therapy manual: A clinical research guide for therapists treating individuals with alcohol abuse and dependence.* National Institute on Alcohol Abuse and Alcoholism.

Kelly, J. F., Humphreys, K., & Ferri, M. (2020). Alcoholics anonymous and other 12-step programs for alcohol use disorder. *Cochrane Database of Systematic Reviews, 3.* https://doi.org/10.1002/14651858.CD012880.pub2

Lundahl, B. W., Kunz, C., Brownell, C., Tollefson, D., & Burke, B. L. (2010). A meta-analysis of motivational interviewing: Twenty-five years of empirical studies. *Research on Social Work Practice, 20*(2), 137–160. https://doi.org/10.1177/1049731509347850

Maguen, S., Lucenko, B. A., Reger, M. A., Gahm, G. A., Litz, B. T., Seal, K. H., Knight, S. J., & Marmar, C. R. (2010). The impact of reported direct and indirect killing on mental health symptoms in Iraq war veterans. *Journal of Traumatic Stress, 23,* 86–90. https://doi.org/10.1002/jts.20434

Manhapra, A., Petrakis, I., & Rosenheck, R. (2017). Three-year retention in buprenorphine treatment for opioid use disorder nationally in the Veterans Health Administration. *The American Journal on Addictions, 26*(6), 572–580. https://doi.org/10.1111/ajad.12553

Manhapra, A., Stefanovics, E., & Rosenheck, R. (2020). Initiating opioid agonist treatment for opioid use disorder nationally in the Veterans Health Administration: Who gets what? *Substance Abuse, 41*(1), 110–120. https://doi.org/10.1080/08897077.2019.1640831

Marshal, M. P. (2003). For better or for worse? The effects of alcohol use on marital functioning. *Clinical Psychology Review, 23*, 959–997. https://doi.org/10.1016/j.cpr.2003.09.002

McCrady, B. S., Wilson, A. D., Muñoz, R. E., Fink, B. C., Fokas, K., & Borders, A. (2016). Alcohol-focused behavioral couple therapy. *Family Process, 55*, 443–459. https://doi.org/10.1111/famp.12231

McPherson, S. M., Burduli, E., Smith, C. L., Herron, J., Oluwoye, O., Hirchak, K., Orr, M. F., McDonell, M. G., & Roll, J. M. (2018). A review of contingency management for the treatment of substance-use disorders: Adaptation for underserved populations, use of experimental technologies, and personalized optimization strategies. *Substance Abuse and Rehabilitation, 9*, 43–57. https://doi.org/10.2147/SAR.S138439

Meadows, S. O., Beckman, R., Engel, C. C., & Jefferey, D. D. (2022). The culture of alcohol in the U.S. military: Correlations with problematic drinking behaviors and negative consequences of alcohol use. *Armed Forced & Society*, 1–25. https://doi.org/10.1177/0095327X211069162

Mercer, D. E., & Woody, G. E. (1999). *Individual drug counseling*. National Institute on Drug Abuse.

Meyers, R. J., Villanueva, M., & Smith, J. E. (2005). The community reinforcement approach: History and new directions. *Journal of Cognitive Psychotherapy, 19*(3), 247–260. https://doi.org/10.1891/jcop.2005.19.3.247

Meyers, R. J., Roozen, H. G., & Smith, J. E. (2011). The community reinforcement approach: An update of the evidence. *Alcohol Research & Health: The Journal of the National Institute on Alcohol Abuse and Alcoholism, 33*(4), 380–388.

Miller, W. R., Zweben, A., DiClemente, C. C., & Rychtarik, R. G. (1995). *Motivational Enhancement Therapy manual: A clinical research guide for therapists treating individuals with alcohol abuse and dependence*. National Institute on Alcohol Abuse and Alcoholism. https://www.motivationalinterviewing.org/sites/default/files/MATCH.pdf

Miller, W. R., Meyers, R. J., & Hiller-Sturmhöfel, S. (1999). The community-reinforcement approach. *Alcohol Research & Health, 23*(2), 116–121.

Nowinski, J., Baker, S., & Carroll, K. (1999). *Twelve-step facilitation therapy manual: A clinical research guide for therapists treating individuals with alcohol abuse and dependence*. National Institute on Alcohol Abuse and Alcoholism.

O'Farrell, T. J. (1993). A behavioral marital therapy couples group program for alcoholics and their spouses. In T. J. O'Farrell (Ed.), *Treating alcohol problems: Marital and family interventions* (pp. 170–209). Guilford Press.

O'Farrell, T. J., & Cutter, H. S. (1984). Behavioral marital therapy couples groups for male alcoholics and their wives. *Journal of Substance Abuse Treatment, 1*, 191–204. https://doi.org/10.1016/0740-5472(84)90022-9

Paris, M., Silva, M., Añez-Nava, L., Jaramillo, Y., Kiluk, B. D., Gordon, M. A., Nich, C., Frankforter, T., Devore, K., Ball, S. A., & Carroll, K. M. (2018). Culturally adapted, web-based cognitive behavioral therapy for Spanish-speaking individuals with substance use disorders: A randomized clinical trial. *American Journal of Public Health, 108*(11), 1535–1542. https://doi.org/10.2105/AJPH.2018.304571

Peltier, M. R., Sofuoglu, M., Petrakis, I., Stefanovics, E., Rosenheck, R. A. (2021). Sex differences in opioid use disorder prevalence and multimorbidity Nationally in the Veterans Health Administration. *Journal of Dual Diagnosis, 17*(2), 124–134.

Petry, N. M., DePhilippis, D., Rash, C. J., Drapkin, M., & McKay, J. R. (2014). Nationwide dissemination of contingency management: the Veterans Administration initiative. *The American Journal on Addictions, 23*(3), 205–210. https://doi.org/10.1111/j.1521-0391.2014.12092.x

Project MATCH Research Group. (1998). Matching alcoholism treatment to client heterogeneity: Project MATCH three-year drinking outcomes. *Alcoholism: Clinical and Experimental Research, 22*, 1300–1311.

Schuler, M. S., Wong, E. C., & Ramchand, R. (2022). Military service branch differences in alcohol use, tobacco use, prescription drug misuse, and mental health conditions. *Drug and Alcohol Dependence, 235*, 1–10. https://doi.org/10.1016/j.drugalcdep.2022.109461

Schumm, J. A., & Renno, S. (2021). Implementing behavioral couple therapy for substance use disorders in real-world clinical practice. *Family Process, 61*, 25–42 https://doi.org/10.1111/famp.12659

Self, K. J., Borsari, B., Ladd, B. O., Nicolas, G., Gibson, C. J., Jackson, K., Manuel, J. (2023). Cultural adaptations of motivational interviewing: A systematic review. *Psychological Services, 20*(1), 7–18.

Substance Abuse and Mental Health Services Administration. (2020). *U.S. Department of Health and Human Services. 2019 National survey on drug use and health: Veteran adults.* Author.

Suris, A., & Lind, L. (2008). Military sexual trauma: A review of prevalence and associated health consequences in veterans. *Trauma, Violence, & Abuse, 9*, 250–269. https://doi.org/10.1177/1524838008324419

Timko, C., Billow, R., & DeBenedetti, A. (2006). Determinants of 12-step group affiliation and moderators of the affiliation-abstinence relationship. *Drug and Alcohol Dependence, 83*(2), 111–121. https://doi.org/10.1016/j.drugalcdep.2005.11.005

Vasilaki, E. I., Hosier, S. G., & Miles Cox, W. (2006). The efficacy of motivational interviewing as a brief intervention for excessive drinking: A meta-analytic review. *Alcohol and Alcoholism, 41*(3), 328–335. https://doi.org/10.1093/alcalc/agl016

Wilk, J. E., Bliese, P. D., Kim, P. Y., Thomas, J. L., McGurk, D., & Hoge, C. W. (2010). Relationship of combat experiences to alcohol misuse among U.S. soldiers returning from the Iraq war. *Drug and Alcohol Dependence, 108*, 115–121. https://doi.org/10.1016/j.drugalcdep.2009.12.003

Witkiewitz, K., Hartzler, B., & Donovan, D. (2010). Matching motivation enhancement treatment to client motivation: Re-examining the Project MATCH motivation matching hypothesis. *Addiction, 105*(8), 1403–1413. https://doi.org/10.1111/j.1360-0443.2010.02954.x

Cannabis Use Disorder in Active-Duty Service Members and Veterans

7

Anthony H. Ecker, Julianna Hogan, Jennifer L. Bryan, and Katharine L. Thomas

Introduction

Cannabis is among the most widely used substances in the United States, following alcohol and tobacco; and cannabis use disorder (CUD) is the most highly prevalent substance use disorder in the United States (Substance Abuse and Mental Health Services Administration, 2020). Current diagnostic criteria classify CUD if at least two of 11 symptoms are met, corresponding with mild CUD. Moderate CUD requires four symptoms, and a severe designation requires six or more. Like other substance use disorders (SUDs), CUD is characterized by continued use of the substance despite negative physical or psychosocial problems (American Psychiatric Association, 2013; Budney et al., 2019). Further, tolerance and withdrawal can occur in CUD. Cannabis withdrawal is characterized by significant discomfort related to anxiety, irritability, depression, difficulty with sleep, and weight and appetite changes following discontinuing cannabis (Budney & Hughes, 2006; Schlienz et al., 2017). CUD,

DOI: 10.4324/9781003185949-7

beyond the impairment and distress characterized by its symptoms, is related to functional impairment related to occupational, educational, and legal domains (Foster et al., 2018; Kosty et al., 2017; Lorenzetti et al., 2020).

CUD in the General Population

Nearly 2% of U.S. adults meet criteria for CUD, with nearly 17% of cannabis users meeting criteria for the disorder (Compton et al., 2019). Further, CUD has been increasing in recent decades (Compton et al., 2019; Hasin et al., 2019; Leung et al., 2018). Strikingly these increases have been more pronounced among historically underrepresented groups, including African Americans and those with lower incomes, with risk also increased for men, young adults, and those living in urban areas (Hasin et al., 2019; Kerridge et al., 2018). Although men may be more likely to be diagnosed with CUD, rates of CUD among women have been rising, narrowing the gap in CUD between men and women previously observed (Chapman et al., 2017).

Several factors may influence the etiology and maintenance of CUD. First, cannabis has been observed to be of higher potency in the United States over time, with concentrations of $\Delta 9$-tetrahydrocannabinol (THC), the active psychoactive ingredient in cannabis rising from 4% on average in 1995 to 12% on average in 2014 (ElSohly et al., 2016). As cannabis potency has risen, so has the likelihood of experiencing CUD symptoms within one year of beginning to use cannabis, with the higher average potency of 12.3% in 2012 being related to nearly four times greater likelihood of experiencing a CUD symptom (Arterberry et al., 2019). Changes in cannabis policies may also be contributing to rising rates of CUD. Jurisdictions with medical marijuana laws and/or decriminalization have been associated with greater rates of CUD than those without (Hasin et al., 2017; McBain et al., 2020).

Veterans and Active-Duty Service Members

Among veteran populations, cannabis is one of the most commonly used illicit drugs (Teeters et al., 2017). In the 2019–2020 National Health and Resilience in Veterans Study, a nationally representative survey of veterans, 11.9% of veterans endorsed cannabis use and 2.7% met the criteria for CUD. These rates are slightly higher than those for the general U.S. adult population, among whom 7.55% endorsed cannabis use, and 2.57% met the criteria for CUD (Hasin et al., 2017; Hill et al., 2021). However, CUD may be underdiagnosed within the Veterans Health Administration (VHA), where many veterans receive their medical and mental health care (Bonn-Miller et al., 2012a). Rates of CUD among veterans increased by over 50% between 2002 and 2009 (Bonn-Miller et al., 2012b). Further, veterans are also more likely to endorse medical cannabis use than the general population, and the increasing availability of medical cannabis in the United States may have had a significant impact on veterans (Davis et al., 2018). Taken together, these findings suggest that veterans may be especially at risk for CUD.

Several factors may compound that risk further. Cannabis use and CUD prevalence rates are higher among younger Veterans, who are likely to have served in recent conflicts, including Operation Enduring Freedom/Operation Iraqi Freedom/Operation New Dawn (OEF/OIF/OND), as well as in those with psychiatric conditions. It is noteworthy that cannabis use and CUD prevalence were significantly lower in older Veterans, age 65+ (6.2% and 0.7%, respectively) (Kline et al., 2009).

Active-duty service members (ADSMs) are also considered a vulnerable population with a high risk for substance use (Norman et al., 2014). Although the Department of Defense (DoD) has enacted programs to combat drug use among service members, and a zero-tolerance policy is maintained in the military, cannabis and other illegal substances are still used by a subsection of active military personnel. One retrospective survey of 80 Veterans found that 3.7% of respondents endorsed cannabis use during active duty, which significantly increased to 26.2% postseparation; however, data on participant age or service era were not collected (Derefinko et al., 2018). In older Veterans, however, an opposite trend was noted, as frequent cannabis use for Vietnam-era veterans was more common during their military service than in their civilian life postwar (23.1% vs 10.3%, respectively). This may be in part due to the fact that stricter drug policies were not enacted by the DoD until the 1970s (Office of the Under Secretary of Defense for Personnel and Readiness, 2011).

In the VHA, specifically, CUD is more prevalent among younger veterans and those with posttraumatic stress disorder (PTSD; Bonn-Miller et al., 2012b) than among older veterans and those without PTSD. Bryan et al. showed that the prevalence of a comorbid PTSD diagnosis among OEF/OIF/OND veterans with a CUD diagnosis was 72.3% (Bryan et al., 2021). Another study found that 22% of OEF/OIF veterans screened positive for alcohol use disorder, in comparison to 14.8% of veterans of all eras and 5.8% of Americans over the age of 18 (Calhoun et al., 2008; Fuehrlein et al., 2016; Substance Abuse and Mental Health Services Administration, 2020). Taken together, these findings suggest that veterans of these recent conflicts may be especially at risk for experiencing substance-related problems such as SUDs.

Cannabis Use Disorder and Mental Health Disorder Comorbidity

PTSD is among the most common mental disorders among veterans (Goldberg et al., 2016; Nichter et al., 2019; Williamson et al., 2018) and one of the highest priorities for treatment by the VHA (Department of Veterans Affairs, 2019). Among veterans with PTSD who presented for treatment in a specialty VA PTSD clinic, nearly 15% reported cannabis use in the past six months. Importantly, greater severity of PTSD, depression, and suicidality was positively related to cannabis use (Gentes et al., 2016).

Veterans with PTSD are more likely to report using cannabis to cope with negative affect than those without PTSD (Boden et al., 2013). Greater PTSD symptom severity was associated with greater cannabis-related problems and withdrawal symptoms, suggesting that PTSD severity may be linked to symptoms of CUD (e.g., withdrawal, psychosocial problems). Although negative affect often precedes cannabis use (Buckner et al., 2014), the relationship between CUD and PTSD may be bidirectional among veterans with PTSD. That is, not only would PTSD symptoms influence cannabis use and CUD, but cannabis use could exacerbate PTSD symptoms. Metrik et al. (2020) found evidence for a prospective influence of PTSD diagnosis to CUD over the course of a year. Further, greater cannabis use frequency was related to stronger PTSD intrusion symptoms, which are hallmark features of the disorder, suggesting cannabis use has a specific link to PTSD as opposed to negative affect or anxiety more broadly. CUD among returning veterans also prospectively predicted more severe PTSD symptomatology (Livingston et al., 2021). Veterans with CUD diagnoses in VHA, compared to those without such diagnoses, have poorer psychosocial functioning, and report greater alcohol use and greater mental health disorder symptoms, including depression, anxiety, and PTSD (Livingston et al., 2021). Notably, veterans in the sample who identified as people of color who had diagnoses of CUD reported more severe mental health symptoms and poorer overall functioning.

Further, veterans with PTSD and CUD had poorer treatment outcomes than those without CUD (Bonn-Miller et al., 2013). In the VHA, specifically, CUD is more prevalent among younger veterans and those with PTSD (Bonn-Miller et al., 2012a) than among older veterans and those without PTSD. Bryan et al. (2021) showed that the prevalence of a comorbid PTSD diagnosis among OEF/OIF/OND veterans with a CUD diagnosis was 72.3% (2021). Taken together, these studies all suggest a complex relationship between cannabis use, CUD, and PTSD that warrants further scientific investigation and consideration in treatment approaches.

CUD among veterans and ADSMs has also been found to co-occur with other mental disorders. Among U.S. Air Force members, airmen with mild traumatic brain injury (mTBI) had greater rates of alcohol and drug abuse, including cannabis, than those with nonbrain injuries (e.g., body, limb injuries; Miller et al., 2013). Veterans of recent conflicts enrolled in VHA health care with co-occurring PTSD and CUD were more likely than veterans with CUD only to also have been diagnosed with panic disorder, alcohol use disorder, opioid use disorder, and insomnia (Bryan et al., 2021).

Treatment

Given that cannabis use continues to be illegal at the federal level, and the military maintains a zero-tolerance policy, very little work on treatment for cannabis use disorders within ADSM has been published, although guidelines have been reviewed and published by DoD in partnership with VA for the management of substance use disorders, which includes CUD (Department of Veteran's Affairs, 2021). Both within and outside VHA, evidence-based behavioral and pharmacological treatments for CUD are limited (Department of Veterans Affairs, 2021; Lee et al., 2019). While there are likely many reasons for a lack of treatments for CUD, it may be partially explained by disinterest in treatment seeking for those using cannabis (Gates et al., 2012; Sherman & McRae-Clark, 2016), diagnostic practices (Bonn-Miller et al., 2012a; Bryan et al., 2021), or system-level issues, such as limited provider training or availability (Martino et al., 2009), although interest in treatment is growing (Browne et al., 2021; Lee et al., 2019). Front-line treatments for cannabis use include targeted interventions that help patients identify strategies to better manage cannabis cravings, as well as to develop coping skills to managing craving and other high-risk situations (i.e., emotional states, social situations; Babor, 2004; Department of Veterans Affairs, 2021; Sherman & McRae-Clark, 2016).

Currently, there are no pharmacotherapies approved for treating CUD (Brezing & Levin, 2018; Department of Veterans Affairs, 2021). Evidence suggests that most who enter treatment for CUD will relapse within one year (Budney et al., 2007). The three behavioral treatments that have a growing evidence base include cognitive behavioral therapy (CBT), Contingency Management (CM), and motivational enhancement therapy (MET).

CBT and evidence-based therapy, often considered a front-line treatment approach, help patients better understand their motivation for cannabis use and ways to manage use behaviors by self-monitoring, developing coping skills, and restructuring unhelpful thought patterns that contribute to continued cannabis use (Chatters et al., 2016; Sherman & McRae-Clark, 2016). CBT often involves elements of relapse prevention (RP), whereby patients will identify high-risk situations for relapse and learn and practice skills to become more resilient to situations in which relapse is likely. Although there is no veteran-specific CBT for CUD treatments, VHA and DoD recognize CBT for CUD as an acceptable approach to treatment (Department of Veterans Affairs, 2021).

CM is an efficacious intervention based on operant conditioning principles, whereby patients are offered tangible (positive) reinforcers to achieve a targeted behavior (i.e., abstinence; treatment engagement); in essence, patients are rewarded for healthy behaviors (DePhilippis et al., 2018). CM is often used as an adjunctive treatment to CBT approaches to augment treatment or encourage engagement in treatment. In VHA, CM has historically been underused (Watkins et al., 2001); however, VHA has begun training, consultation, and coaching initiatives to support CM for substance use disorders among veterans (Rash & DePhilippis, 2019).

MET is an approach that helps patients identify and resolve ambivalence about cannabis use, thus increasing commitment to treatment and cessation of cannabis use (National Institutes of Drug Abuse, 2020). Similar to CM, MET can be combined with other types of behavioral treatment to create a more robust approach to manage cannabis use (Walker et al., 2015). MET is an effective approach that may be more acceptable to some patients than more intensive behavioral therapies.

Age of first use of cannabis and onset of CUD can impact treatment outcomes. For example, if cannabis use was initiated in teenage years and has led to chronic use patterns, treatment may need to target multiple approaches to manage use (Stephens et al., 1993). Additionally, poorer treatment outcomes are generally observed for those whose onset of CUD occurred in adolescence. Careful assessment of use history is important to the outcome of treatment. A combination of behavioral treatments (CBT, CM, and MET) often produces the best abstinence outcomes, yet abstinence rates remain modest and decline after treatment in most published trials (Stephens et al., 2000).

Conclusion

Veterans and ADSMs are groups especially at risk for cannabis-related problems and CUD. Given rises in CUD diagnoses among veterans, growing availability and strength of cannabis, and high rates of co-occurrence with mental health conditions like PTSD, continued research on public health and clinical interventions to address CUD in these populations is warranted. A particular weakness of the extant literature on cannabis use among ADSMs is examination of racial and ethnic differences in cannabis use and response to treatment. Although many of the studies reviewed included race and/or ethnicity as a covariate in analyses, very few examined such factors' relation to prevalence of CUD or response to treatments. Such work will be crucial for expanding our understanding of how to best assess and treat CUD among diverse ADSMs. Further, as CUD prevalence grows, systematic approaches to screening, assessment, and treatment within veteran and ADSM–serving institutions are needed to better serve these individuals. Particular attention is needed to provide comprehensive care in the context of multimorbidity.

References

American Psychiatric Association [APA]. (2013). *Diagnostic and statistical manual of mental disorders* (5th ed.) [Non-fiction]. American Psychiatric Association. http://libezp.lib.lsu.edu/login?url=http://search.ebscohost.com/login.aspx?direct=true&db=cat00252a&AN=lalu.3913149&site=eds-live&scope=site, http://www.psychiatryonline.org/

Arterberry, B. J., Treloar Padovano, H., Foster, K. T., Zucker, R. A., & Hicks, B. M. (2019, February 1). Higher average potency across the United States is associated with progression to first cannabis use disorder symptom. *Drug and Alcohol Dependence*, 195, 186–192. https://doi.org/10.1016/j.drugalcdep.2018.11.012

Babor, T. F. (2004). Brief treatments for cannabis dependence: Findings from a randomized multisite trial. *Journal of Consulting and Clinical Psychology*, 72(3), 455–466. https://doi.org/10.1037/0022-006x.72.3.455

Boden, M. T., Babson, K. A., Vujanovic, A. A., Short, N. A., & Bonn-Miller, M. O. (2013, May 1). Posttraumatic stress disorder and cannabis use characteristics among military veterans with cannabis dependence. *The American Journal on Addictions*, 22(3), 277–284. https://doi.org/10.1111/j.1521-0391.2012.12018.x

Bonn-Miller, M. O., Bucossi, M. M., & Trafton, J. A. (2012a, July). The underdiagnosis of cannabis use disorders and other Axis-I disorders among military veterans within VHA. *Military Medicine*, 177(7), 786–788.

Bonn-Miller, M. O., Harris, A. H. S., & Trafton, J. A. (2012b, November). Prevalence of cannabis use disorder diagnoses among veterans in 2002, 2008, and 2009. *Psychological Services*, 9(4), 404–416. https://doi.org/10.1037/a0027622

Bonn-Miller, M. O., Boden, M. T., Vujanovic, A. A., & Drescher, K. D. (2013). Prospective investigation of the impact of cannabis use disorders on posttraumatic stress disorder symptoms among veterans in residential treatment. *Psychological Trauma: Theory, Research, Practice, and Policy*, 5(2), 193.

Brezing, C. A., & Levin, F. R. (2018, January). The current state of pharmacological treatments for cannabis use disorder and withdrawal. *Neuropsychopharmacology*, 43(1), 173–194. https://doi.org/10.1038/npp.2017.212

Browne, K. C., Stohl, M., Bohnert, K. M., Saxon, A. J., Fink, D. S., Olfson, M., Cerda, M., Sherman, S., Gradus, J. L., Martins, S. S., & Hasin, D. S. (2021, Aug 19). Prevalence and correlates of cannabis use and cannabis use disorder among U.S. veterans: Results from the national epidemiologic survey on alcohol and related conditions (NESARC-III). *American Journal of Psychiatry.* https://doi.org/10.1176/appi.ajp.2021.20081202

Bryan, J. L., Hogan, J., Lindsay, J. A., & Ecker, A. H. (2021, March). Cannabis use disorder and post-traumatic stress disorder: The prevalence of comorbidity in veterans of recent conflicts. *Journal of Substance Abuse Treatment, 122,* 108254. https://doi.org/10.1016/j.jsat.2020.108254

Buckner, J. D., Zvolensky, M. J., Crosby, R. D., Wonderlich, S. A., Ecker, A. H., & Richter, A. (2014). Antecedents and consequences of cannabis use among racially diverse cannabis users: An analysis from ecological momentary assessment. *Drug and Alcohol Dependence.* http://libezp.lib.lsu.edu/login?url=http://search.ebscohost.com/login.aspx?direct=true&db=psyh&AN=2015-00807-001&site=ehost-live&scope=site

Budney, A. J., & Hughes, J. R. (2006, May). The cannabis withdrawal syndrome. *Current Opinion in Psychiatry, 19*(3), 233–238. https://doi.org/10.1097/01.yco.0000218592.00689.e5

Budney, A. J., Roffman, R., Stephens, R. S., & Walker, D. (2007, December). Marijuana dependence and its treatment. *Addiction Science & Clinical Practice, 4*(1), 4–16. https://doi.org/10.1151/ascp07414

Budney, A. J., Sofis, M. J., & Borodovsky, J. T. (2019, February). An update on cannabis use disorder with comment on the impact of policy related to therapeutic and recreational cannabis use. *European Archives of Psychiatry and Clinical Neuroscience, 269*(1), 73–86. https://doi.org/10.1007/s00406-018-0976-1

Calhoun, P. S., Elter, J. R., Jones, E. R., Jr., Kudler, H., & Straits-Tröster, K. (2008, November). Hazardous alcohol use and receipt of risk-reduction counseling among U.S. veterans of the wars in Iraq and Afghanistan. *The Journal of Clinical Psychiatry, 69*(11), 1686–1693. https://doi.org/10.4088/jcp.v69n1103

Chapman, C., Slade, T., Swift, W., Keyes, K., Tonks, Z., & Teesson, M. (2017, May 1). Evidence for sex convergence in prevalence of cannabis use: A systematic review and meta-regression. *Journal of Studies on Alcohol and Drugs, 78*(3), 344–352. https://doi.org/10.15288/jsad.2017.78.344

Chatters, R., Cooper, K., Day, E., Knight, M., Lagundoye, O., Wong, R., & Kaltenthaler, E. (2016). Psychological and psychosocial interventions for cannabis cessation in adults: A systematic review. *Addiction Research & Theory, 24*(2), 93–110.

Compton, W. M., Han, B., Jones, C. M., & Blanco, C. (2019, November 1). Cannabis use disorders among adults in the United States during a time of increasing use of cannabis. *Drug and Alcohol Dependence, 204,* 107468. https://doi.org/10.1016/j.drugalcdep.2019.05.008

Davis, A. K., Lin, L. A., Ilgen, M. A., & Bohnert, K. M. (2018, Jan). Recent cannabis use among Veterans in the United States: Results from a national sample. *Addictive Behaviors, 76,* 223–228. https://doi.org/10.1016/j.addbeh.2017.08.010

Department of Veterans Affairs. (2019). *FY 2018-2024 Strategic Plan.* https://www.va.gov/oei/docs/VA2018-2024strategicPlan.pdf

Department of Veterans Affairs. (2021). *VA/DoD clinical practice guideline for management of substance use disorders, Version 4.0.*

DePhilippis, D., Petry, N. M., Bonn-Miller, M. O., Rosenbach, S. B., & McKay, J. R. (2018, April 1). The national implementation of Contingency Management (CM) in the Department of veterans affairs: Attendance at CM sessions and substance use outcomes. *Drug and Alcohol Dependence, 185*, 367–373. https://doi.org/10.1016/j.drugalcdep.2017.12.020

Derefinko, K. J., Hallsell, T. A., Isaacs, M. B., Salgado Garcia, F. I., Colvin, L. W., Bursac, Z., McDevitt-Murphy, M. E., Murphy, J. G., Little, M. A., Talcott, G. W., & Klesges, R. C. (2018, May 1). Substance use and psychological distress before and after the military to civilian transition. *Military Medicine, 183*(5–6), e258–e265. https://doi.org/10.1093/milmed/usx082

ElSohly, M. A., Mehmedic, Z., Foster, S., Gon, C., Chandra, S., & Church, J. C. (2016, April 1). Changes in cannabis potency over the last 2 decades (1995–2014): Analysis of current data in the United States. *Biological Psychiatry, 79*(7), 613–619. https://doi.org/10.1016/j.biopsych.2016.01.004

Foster, K. T., Arterberry, B. J., Iacono, W. G., McGue, M., & Hicks, B. M. (2018, Aug). Psychosocial functioning among regular cannabis users with and without cannabis use disorder. *Psychological Medicine, 48*(11), 1853–1861. https://doi.org/10.1017/s0033291717003361

Fuehrlein, B. S., Mota, N., Arias, A. J., Trevisan, L. A., Kachadourian, L. K., Krystal, J. H., Southwick, S. M., & Pietrzak, R. H. (2016, Oct). The burden of alcohol use disorders in US military veterans: Results from the national health and resilience in veterans study. *Addiction, 111*(10), 1786–1794. https://doi.org/10.1111/add.13423

Gates, P., Copeland, J., Swift, W., & Martin, G. (2012, May). Barriers and facilitators to cannabis treatment. *Drug and Alcohol Review, 31*(3), 311–319. https://doi.org/10.1111/j.1465-3362.2011.00313.x

Gentes, E. L., Schry, A. R., Hicks, T. A., Clancy, C. P., Collie, C. F., Kirby, A. C., Dennis, M. F., Hertzberg, M. A., Beckham, J. C., & Calhoun, P. S. (2016, May). Prevalence and correlates of cannabis use in an outpatient VA posttraumatic stress disorder clinic. *Psychology of Addictive Behaviors: Journal of the Society of Psychologists in Addictive Behaviors, 30*(3), 415–421. https://doi.org/10.1037/adb0000154

Goldberg, J., Magruder, K. M., Forsberg, C. W., Friedman, M. J., Litz, B. T., Vaccarino, V., Heagerty, P. J., Gleason, T. C., Huang, G. D., & Smith, N. L. (2016, March). Prevalence of post-traumatic stress disorder in aging Vietnam-era veterans: Veterans administration cooperative study 569: Course and consequences of post-traumatic stress disorder in Vietnam-era veteran twins. *The American Journal of Geriatric Psychiatry, 24*(3), 181–191. https://doi.org/10.1016/j.jagp.2015.05.004

Hasin, D. S., Sarvet, A. L., Cerdá, M., Keyes, K. M., Stohl, M., Galea, S., & Wall, M. M. (2017, June 1). US adult illicit cannabis use, cannabis use disorder, and medical marijuana laws: 1991–1992 to 2012–2013. *JAMA Psychiatry, 74*(6), 579–588. https://doi.org/10.1001/jamapsychiatry.2017.0724

Hasin, D. S., Shmulewitz, D., & Sarvet, A. L. (2019, November 2). Time trends in US cannabis use and cannabis use disorders overall and by sociodemographic subgroups: a narrative review and new findings. *The American Journal of Drug and Alcohol Abuse, 45*(6), 623–643. https://doi.org/10.1080/00952990.2019.1569668

Hill, M. L., Loflin, M., Nichter, B., Norman, S. B., & Pietrzak, R. H. (2021, September). Prevalence of cannabis use, disorder, and medical card possession in U.S. military veterans: Results from the 2019-2020 national health and resilience in veterans study. *Addictive Behaviors, 120*, 106963. https://doi.org/10.1016/j.addbeh.2021.106963

Kerridge, B. T., Pickering, R., Chou, P., Saha, T. D., & Hasin, D. S. (2018, January 1). DSM-5 cannabis use disorder in the national epidemiologic survey on alcohol and related conditions-III: Gender-specific profiles. *Addictive Behaviors, 76,* 52–60. https://doi.org/10.1016/j.addbeh.2017.07.012

Kline, A., Callahan, L., Butler, M., St. Hill, L., Losonczy, M. F., & Smelson, D. A. (2009, November 24). The relationship between military service eras and psychosocial treatment needs among homeless veterans with a co-occurring substance abuse and mental health disorder. *Journal of Dual Diagnosis, 5*(3–4), 357–374. https://doi.org/10.1080/15504260903175882

Kosty, D. B., Seeley, J. R., Farmer, R. F., Stevens, J. J., & Lewinsohn, P. M. (2017, February). Trajectories of cannabis use disorder: Risk factors, clinical characteristics and outcomes. *Addiction, 112*(2), 279–287. https://doi.org/10.1111/add.13557

Lee, D. C., Schlienz, N. J., Peters, E. N., Dworkin, R. H., Turk, D. C., Strain, E. C., & Vandrey, R. (2019, January 1). Systematic review of outcome domains and measures used in psychosocial and pharmacological treatment trials for cannabis use disorder. *Drug and Alcohol Dependence, 194,* 500–517. https://doi.org/10.1016/j.drugalcdep.2018.10.020

Leung, J., Chiu, C. Y. V., Stjepanović, D., & Hall, W. (2018, December 1). Has the legalisation of medical and recreational cannabis use in the USA affected the prevalence of cannabis use and cannabis use disorders? *Current Addiction Reports, 5*(4), 403–417. https://doi.org/10.1007/s40429-018-0224-9

Livingston, N. A., Farmer, S. L., Mahoney, C. T., Marx, B. P., & Keane, T. M. (2021, August 5). Longitudinal course of mental health symptoms among veterans with and without cannabis use disorder. *Psychology of Addictive Behaviors : Journal of the Society of Psychologists in Addictive Behaviors.* https://doi.org/10.1037/adb0000736

Lorenzetti, V., Hoch, E., & Hall, W. (2020, July). Adolescent cannabis use, cognition, brain health and educational outcomes: A review of the evidence. *European Neuropsychopharmacology, 36,* 169–180. https://doi.org/10.1016/j.euroneuro.2020.03.012

Martino, S., Ball, S. A., Nich, C., Frankforter, T. L., & Carroll, K. M. (2009, June). Informal discussions in substance abuse treatment sessions. *Journal of Substance Abuse Treatment, 36*(4), 366–375. https://doi.org/10.1016/j.jsat.2008.08.003

McBain, R. K., Wong, E. C., Breslau, J., Shearer, A. L., Cefalu, M. S., Roth, E., Burnam, M. A., & Collins, R. L. (2020, October 1). State medical marijuana laws, cannabis use and cannabis use disorder among adults with elevated psychological distress. *Drug and Alcohol Dependence, 215,* 108191. https://doi.org/10.1016/j.drugalcdep.2020.108191

Metrik, J., Stevens, A. K., Gunn, R. L., Borsari, B., & Jackson, K. M. (2020). Cannabis use and posttraumatic stress disorder: Prospective evidence from a longitudinal study of veterans. *Psychological Medicine,* 1–11. https://doi.org/10.1017/S003329172000197X

Miller, S. C., Baktash, S. H., Webb, T. S., Whitehead, C. R., Maynard, C., Wells, T. S., Otte, C. N., & Gore, R. K. (2013, April 1). Risk for addiction-related disorders following mild traumatic brain injury in a large cohort of active-duty U.S. Airmen. *American Journal of Psychiatry, 170*(4), 383–390. https://doi.org/10.1176/appi.ajp.2012.12010126

National Institutes of Drug Abuse. (2020). *Motivational Enhancement Therapy (Alcohol, Marijuana, Nicotine).* https://www.drugabuse.gov/publications/principles-drug-addiction-treatment-research-based-guide-third-edition/evidence-based-approaches-to-drug-addiction-treatment/behavioral-therapies/motivational-enhancement-therapy

Nichter, B., Norman, S., Haller, M., & Pietrzak, R. H. (2019, September 1). Psychological burden of PTSD, depression, and their comorbidity in the U.S. veteran population:

Suicidality, functioning, and service utilization. *Journal of Affective Disorders*, *256*, 633–640. https://doi.org/10.1016/j.jad.2019.06.072

Norman, S. B., Schmied, E., & Larson, G. E. (2014, July). Predictors of continued problem drinking and substance use following military discharge. *Journal of Studies on Alcohol and Drugs*, *75*(4), 557–566. https://doi.org/10.15288/jsad.2014.75.557

Office of the Under Secretary of Defense for Personnel and Readiness. (2011). *Status of Drug Use in the Department of Defense Personnel: Fiscal Year 2011 Drug Testing Statistical Report.* https://prhome.defense.gov/Portals/52/Documents/RFM/Readiness/DDRP/docs/6b%20FY%202011%20Annual%20Drug%20Use%20Status%20Report.pdf

Rash, C. J., & DePhilippis, D. (2019, September). Considerations for implementing contingency management in substance abuse treatment clinics: The Veterans Affairs initiative as a model. *Perspectives on Behavior Science*, *42*(3), 479–499. https://doi.org/10.1007/s40614-019-00204-3

Schlienz, N. J., Budney, A. J., Lee, D. C., & Vandrey, R. (2017, June). Cannabis withdrawal: A review of neurobiological mechanisms and sex differences. *Current Addiction Reports*, *4*(2), 75–81. https://doi.org/10.1007/s40429-017-0143-1

Sherman, B. J., & McRae-Clark, A. L. (2016, May). Treatment of cannabis use disorder: current science and future outlook. *Pharmacotherapy*, *36*(5), 511–535. https://doi.org/10.1002/phar.1747

Stephens, R. S., Roffman, R. A., & Simpson, E. E. (1993, December). Adult marijuana users seeking treatment. *Journal of Consulting and Clinical Psychology*, *61*(6), 1100–1104. https://doi.org/10.1037//0022-006x.61.6.1100

Stephens, R. S., Roffman, R. A., & Curtin, L. (2000). Comparison of extended versus brief treatments for marijuana use. *Journal of Consulting and Clinical Psychology*, *68*(5), 898–908. https://doi.org/10.1037/0022-006x.68.5.898

Substance Abuse and Mental Health Services Administration. (2020). *Key Substance Use and Mental Health Indicators in the United States: Results from the 2019 National Survey on Drug Use and Health*. https://www.samhsa.gov/data/

Teeters, J. B., Lancaster, C. L., Brown, D. G., & Back, S. E. (2017). Substance use disorders in military veterans: Prevalence and treatment challenges. *Substance Abuse and Rehabilitation*, *8*, 69–77. https://doi.org/10.2147/sar.S116720

Watkins, K. E., Burnam, A., Kung, F. Y., & Paddock, S. (2001, August). A national survey of care for persons with co-occurring mental and substance use disorders. *Psychiatric Services*, *52*(8), 1062–1068. https://doi.org/10.1176/appi.ps.52.8.1062

Walker, D. D., Stephens, R. S., Towe, S., Banes, K., & Roffman, R. (2015, September). Maintenance check-ups following treatment for cannabis dependence. *Journal of Substance Abuse Treatment*, *56*, 11–15. https://doi.org/10.1016/j.jsat.2015.03.006

White, J., Mortensen, L. H., & Batty, G. D. (2012, September 1). Cognitive ability in early adulthood as a predictor of habitual drug use during later military service and civilian life: The Vietnam experience study. *Drug and Alcohol Dependence*, *125*(1–2), 164–168. https://doi.org/10.1016/j.drugalcdep.2012.03.024

Williamson, V., Stevelink, S. A. M., Greenberg, K., & Greenberg, N. (2018, May). Prevalence of mental health disorders in elderly U.S. military veterans: A meta-analysis and systematic review. *The American Journal of Geriatric Psychiatry*, *26*(5), 534–545. https://doi.org/10.1016/j.jagp.2017.11.001

8 Treating Nightmares, Sleep, and Insomnia Disturbances in Active-Duty Service Members and Veterans

Elaine Boland and Katharine E. Miller

Introduction

Sleep disturbances are prevalent in U.S. active-duty service members (ADSMs) and veterans (Folmer et al., 2020; Moore et al., 2021). Poor sleep is associated with worsened physical and mental health outcomes; however significant gender, racial, and socioeconomic disparities exist that may place some veterans and ADSMs at greater risk. This chapter discusses three prominent sleep disruptions in veterans and ADSMs: insomnia, nightmares, and obstructive sleep apnea (OSA), highlighting the latest treatment and research advances and the work still needed to eliminate health and treatment disparities in these populations.

DOI: 10.4324/9781003185949-8

Insomnia

Insomnia is characterized by difficulty falling and staying asleep and/or waking too early, accompanied by significant distress or impairment (APA, 2013). Most theoretical models point to a "stress-diathesis" conceptualization whereby insomnia develops through the interaction of underlying predispositions and active stressors (e.g., active duty/post-deployment adjustment) (Drake et al., 2003). Insomnia disorder rates in veterans rose from 4.4% in 2012 to 11.8% in 2018 (Folmer et al., 2020), while insomnia symptoms have been reported in up to 57% of veterans across military eras (Hughes et al., 2018). Similar rates and increases are observed in ADSMs: Between 2005 and 2015, insomnia incidence jumped from approximately 5.7–272 cases per 10,000 (Moore et al., 2021), while approximately 69% reported insomnia symptoms either before, during, or after deployment (Miller et al., 2021).

Insomnia is associated with medical conditions such as dementia, cardiovascular disease, and metabolic syndrome (e.g., hypertension, hyperglycemia, and hyperlipidemia; Lovato & Lack, 2019), conditions that greatly impact quality of life and overall mortality. Insomnia is also frequently observed in posttraumatic stress disorder (PTSD), depression, and traumatic brain injury (TBI), all of which are prevalent health issues in veterans and ADSMs (Colvonen et al., 2020), and has been independently associated with suicidality (Simmons et al., 2020). Given the high suicide rates among veterans and ADSMs (VA/DoD, 2019a), adequate treatment of insomnia is critical.

These known risks and associations may differentially impact diverse veterans and ADSMs. Higher rates of insomnia are observed in all races other than White veterans (Colvonen et al., 2020), and Black ADSMs have presented with higher-than-expected rates of diagnosed insomnia (Moore et al., 2021). Notably, Black individuals are more likely to experience insomnia in combination with short sleep duration, a particularly severe phenotype with greater links to poor physical and mental health outcomes (Kalmbach et al., 2016). Higher insomnia rates are also observed in women veterans (Martin et al., 2017), although research suggests insomnia is underdiagnosed in women ADSMs (Moore et al., 2021), potentially delaying intervention. Socioeconomic status (SES) can also contribute to risk for insomnia. One study of Iraq and Afghanistan veterans found low SES was significantly associated with shorter sleep duration after adjusting for health behaviors and PTSD (Widome et al., 2015). Among women veterans, those with insomnia have reported lower SES than those without (Babson et al., 2018).

Despite these well-documented disparities, studies investigating their underlying mechanisms are sparse. One study suggests self-reported racial discrimination may mediate associations of race and insomnia symptom severity (Cheng et al., 2020), while another investigation of gender disparities found no gender differences after adjusting for work and family responsibilities, suggesting these stressors may drive disparate prevalence rates (Yoshioka et al., 2012). Research into military-specific drivers of sleep disparities in diverse veterans and ADSMs is lacking.

Although insomnia is a prominent health concern, there are effective treatments. Cognitive behavioral therapy for insomnia (CBT-I), a skills-focused psychotherapy focusing on sleep/wake regulation and reducing hyperarousal, has the strongest evidence base and is considered the frontline treatment by the VA/DoD clinical practice guidelines (VA/DoD, 2019b). CBT-I in ADSM and veteran samples has been associated with significant decreases in self-reported insomnia severity (Pruiksma et al., 2020a; Trockel et al., 2014), and a condensed version known as brief behavioral treatment for insomnia (BBT-I) has shown promise in veterans (Bramoweth et al., 2020). In cases where CBT-I is contraindicated or ineffective, the guidelines support short-course, pharmacologic treatment of insomnia using low doses of doxepin or nonbenzodiazepine benzodiazepine-receptor agonists (e.g., zolpidem), although long-term pharmacologic management is generally not recommended (VA/DoD, 2019b) due to risks for dependence and relapse when discontinued.

There is a paucity of research investigating whether insomnia treatments are equally effective across diverse groups of veterans and ADSMs. A meta-analysis of CBT-I did not show robust effects on objectively measured sleep (i.e., with actigraphy or polysomnography), but rather self-reports of insomnia improvement (Mitchell et al., 2019). The analysis did not specifically examine effects of race or gender; however, treatments that do not improve the shorter total sleep time observed in Black individuals and those of lower SES may not effectively reduce sleep disparities.

Nightmares

Nightmares are best understood as story-like sequences of dream imagery with dysphoric emotions, typically causing a complete awakening accompanied by physiological arousal (e.g., heart palpitations) with well-remembered content (APA, 2013). Nightmares following trauma exposure may closely resemble the event(s) or include related themes. Nightmares occurring at least weekly are reported in 1%–2% of the general adult population (APA,

2013), but are significantly higher among veterans and ADSMs in response to trauma exposure (e.g., military deployments). In U.S. ADSMs (Creamer et al., 2018) and National Guard personnel (Pruiksma et al., 2021), 31.2%–32%, respectively, had clinically significant nightmares, with trauma-related nightmares being more likely in those who deployed. In veterans, rates of distressing nightmares range between 51% (Gellis et al., 2010) and 88% (Richardson et al., 2018). Studies are limited by predominantly male samples and a lack of reporting on, or limited power to detect, differences among other demographic variables. Given known race/ethnicity differences in PTSD diagnosis (Koo et al., 2016), including higher rates of re-experiencing symptoms endorsed in Black vs. White veterans (Coleman et al., 2019), there likely are unobserved group differences.

Cultural and individual differences regarding nightmares may impact these rates. One study of Native Northern Plains American veterans found notably high nightmare rates (97% of those with combat-related PTSD; Shore et al., 2009). While speculative, the authors suggest the importance of dreams in the indigenous culture may increase awareness and reporting of nightmares. In contrast, nightmares are infrequently disclosed to clinical providers and may not be recognized by patients as a treatable clinical condition (Nadorff et al., 2015). Indeed, in one study only 3.9% of ADSMs meeting criteria for nightmare disorder reported nightmares as a reason for evaluation (Creamer et al., 2018).

While often associated with PTSD, nightmares may present without PTSD diagnosis, can contribute to its development (van Liempt et al., 2013), and may remain following PTSD-focused interventions (Pruiksma et al., 2016). Nightmares also are linked to greater levels of depression, perceived stress, substance use, and physical health complaints (Pruiksma et al., 2021). Notably, nightmares have been associated with a five-fold increase for high suicidality (Sjöström et al., 2007) and remained a prospective risk factor for repeat attempts (Sjöström et al., 2009).

Unlike insomnia, there is inconsistent support for effective nightmare treatment in veterans and ADSMs. CBT for nightmares, a term encompassing protocols including imagery rehearsal therapy (IRT) and exposure, relaxation, and rescripting therapy (ERRT), has the most empirical support in civilians. Currently, the American Academy of Sleep Medicine (AASM) recommends only IRT for treating trauma-related nightmares and nightmare disorder (Morgenthaler et al., 2018), with mixed support in veterans. IRT is a psychotherapy in which individuals choose a nightmare and rehearse a revised dream in the nightmare's place. An uncontrolled study with Australian veterans showed significant improvement in nightmare frequency and intensity (Forbes et al., 2003), whereas another trial with U.S. veterans reported no symptom reductions (Lu et al., 2009). In Vietnam veterans, no significant group differences were observed in nightmare frequency, PTSD severity, or sleep quality in IRT vs. a control condition (Cook et al., 2010). A randomized controlled trial of CBT-I+IRT or IRT alone found significant reductions in nightmare frequency and distress in veterans with PTSD (Harb et al., 2019); however, the addition of IRT did not contribute to treatment benefits, and neither race nor gender modified effects. Only uncontrolled trials of ERRT have been conducted in veterans, and show significant improvements in nightmare variables (e.g., Balliett et al., 2015). In ADSMs, ERRT resulted in within-group reductions in nightmare measures compared to control condition, but no significant between-group differences (Pruiksma et al., 2020b). Additional controlled trials in military samples are needed, particularly ones that examine efficacy across racial and gender groups.

Pharmacological treatment is typically approached with prazosin, a generic alpha-1 adrenergic antagonist. A meta-analysis of placebo-controlled studies found significant improvements in nightmare frequency and sleep quality in favor of prazosin (Khachatryan et al., 2016); however, a subsequent large multisite study in veterans with combat-related PTSD found no benefit over placebo (Raskind et al., 2018). As such, the VA/DoD (2017) and AASM clinical practice guidelines (Morgenthaler et al., 2018) give no specific recommendation for prazosin, although it continues to be used widely in veterans.

Questions remain regarding which nightmare treatments work best and for whom. One study found that women veterans received lower therapeutic prazosin doses and the strongest risk factor for non-adherence was underrepresented race/ethnicity (Rubin et al., 2020), potentially due to perceived discrimination and mistrust in health-care providers. Noticeably, few efficacy trials of nightmare treatments are focused within demographically diverse groups (Alcántara et al., 2021), and there is little research on cultural beliefs regarding nightmares in the clinical context. Collaborations between Western medicine and culturally sanctioned approaches may improve treatment outcomes (Shore et al., 2009).

Obstructive Sleep Apnea

Obstructive sleep apnea (OSA) is a serious breathing disorder characterized by repeated breathing pauses (i.e., apneas) caused by intermittent relaxation of throat muscles obscuring the airway. This results in numerous nocturnal arousals, leading to inadequate sleep depth/continuity and excessive daytime sleepiness. Prevalence varies based on apnea-hypopnea index (AHI), which estimates the number of arousals per hour: one systematic review estimated population prevalence of 9% to 38% for AHI ≥5 (<5 being the normal range), but when using the minimal threshold for moderate OSA (≥15), prevalence ranged from 6% to 17% (Senaratna et al., 2017). ADSMs and veterans, particularly those with PTSD, may be at increased risk for OSA. From 2005 to 2016, rates in ADSMs increased from 11.8 to 333.8 out of every 10,000 (Moore et al., 2021), and approximately 69% of Iraq and Afghanistan veterans who presented to an outpatient PTSD clinic were found to be at high risk for OSA (Colvonen et al., 2015).

Impairments in mood and cognitive functions have been observed in untreated OSA, particularly depression/anxiety symptoms and deficits in attention, memory, and executive functions (Vanek et al., 2020). Untreated moderate/severe OSA is also linked to cardiovascular disease, mortality risk, and metabolic syndrome (Kendzerska et al., 2014). Importantly, OSA is often comorbid with insomnia, increasing risk for excessive daytime sleepiness, mental health problems, and poor quality of life compared to OSA alone (Cho et al., 2018). An estimated 33% of ADSMs have comorbid insomnia/OSA (Mysliwiec et al., 2013), and a separate analysis showed that 74% of veterans diagnosed with OSA also reported clinical insomnia (Wallace & Wohlgemuth, 2019).

Racial disparities in OSA are well documented. OSA rates are higher in both Black and Hispanic adults in the general population, and a recent study noted greater than expected increases in OSA among Black service members (Moore et al., 2021). These disparities may be due to physical characteristics that impact the airway (e.g., maxillary-mandibular shape, cranial base) or due to the contributions of obesity, rates of which are higher among Black individuals (Dudley & Patel, 2016). Although women are less frequently diagnosed with OSA, women with OSA demonstrate greater impairment in daytime functioning compared to men (Ye et al., 2009). Older age, Black racial/ethnic identity, and unemployment were predictors of OSA among women veterans receiving VA health care (Martin et al., 2021), although mechanisms driving these associations are unclear.

The frontline treatment for OSA is continuous positive airway pressure (CPAP), a device that moves air steadily through the airway to push against blockages, albeit with documented treatment disparities. Both lower SES and Black race have been associated with reduced CPAP adherence in the general population (Billings et al., 2011), while a separate study of over 2,500 veterans with OSA found associations between Black race and reduced CPAP adherence even when adjusting for SES (Hsu et al., 2020). Similar comparative reductions in CPAP adherence among Black veterans were reported in a separate study that adjusted for additional factors (e.g., BMI, age, gender, and OSA severity) (Schwartz et al., 2016).

To date, mechanisms underlying these treatment disparities remain speculative and in need of further research. Adults from underrepresented racial groups may engage in follow-up care less frequently, which can impact adherence (Greenberg et al., 2004). Indeed, the proportion of Black and Hispanic veterans diagnosed with sleep disorders between 2012 and 2018 was higher than the percentage of Black and Hispanic veterans seeking VHA health care, possibly reflecting differences in health-care utilization (Folmer et al., 2020). Racial disparities in CPAP adherence also may be mediated by sleep duration, as shorter sleep duration is associated with worse CPAP adherence (Billings et al., 2013).

Conclusion

Sleep disorders such as insomnia, nightmare disorder, and OSA are highly prevalent in diverse veterans and ADSMs. Marked disparities in sleep health exist across race and gender groups, and while effective interventions are available, there is much work to be done to better understand the mechanisms of these sleep disparities to enhance treatments. Notably, we observed a paucity of research on sleep disparities in sexual minority and gender-diverse veterans and ADSMs. Sexual minority status has been associated with shorter sleep duration and poorer sleep quality (Patterson & Potter, 2019); however, few if any studies have explored these disparities in veterans or ADSMs. To ensure effective sleep treatment for current and former military personnel, studies must investigate the full range of racial, gender, socioeconomic, and sexual diversity.

References

Alcántara, C., Cosenzo, L. G., McCullough, E., Vogt, T., Falzon, A. L., & Ibarra, I. P. (2021). Cultural adaptations of psychological interventions for prevalent sleep disorders and sleep disturbances: A systematic review of randomized controlled trials in the United States. *Sleep Medicine Reviews*, 101455. https://doi.org/10.1016/j.smrv.2021.101455

American Psychiatric Association [APA]. (2013). *Diagnostic and statistical manual of mental disorders* (5th ed.). American Psychiatric Publishing. https://doi.org/10.1176/appi.books.9780890425596

Babson, K. A., Wong, A. C., Morabito, D., & Kimerling, R. (2018). Insomnia symptoms among female veterans: Prevalence, risk factors, and the impact on psychosocial functioning and health care utilization. *Journal of Clinical Sleep Medicine*, 14(6), 931–939. https://doi.org/10.5664/jcsm.7154

Balliett, N. E., Davis, J. L., & Miller, K. E. (2015). Efficacy of a brief treatment for nightmares and sleep disturbances for veterans. *Psychological Trauma: Theory, Research, Practice, and Policy*, 7(6), 507–515. https://doi.org/10.1037/tra0000055

Billings, M. E., Auckley, D., Benca, R., Foldvary-Schaefer, N., Iber, C., Redline, S., Rosen, C. L., Zee, P., & Kapur, V. K. (2011). Race and residential socioeconomics as predictors of CPAP adherence. *Sleep, 34*(12), 1653–1658. https://doi.org/10.5665/sleep.1428

Billings, M. E., Rosen, C. L., Wang, R., Auckley, D., Benca, R., Foldvary-Schaefer, N., Iber, C., Zee, P., Redline, S., & Kapur, V. K. (2013). Is the relationship between race and continuous positive airway pressure adherence mediated by sleep duration? *Sleep, 36*(2), 221–227. https://doi.org/10.5665/sleep.2376

Bramoweth, A. D., Lederer, L. G., Youk, A. O., Germain, A., & Chinman, M. J. (2020). Brief behavioral treatment for insomnia vs. cognitive behavioral therapy for insomnia: Results of a randomized noninferiority clinical trial among veterans. *Behavior Therapy, 51*(4), 535–547. https://doi.org/10.1016/j.beth.2020.02.002

Cheng, P., Cuellar, R., Johnson, D. A., Kalmbach, D. A., Joseph, C. L., Castelan, A. C., Sagong, C., Casement, M. D., & Drake, C. L. (2020). Racial discrimination as a mediator of racial disparities in insomnia disorder. *Sleep Health, 6*(5), 543–549. https://doi.org/10.1016/j.sleh.2020.07.007

Cho, Y. W., Kim, K. T., Moon, H.-J., Korostyshevskiy, V. R., Motamedi, G. K., & Yang, K. I. (2018). Comorbid insomnia with obstructive sleep apnea: Clinical characteristics and risk factors. *Journal of Clinical Sleep Medicine, 14*(3), 409–417. https://doi.org/10.5664/jcsm.6988

Coleman, J. A., Ingram, K. M., & Sheerin, C. M. (2019). Racial differences in posttraumatic stress disorder symptoms among African American and Caucasian male veterans. *Traumatology, 25*(4), 297. https://doi.org/10.1037/trm0000201

Colvonen, P. J., Almklov, E., Tripp, J. C., Ulmer, C. S., Pittman, J. O. E., & Afari, N. (2020). Prevalence rates and correlates of insomnia disorder in post-9/11 veterans enrolling in VA healthcare. *Sleep, 43*(12). https://doi.org/10.1093/sleep/zsaa119

Colvonen, P. J., Masino, T., Drummond, S. P., Myers, U. S., Angkaw, A. C., & Norman, S. B. (2015). Obstructive sleep apnea and posttraumatic stress disorder among OEF/OIF/OND veterans. *Journal of Clinical Sleep Medicine, 11*(5), 513–518. https://doi.org/10.5664/jcsm.4692

Cook, J. M., Harb, G. C., Gehrman, P. R., Cary, M. S., Gamble, G. M., Forbes, D., & Ross, R. J. (2010). Imagery rehearsal for posttraumatic nightmares: A randomized controlled trial. *Journal of Traumatic Stress, 23*(5), 553–563. https://doi.org/10.1002/jts.20569

Creamer, J. L., Brock, M. S., Matsangas, P., Motamedi, V., & Mysliwiec, V. (2018). Nightmares in United States military personnel with sleep disturbances. *Journal of Clinical Sleep Medicine, 14*(3), 419–426. https://doi.org/10.5664/jcsm.6990

Department of Veterans Affairs, & Department of Defense. (2017). *VA/DoD clinical practice guideline for the management of posttraumatic stress disorder and acute stress disorder.* https://www.healthquality.va.gov/guidelines/MH/ptsd/VADoDPTSDCPGFinal012418.pdf

Department of Veterans Affairs & Department of Defense. (2019a). *VA/DoD clinical practice guideline for the assessment and management of patients at risk for suicide.* https://www.healthquality.va.gov/guidelines/MH/srb/VADoDSuicideRiskFullCPGFinal5088212019.pdf

Department of Veterans Affairs & Department of Defense. (2019b). *VA/DoD clinical practice guideline for the management of chronic insomnia disorder and obstructive sleep apnea.* https://www.healthquality.va.gov/guidelines/CD/insomnia/VADoDSleepCPGFinal508.pdf

Drake, C. L., Roehrs, T., & Roth, T. (2003). Insomnia causes, consequences, and therapeutics: An overview. *Depression and Anxiety*, *18*(4), 163–176. https://doi.org/10.1002/da.10151

Dudley, K. A., & Patel, S. R. (2016). Disparities and genetic risk factors in obstructive sleep apnea. *Sleep Medicine*, *18*, 96–102. https://doi.org/10.1016/j.sleep.2015.01.015

Folmer, R. L., Smith, C. J., Boudreau, E. A., Hickok, A. W., Totten, A. M., Kaul, B., Stepnowsky, C. J., Whooley, M. A., & Sarmiento, K. F. (2020). Prevalence and management of sleep disorders in the Veterans Health Administration. *Sleep Medicine Reviews*, *54*, 101358. https://doi.org/10.1016/j.smrv.2020.101358

Forbes, D., Phelps, A. J., McHugh, A. F., Debenham, P., Hopwood, M., & Creamer, M. (2003). Imagery rehearsal in the treatment of posttraumatic nightmares in Australian veterans with chronic combat-related PTSD: 12-month follow-up data. *Journal of Traumatic Stress*, *16*(5), 509–513. https://doi.org/10.1023/A:1025718830026

Gellis, L. A., Gehrman, P. R., Mavandadi, S., & Oslin, D. W. (2010). Predictors of sleep disturbances in Operation Iraqi Freedom/Operation Enduring Freedom veterans reporting a trauma. *Military Medicine*, *175*(8), 567–573. http://www.ncbi.nlm.nih.gov/pubmed/20731260

Greenberg, H., Fleischman, J., Gouda, H. E., Angel, E., Lopez, R., Mrejen, K., Web, A., & Feinsilver, S. (2004). Disparities in obstructive sleep apnea and its management between a minority-serving institution and a voluntary hospital. *Sleep and Breathing*, *8*(4), 185–192. https://doi.org/10.1055/s-2004-860895

Harb, G. C., Cook, J. M., Phelps, A. J., Gehrman, P. R., Forbes, D., Localio, R., Harpaz-Rotem, I., Gur, R. C., & Ross, R. J. (2019). Randomized controlled trial of imagery rehearsal for posttraumatic nightmares in combat veterans. *Journal of Clinical Sleep Medicine*, *15*(5), 757–767. https://doi.org/10.5664/jcsm.7770

Hsu, N., Zeidler, M. R., Ryden, A. M., & Fung, C. H. (2020). Racial disparities in positive airway pressure therapy adherence among veterans with obstructive sleep apnea. *Journal of Clinical Sleep Medicine*, *16*(8), 1249–1254. https://doi.org/10.5664/jcsm.8476

Hughes, J. M., Ulmer, C. S., Gierisch, J. M., Nicole Hastings, S., & Howard, M. O. (2018). Insomnia in United States military veterans: An integrated theoretical model. *Clinical Psychology Review*, *59*, 118–125. https://doi.org/10.1016/j.cpr.2017.11.005

Kalmbach, D. A., Pillai, V., Arnedt, J. T., & Drake, C. L. (2016). DSM-5 insomnia and short sleep: Comorbidity landscape and racial disparities. *Sleep*, *39*(12), 2101–2111. https://doi.org/10.5665/sleep.6306

Kendzerska, T., Mollayeva, T., Gershon, A. S., Leung, R. S., Hawker, G., & Tomlinson, G. (2014). Untreated obstructive sleep apnea and the risk for serious long-term adverse outcomes: A systematic review. *Sleep Medicine Reviews*, *18*(1), 49–59. https://doi.org/10.1016/j.smrv.2013.01.003

Khachatryan, D., Groll, D., Booij, L., Sepehry, A. A., & Schütz, C. G. (2016). Prazosin for treating sleep disturbances in adults with posttraumatic stress disorder: A systematic review and meta-analysis of randomized controlled trials. *General Hospital Psychiatry*, *39*, 46–52. https://doi.org/10.1016/j.genhosppsych.2015.10.007

Koo, K. H., Hebenstreit, C. L., Madden, E., & Maguen, S. (2016). PTSD detection and symptom presentation: Racial/ethnic differences by gender among veterans with PTSD returning from Iraq and Afghanistan. *Journal of Affective Disorders*, *189*, 10–16. https://doi.org/10.1016/j.psychres.2015.08.013

Lovato, N., & Lack, L. (2019). Insomnia and mortality: A meta-analysis. *Sleep Medicine Reviews*, *43*, 71–83. https://doi.org/10.1016/j.smrv.2018.10.004

Lu, M., Wagner, A., Van Male, L., Whitehead, A., & Boehnlein, J. (2009). Imagery rehearsal therapy for posttraumatic nightmares in U.S. veterans. *Journal of Traumatic Stress, 22*(3), 236–239. https://doi.org/10.1002/jts.20407

Martin, J. L., Schweizer, C. A., Hughes, J. M., Fung, C. H., Dzierzewski, J. M., Washington, D. L., Kramer, B. J., Jouldjian, S., Mitchell, M. N., & Josephson, K. R. (2017). Estimated prevalence of insomnia among women veterans: Results of a postal survey. *Women's Health Issues, 27*(3), 366–373. https://doi.org/10.1016/j.whi.2016.12.003

Martin, J. L., Carlson, G., Kelly, M., Fung, C. H., Song, Y., Mitchell, M. N., Zeidler, M. R., Josephson, K. R., Badr, M. S., & Zhu, R. (2021). Sleep apnea in women veterans: Results of a national survey of VA health care users. *Journal of Clinical Sleep Medicine, 17*(3), 555–565. https://doi.org/10.5664/jcsm.8956

Miller, K. E., Ramsey, C. M., Boland, E. M., Klingaman, E. A., & Gehrman, P. (2021). Identifying and characterizing longitudinal patterns of insomnia across the deployment cycle in active duty Army soldiers. *Sleep, 44*(7). https://doi.org/10.1093/sleep/zsab004

Mitchell, L. J., Bisdounis, L., Ballesio, A., Omlin, X., & Kyle, S. D. (2019). The impact of cognitive behavioural therapy for insomnia on object sleep parameters: A meta-analysis and systematic review. *Sleep Medicine Reviews, 47*, 90–102.

Moore, B. A., Tison, L. M., Palacios, J. G., Peterson, A. L., & Mysliwiec, V. (2021). Incidence of insomnia and obstructive sleep apnea in active duty United States military service members. *Sleep, 44*(7). https://doi.org/10.1093/sleep/zsab024

Morgenthaler, T. I., Auerbach, S., Casey, K. R., Kristo, D., Maganti, R., Ramar, K., Zak, R., & Kartje, R. (2018). Position paper for the treatment of nightmare disorder in adults: An American Academy of Sleep Medicine position paper. *Journal of Clinical Sleep Medicine, 14*(6), 1041–1055. https://doi.org/10.5664/jcsm.7178

Mysliwiec, V., Gill, J., Lee, H., Baxter, T., Pierce, R., Barr, T. L., Krakow, B., & Roth, B. J. (2013). Sleep disorders in US military personnel: A high rate of comorbid insomnia and obstructive sleep apnea. *CHEST Journal, 144*(2), 549–557. https://doi.org/10.1378/chest.13-0088

Nadorff, M. R., Nadorff, D. K., & Germain, A. (2015). Nightmares: Under-reported, undetected, and therefore untreated. *Journal of Clinical Sleep Medicine, 11*(7), 747–750. https://doi.org/10.5664/jcsm.4850

Patterson, C. J., & Potter, E. C. (2019). Sexual orientation and sleep difficulties: A review of research. *Sleep Health, 5*(3), 227–235. https://doi.org/10.1016/j.sleh.2019.02.004

Pruiksma, K. E., Taylor, D. J., Wachen, J. S., Mintz, J., Young-McCaughan, S., Peterson, A. L., Yarvis, J. S., Borah, E. V., Dondanville, K. A., Litz, B. T., Hembree, E. A., & Resick, P. A. (2016). Residual sleep disturbances following PTSD treatment in active duty military personnel. *Psychological Trauma: Theory, Research, Practice, and Policy, 8*(6), 697–701. https://doi.org/10.1037/tra0000150

Pruiksma, K. E., Hale, W. J., Mintz, J., Peterson, A. L., Young-McCaughan, S., Wilkerson, A., Nicholson, K., Dondanville, K. A., Fina, B. A., & Borah, E. V. (2020a). Predictors of Cognitive Behavioral Therapy for Insomnia (CBTi) outcomes in active-duty US Army Personnel. *Behavior Therapy, 51*(4), 522–534. https://doi.org/10.1016/j.beth.2020.02.001

Pruiksma, K. E., Taylor, D. J., Mintz, J., Nicholson, K. L., Rodgers, M., Young-McCaughan, S., Hall-Clark, B. N., Fina, B. A., Dondanville, K. A., & Cobos, B. (2020b). A pilot randomized controlled trial of cognitive behavioral treatment for trauma-related nightmares in active duty military personnel. *Journal of Clinical Sleep Medicine, 16*(1), 29–40. https://doi.org/10.5664/jcsm.8116

Pruiksma, K. E., Slavish, D. C., Taylor, D. J., Dietch, J. R., Tyler, H., Dolan, M., Bryan, A. O., & Bryan, C. J. (2021). Nightmares and insomnia in the US National Guard: Mental and physical health correlates. *International Journal of Behavioral Medicine, 28*, 238–249. https://doi.org/10.1007/s12529-020-09889-2

Raskind, M. A., Peskind, E. R., Chow, B., Harris, C., Davis-Karim, A., Holmes, H. A., Hart, K. L., McFall, M., Mellman, T. A., & Reist, C. (2018). Trial of prazosin for posttraumatic stress disorder in military veterans. *New England Journal of Medicine, 378*(6), 507–517. https://doi.org/10.1056/NEJMoa1507898

Richardson, J. D., King, L., Cyr, K. S., Shnaider, P., Roth, M. L., Ketcheson, F., Balderson, K., & Elhai, J. D. (2018). Depression and the relationship between sleep disturbances, nightmares, and suicidal ideation in treatment-seeking Canadian Armed Forces members and veterans. *BMC Psychiatry, 18*(1), 1–8. https://doi.org/10.1186/s12888-018-1782-z

Rubin, M. L., Copeland, L. A., Kroll-Desrosiers, A. R., & Knittel, A. G. (2020). Demographic variation in the use of prazosin for treatment of sleep disturbance in combat veterans with PTSD. *Psychopharmacology Bulletin, 50*(2), 26. PMCID: PMC7255837

Schwartz, S. W., Sebastião, Y., Rosas, J., Iannacone, M. R., Foulis, P. R., & Anderson, W. M. (2016). Racial disparity in adherence to positive airway pressure among US veterans. *Sleep and Breathing, 20*(3), 947–955. https://doi.org/10.1007/s11325-016-1316-1

Senaratna, C. V., Perret, J. L., Lodge, C. J., Lowe, A. J., Campbell, B. E., Matheson, M. C., Hamilton, G. S., & Dharmage, S. C. (2017). Prevalence of obstructive sleep apnea in the general population: A systematic review. *Sleep Medicine Reviews, 34*, 70–81. https://doi.org/10.1016/j.smrv.2016.07.002

Shore, J. H., Orton, H., & Manson, S. M. (2009). Trauma-related nightmares among American Indian veterans: Views from the dream catcher. *American Indian and Alaska Native Mental Health Research: The Journal of the National Center, 16*(1), 25–38. https://doi.org/10.5820/aian.1601.2009.25

Simmons, Z., Erickson, L. D., Hedges, D., & Kay, D. B. (2020). Insomnia is associated with frequency of suicidal ideation independent of depression: A replication and extension of findings from the National Health and Nutrition Examination Survey. *Frontiers in Psychiatry, 11*. https://doi.org/10.3389/fpsyt.2020.561564

Sjöström, N., Waern, M., & Hetta, J. (2007). Nightmares and sleep disturbances in relation to suicidality in suicide attempters. *Sleep, 30*(1), 91–95. https://doi.org/10.1093/sleep/30.1.91

Sjöström, N., Hetta, J., & Waern, M. (2009). Persistent nightmares are associated with repeat suicide attempt: A prospective study. *Psychiatry Research, 170*(2–3), 208–211. https://doi.org/10.1016/j.psychres.2008.09.006

Trockel, M., Karlin, B. E., Taylor, C. B., & Manber, R. (2014). Cognitive behavioral therapy for insomnia with veterans: Evaluation of effectiveness and correlates of treatment outcomes. *Behaviour Research and Therapy, 53*, 41–46. https://doi.org/10.1016/j.brat.2013.11.006

van Liempt, S., van Zuiden, M., Westenberg, H., Super, A., & Vermetten, E. (2013). Impact of impaired sleep on the development of PTSD symptoms in combat veterans: A prospective longitudinal cohort study. *Depression and Anxiety, 30*(5), 469–474. https://doi.org/10.1002/da.22054

Vanek, J., Prasko, J., Genzor, S., Ociskova, M., Kantor, K., Holubova, M., Slepecky, M., Nesnidal, V., Kolek, A., & Sova, M. (2020). Obstructive sleep apnea, depression and cognitive impairment. *Sleep Medicine, 72*, 50–58. https://doi.org/10.1016/j.sleep.2020.03.017

Wallace, D. M., & Wohlgemuth, W. K. (2019). Predictors of Insomnia Severity Index profiles in United States veterans with obstructive sleep apnea. *Journal of Clinical Sleep Medicine*, *15*(12), 1827–1837. https://doi.org/10.5664/jcsm.8094

Widome, R., Jensen, A., & Fu, S. S. (2015). Socioeconomic disparities in sleep duration among veterans of the US wars in Iraq and Afghanistan. *American Journal of Public Health*, *105*(2), e70–e74. https://doi.org/10.2105/AJPH.2014.302375

Ye, L., Pien, G. W., & Weaver, T. E. (2009). Gender differences in the clinical manifestation of obstructive sleep apnea. *Sleep Medicine*, *10*(10), 1075–1084. https://doi.org/10.1016/j.sleep.2009.02.006

Yoshioka, E., Saijo, Y., Kita, T., Satoh, H., Kawaharada, M., Fukui, T., & Kishi, R. (2012). Gender differences in insomnia and the role of paid work and family responsibilities. *Social Psychiatry and Psychiatric Epidemiology*, *47*(4), 651–662. https://doi.org/10.1007/s00127-011-0370-z

Couples Therapy with Active-Duty Service Members and Veterans

9

Amber M. Jarnecke, Jessica H. Kansky, Karen Petty, and Jenna B. Teves

Introduction

Active-duty service members (ADSM) and military veterans, overall, represent a group of highly resilient and adaptable individuals. Yet, they may encounter many distinct experiences and stressors that can have an impact on their wellbeing and intimate relationships. For instance, ADSM and veterans may experience frequent relocation, deployments, reintegration, and military-related trauma (e.g., combat trauma, military sexual trauma [MST]); they are also at increased risk for traumatic brain injury (TBI), chronic pain, posttraumatic stress disorder (PTSD), depression, and substance use disorders (SUD) relative to the general population (Campbell & Nobel, 2009; Olenick et al., 2015). These contexts and factors can affect intimate relationship functioning; however, risks of these experiences as well as their effects on intimate relationships are not equivalent across all ADSM and veteran subpopulations.

DOI: 10.4324/9781003185949-9

Disparities by military branch and rank, race and ethnicity, gender, sexual orientation, socioeconomic status, and length of deployment may all have implications on how military life impacts intimate relationships (Coughlin, 2021; Schuyler et al., 2020; Turchik & Wilson, 2010; Wilson, 2016). As such, when clinicians work with ADSM and veteran couples, it is crucial that the unique presenting problem, background, history, and circumstances of the ADSM or veteran couple are examined throughout the assessment, case conceptualization, and therapeutic processes. To that end, this chapter will discuss considerations clinicians can take when working with ADSM and veteran couples, specific couples therapy protocols that could be used with this population, and future directions for clinical care with ADSM and veteran couples.

Considerations for Working with ADSM and Veteran Couples

Military Culture

Although ADSM and veteran couples are not a homogenous group, a working knowledge of military culture is necessary for clinicians working with these couples to build rapport, increase understanding of their unique stressors, and strive towards cultural competency. Key tenets of military workplace culture include an emphasis on cohesion, strength, commitment, obedience, self-sacrifice, and the overall warrior ethos (e.g., mindset of mission first and never leaving fellow Americans behind). Redmond et al. (2015) highlight important variations in military culture based on specific experiences (e.g., rank, occupation, demographics, branch, combat exposure, deployments) that are important to assess and include in case conceptualization to develop a deeper understanding of individual experiences. Oftentimes, military culture may be referenced as a barrier towards reintegration into civilian life, including reintegration within family life (Sayers, 2011). The BATTLEMIND program helps to increase awareness of the links between the mindset, attitude, and behaviors that are valued within the military and some of the common problematic ways these behaviors may present if overutilized in the home environment (Adler et al., 2011). For example, while it is beneficial to follow orders and maintain emotional distance from challenges while serving, this may present as inflexibility or avoidance of close relationships upon returning home. Developing a deeper understanding of the mindset that is valued within the military and how this may relate to difficulties with close relationships and reintegration is essential for providing quality care.

Military Work-related Stressors

Military life entails a variety of stressors that impact ADSMs, veterans, and their families: deployments and combat exposure, lengthy separations from family, long hours, and frequent relocation, among others. While many couples and families are resilient in the face of these stressors, others may struggle. For instance, research has shown that ADSM couples have a range of relationship experiences from pre-deployment to post-deployment. Some partners report that their relationship satisfaction is relatively stable over time, some report increased relationship satisfaction, and others report decreases or instability in their relationship satisfaction (Parcell & Maguire, 2014). During reintegration, some couples report challenges with the ADSM reconnecting with their partner or children, difficulty communicating about family routines, or trouble redistributing household tasks (Knobloch et al., 2016). For clinicians working with ADSM and veteran couples, it is necessary to consider how the unique experiences and perceptions of these potential stressors influence the dyadic context and home environment.

Psychopathology

The impact of military-related stressors can be amplified when an ADSM or veteran suffers from psychopathology (e.g., depression, PTSD, SUD) (Sayers, 2011). Conversely, stress at home and in important relationships puts individuals at greater risk of developing psychological symptoms, including posttraumatic stress symptoms and other mood, anxiety, and substance use disorder symptoms (Interian et al., 2014; Whisman et al., 2020). Given the increased risk of individual *and* interpersonal distress, ADSMs and veterans may become stuck in dysfunctional patterns that exacerbate stress across both domains. A wealth of literature in both ADSMs and veterans as well as civilians has shown that psychopathology can contribute to increased withdrawal, conflict, or criticism between partners in a couple as well as an increased risk of relationship dissolution (Whisman & Robustelli, 2016). In particular, PTSD, which can be associated with military-related trauma exposure (e.g., combat, MST), can be associated with fewer self-disclosures and emotional expression in intimate relationships, greater anxiety associated with intimacy, and more aggression (Monson et al., 2009). As such, couples interventions focused on targeting psychopathology may be indicated for ADSMs and veterans with significant psychopathological symptoms (see below for more on these interventions).

Injury, Chronic Pain, and TBI

ADSMs and veterans may also be at risk for injury related to their military service. This has the potential to result in changes in physical performance and ability that may impact mental health as well as functioning and responsibilities in relationships and at home. For ADSM and veterans with chronic pain, partners' behaviors and perceptions of the other's pain can impact both pain levels and relationship functioning. For example, in a sample of veteran couples, partners' understanding toward the veteran was associated with increased positive affect and decreased veteran pain (O'Neill et al., 2020). Other research shows when partners are uncertain about the source of the other's pain or when they attribute the other's pain behavior as within their control, they display more hostile, critical, and invalidating behaviors toward their partner (Burns et al., 2018, 2019). TBI, a key injury of the OIF/OEF/OND conflict, is also associated with decreased family and couple functioning years after returning home from deployment (Pugh et al., 2018). TBI in civilian populations has been associated with decreased relationship satisfaction, intimacy, sexual functioning, and sexual satisfaction (e.g., Gill et al., 2011; Ponsford, 2003). Although fewer studies have assessed the impact of military-related TBI on intimate relationships, there is some evidence suggesting a link between TBI and relationship status change (e.g., divorce or separation) (Stevens et al., 2017; Vanderploeg et al., 2003). Given the association between TBI and functioning in key areas such as cognitive, emotional, and relational expression, it is likely ADSMs and veterans with a TBI history may seek services for relationship distress.

Infidelity and Intimate Partner Violence

Infidelity and intimate partner violence (IPV) are major causes of relationship distress and treatment seeking among both military and civilian couples. By some estimates, infidelity is at least as frequent in military couples as compared to the general population, while recent studies suggest the largest discrepancy in infidelity rates exist between deployed ADSM (22.6%) and civilian community members (1.5–4%) (Allen & Atkins, 2005; Balderrama-Durbin et al., 2017). IPV tends to be more severe and more prevalent in military couples than in civilian couples (Klostermann et al., 2012). These high infidelity and IPV rates in ADSM and veteran couples are occurring despite both IPV and infidelity being violations of military regulations with penalties for ADSMs' careers if they are reported (see Klostermann et al., 2012). Perhaps given the military consequences for these relationship transgressions, military couples are more likely than civilian couples to seek couples therapy for infidelity (Atkins et al., 2005).

Identity and Intersectionality

An intersectional framework can help clinicians assess their ADSM and veteran couples' access or lack of access to privilege and sociocultural power as well as the challenges and vulnerabilities to adverse outcomes that they face. ADSM and veterans' identities and the intersections of these identities (e.g., age/cohort, race/ethnicity, gender, gender identity and sexuality) impact their experiences of military service and family life. ADSMs and veterans (women and underserved groups) with less access to privilege and sociocultural power are most at risk for adverse events during military service (e.g., MST, sexual harassment, physical assault, race or gender discrimination, and racism) (Coughlin, 2021; Schuyler et al., 2020; Turchik & Wilson, 2010; Wilson, 2016). These individuals may also subsequently face greater barriers to successful reintegration, such as difficulty obtaining civilian employment and housing, limited gender-specific medical care (e.g., lack of gynecological care or family planning), and challenges transitioning to changing family roles especially in dual military families.

ADSMs and veterans with multiple intersecting stressors from their military and readjustment experiences may also be at increased risk for interpersonal impairments such as sexual and relationship functioning. For example, veterans with a history of MST who subsequently report sexual dissatisfaction and unsatisfactory functioning with a partner are also more likely to report lower relationship satisfaction overall (Blais, 2020). The high comorbidity rates between one military-related stressor, such as MST, and other stressors including SUD, PTSD, or depression remains high (Gilmore et al., 2016; Goldberg et al., 2019), suggesting veterans may face compounding challenges that continue adding to both individual and relationship distress over time. Furthermore, dual military couples have additional/different stressors that impact relationship satisfaction, compared to nondual military or civilian couples, with relationship satisfaction lowest for women in dual-military couples (Woodall et al., 2020). The age and service era (e.g., Vietnam era vs. OEF/OIF/OND) of partners in a couple will impact relationship challenges as well. Presently, Vietnam-era veterans and their spouses/partners may be navigating the challenges of aging and retirement together, which, for many veterans, is associated with declines in physical health and increases in combat PTSD symptoms (Marmar et al., 2015). At the intersection of age and sexual orientation, older LGBTQIA+ couples have a longer history of exposure to discriminatory institutional practices, including military policies (e.g., "Don't Ask, Don't Tell"), and may be more reticent about seeking treatment (Hinrichs & Christie, 2019).

DOD and VA Initiatives to Serve Couples

Both the Department of Defense (DOD) and the Department of Veterans Affairs (VA) have developed strong initiatives to integrate partners and families into treatment for ADSMs and veterans. The DOD provides multiple programs focused on providing short-term skills-based and problem-focused counseling services to assist ADSMs with family difficulties. Two primary DOD counseling programs, Military and Family Life Counseling (MFLC) and Military OneSource, have been utilized by ADSMs to address common family and interpersonal challenges including financial hardship, parenting and relationship difficulties, and other life stressors in addition to military-specific difficulties such as deployments and time away from family. In a recent effectiveness analysis of these programs, most individuals utilizing the DOD family-focused counseling programs reported decreases in problem severity, anxiety, and stress, and a lower negative impact on work and daily life from their original stressors (Tanielian et al., 2018). Further, 90% of individuals reported high satisfaction with these programs, and 81% reported satisfaction with their program counselor regarding follow-up for outside services.

The VA also provides short-term family education programs to assist with family and relationship stressors (Makin-Byrd et al., 2011). Like the DOD counseling programs, the VA's SAFE program (Sherman, 2006) is led by trained professionals with a particular focus on PTSD. The VA also offers other services (e.g., National Alliance on Mental Illness Family-to-Family Education Program; FFEP) led by trained family member volunteers, which allows a greater reach of programs available for veterans and caregivers. The VA has expanded the breadth of evidence-based mental health treatments available to include short-term interventions focused on family psychoeducation for veterans with serious mental illness (e.g., behavioral family therapy; Mueser & Glynn, 1999); multifamily group psychoeducation; McFarlane, 2002) as well national rollouts of couples-focused treatments including both integrative behavioral couple therapy (IBCT) for general relationship functioning (Christensen et al., 2020; Jacobson & Christensen, 1996) and conjoint behavioral couples therapy (CBCT) for PTSD (Monson & Fredman, 2012) to target both relationship functioning and PTSD symptoms.

Evidence-based Couples Protocols for ADSMs and Veterans

There is a range of evidence-based couples therapy protocols available that can be used with ADSM and veteran couples. Research among veteran couples shows that there can be a wide variety of reasons couples seek therapy (Jarnecke et al., 2020). Therefore, before selecting a particular protocol, a couples assessment phase can inform the clinician about the reasons the couple is seeking treatment and their presenting concerns. Protocols exist that can target more general relationship concerns, such as poor communication patterns or lack of empathetic understanding between partners. Alternatively, other couples therapy protocols may be used to target more specific issues (e.g., psychopathology, infidelity, IPV).

Regardless of the couples therapy approach selected, recommendations for delivering culturally competent couples therapy include therapist recognition of their own assumptions and biases, acknowledging and attending to similarities and differences in diversity-related factors (e.g., identity, cultural upbringing and experiences) between therapist and couple and between partners within a couple, and addressing couples' experiences of oppression (Kelly & Iwamasa, 2005; LaTaillade, 2006). Integrating these recommendations across couples therapy protocols is essential to providing quality care among diverse ADSMs and veteran couples.

General Couples Therapy Protocols

As described previously, the primary rollout for evidence-based couples therapy in the VA is IBCT, developed by Jacobson and Christensen (1996) and later refined by Christensen et al. (2020). IBCT utilizes the "DEEP" conceptualization of couple distress with four primary themes (Differences, Emotional Sensitivities, External Stressors, and Patterns of Interaction), which is likely flexible enough to be used for diverse couples presenting to therapy. Primary initial goals of IBCT include emotional acceptance and learning to "let go of the struggle to change each other," while also incorporating change strategies later in therapy. Reports demonstrate how IBCT can be appropriately tailored for intercultural couples (i.e., by using the DEEP formulation to help partners accept differences bound in culture) (Kalai & Eldridge, 2021), and how treatment effects do not seem to vary substantially by gender, race, ethnicity, or income level (Doss et al., 2022), though more research is needed. Research among veteran couples suggests that they tend to average fewer IBCT sessions

(10) than non-veteran couples (12–20), and they also tend to show significant improvement with as few as four sessions (Christensen & Glynn, 2019).

Emotion focused therapy (EFT) is another therapy for targeting more general relationship concerns (Johnson, 2004). The focus of EFT is for couples to create attachment security in their relationship. EFT has a strong evidence base in the literature, and given its focus on attachment, it is theoretically a good fit for ADSMs or veterans and their families dealing with combat trauma and reintegration difficulties (Blow et al., 2015). For example, if an ADSM or veteran is struggling to respond to the emotional bids of their partner or not participating in family life, EFT can help partners create a safe emotional connection to share and respond to different emotional experiences. This can then foster safety, responsiveness, and engagement between partners. Weisman et al. (2013) piloted EFT with 15 veteran couples and noted significant improvements in PTSD symptoms, general life satisfaction, and relationship satisfaction for both veterans and their partners. EFT may also be culturally adapted for couples by utilizing culturally informed models of care or integrating narrative therapy to deconstruct dominant cultural narratives and promote therapeutic alliance (Linhof & Allan, 2019; Nightingale et al., 2019; Rastogi & Thomas, 2009).

Finally, traditional or enhanced cognitive behavioral couples therapy (TBCT) (Baucom & Epstein, 1990; Dattilio, 2010) is a combination of cognitive and behavioral interventions, with cognitive processes being the backbone of understanding relationship dysfunction. As the model has progressed, it has come to incorporate three domains of relationship functioning, including cognitions, emotional responses, and behavioral interactions, and focus more on contextual factors as well (Epstein et al., 2016). Interventions within TBCT can include teaching partners to recognize antecedents or triggers to disagreements (cognitive), then changing their behaviors. A randomized controlled trial found relatively similar effectiveness when comparing TBCT and IBCT, though further gains were made over time with IBCT versus TBCT (71% of IBCT couples and 59% of TBCT couples were reliably improved or recovered) (Christensen et al., 2004, 2010). Work is underway to adapt TBCT to certain populations (e.g., integrating TBCT with the sexual minority stress model for same-sex couples) (Pentel et al., 2021). There are currently no studies to date of TBCT specifically with ADSMs or veterans, however.

Disorder/Issue-specific Protocols

In addition to the more general couples therapy treatments, there are also several evidence-based couples treatment options for more specific issues that might be relevant to working with ADSM and veteran couples. Introducing a couples-focused treatment for individual psychopathology can be useful when partners are engaging in dysfunctional patterns that may exacerbate both individual symptoms and relationship distress. Behavioral couples therapy for depression (BCT-Depression) is closely related to TBCT (Fadden, 1991; Snyder & Whisman, 2004); however, this treatment adds a focus on helping the couple develop a sense of collaboration against depressive symptoms and identify ways to lower aspects of couple distress that may be impacting symptoms of depression. Cognitive-behavioral conjoint therapy (CBCT) for PTSD is another evidence-based treatment that targets both individual PTSD symptoms as well as relationship distress (Monson & Fredman, 2012). This treatment typically involves 15 sessions that incorporate psychoeducation on PTSD as well as behavioral and cognitive interventions for both PTSD and relationship distress. Randomized controlled trials have found strong evidence for CBCT decreasing PTSD symptoms and increasing relationship satisfaction among veteran couples (Liebman et al., 2020).

There are two behavioral couples therapy (BCT) protocols that exist for targeting alcohol and drug use disorders (McCrady & Epstein, 2009; O'Farrell & Fals-Stewart, 2006). Both protocols are grounded in research demonstrating a bi-directional association between relationship functioning and substance use (McCrady et al., 2016; O'Farrell & Schein, 2011). Though each protocol utilizes some different interventions, they both focus on reducing or eliminating hazardous alcohol or drug use by evoking partner support and encouraging communication patterns that promote continued harm reduction or abstinence. Multiple investigations have shown that BCT for alcohol and drug use disorders produces better substance-related and relationship outcomes relative to individual therapy for substance use (Meis et al., 2013; Powers et al., 2008). There is also a preliminary couples-based protocol that combines BCT for alcohol and drug use disorders with CBCT for PTSD. In a veteran sample, this protocol showed promising support for reducing alcohol use and PTSD symptoms while increasing relationship satisfaction (Schumm et al., 2015).

Beyond evidence-based treatments for couples where one or both partners suffer from individual psychopathology, there is also a range of interventions specific to other common relationship issues, such as infidelity or IPV. *Getting Past the Affair* and *Helping Couples Get Past the Affair* (Baucom et al., 2011; Snyder et al., 2007) are companion books for clinicians and couples working on any type of infidelity in a relationship. These books outline a three-step approach to address the initial effect of the infidelity, identify the factors that contributed to the infidelity, and help partners decide how they want to move forward. An early study examining an integrative treatment to help couples recover from infidelity found that most couples enrolled were less distressed at the end of treatment, and the injured partner reported greater levels of forgiveness (Gordon et al., 2004). To date, this is the only evidence-based treatment centered on infidelity and can be used in conjunction with any of the three general, evidence-based couples therapies reviewed earlier.

The Strength at Home Couples Program aims to prevent IPV among ADSMs and veterans (Taft et al. 2016c). It is a trauma-informed program for relationship enhancement and IPV prevention and cessation. There are two cognitive behavioral group interventions for IPV: one is the perpetrator intervention program for those who are self- or court-identified as having difficulties with IPV and the other is a couples program targeting IPV prevention. The program has been found effective in civilian, military, and veteran populations, and it is currently used in the VA (Taft et al., 2016a, 2016b).

Future Directions for Couples Therapy with ADSM/Veterans

Although there are substantial resources and treatment options for ADSM and veteran couples, there are also areas for improved clinical care that warrant future research and attention. As described previously, clinicians must be mindful of the unique intersectionality of each individual and couple to provide the best possible care. However, guidance on how to inform and provide culturally relevant and sensitive practice among ADSMs and veterans is an understudied area ripe for further research. For instance, most treatment outcome studies have utilized homogenous samples of couples (e.g., White, middle-aged, different-sex married couples). Extending the empirical support of existing treatments to a greater diversity of ADSM and veteran couples is necessary to inform efforts to adapt or develop new treatments for specific cultures or identities. Further, some evidence-based couples therapy protocols lack information or language considerations for ADSMs and veterans. Supplements to existing protocols can be developed to address these needs. Additionally, while there are a number of evidence-based therapies for couples (e.g., IBCT, CBCT for PTSD), future work may seek to adapt a wider range of existing therapies for couples, such as dialectical behavioral therapy (Linehan, 2014) or mindfulness and acceptance-based therapies, to reach or meet other needs of couples.

More work is also needed to increase access to clinical care for ADSM and veteran couples. The DOD and VA both have programs and initiatives prioritizing the inclusion of families into ADSM and veteran care; however, further dissemination of these programs as well as additional funding and resources to open more couples and family clinics across VA medical centers, for instance, could further increase access. The DOD and VA have also been leaders in implementing and delivering telehealth services to ADSM and veterans, and use of these services only increased during the COVID-19 pandemic (Connolly et al., 2020). Although there are no well-controlled studies to date examining the effectiveness of telehealth couples therapy versus in-person couples therapy, use of telehealth technologies may be integral for couples who are geographically separated due to the ADSM's work, who live in rural locations, or who have difficulty accessing reliable transportation or childcare.

Many couples make attempts at repairing their relationship before pursuing therapy, although the resources they utilize on their own might not always be evidence based (Jarnecke et al., 2020). Thus, the further development of stepped-care models for couples' treatment may increase accessibility to efficacious relationship resources. That is, if clinicians start with providing couples recommendations for the least intensive services (as appropriate), it may be more feasible for couples to pursue avenues that successfully enhance their relationship. For instance, the use of couples-focused mHealth applications or adjunctive technologies may be beneficial for some couples, particularly those who need lower or less-intensive levels of care. OurRelationship, an online relationship program with a strong evidence base, has already been proposed as being an early step in a stepped-care approach for couples therapy (Le et al., 2021). Additionally, the VA has released Couples Coach, a tool that can be used by couples to complete relationship assessments, improve communication skills, and access information about local couples clinicians (Owen et al., 2020). These technologies hold great promise for providing ADSM and veteran couples with support to improve their relationship and can be used as brief and affordable ways to introduce couples to evidence-based care.

Conclusions

ADSM and veteran couples are highly resilient and even though no two couples are alike, careful considerations should be made when working with this unique population. There are many couple programs and therapy protocols that can be implemented with ADSM and veteran couples, though further work is needed to create and test culturally informed and inclusive protocols for various ADSM and veteran subpopulations. Finally, continued efforts for promoting and increasing accessibility to couples-based resources, including fitting them within a stepped-care model, is an important future direction.

References

Adler, A. B., Bliese, P. D., McGurk, D., Hoge, C. W., & Castro, C. A. (2011). Battlemind debriefing and battlemind training as early interventions with soldiers returning from Iraq: Randomization by platoon. *Journal of Consulting and Clinical Psychology, 77*(5), 928–940.

Allen, E. S., & Atkins, D. C. (2005). The multidimensional and developmental nature of infidelity: Practical applications. *Journal of Clinical Psychology, 61*(11), 1371–1382.

Atkins, D. C., Yi, J., Baucom, D. H., & Christensen, A. (2005). Infidelity in couples seeking marital therapy. *Journal of Family Psychology, 19*(3), 470.

Balderrama-Durbin, C., Stanton, K., Snyder, D. K., Cigrang, J. A., Talcott, G. W., Smith Slep, A. M., Heyman, R. E., & Cassidy, D. G. (2017). The risk for marital infidelity across a year-long deployment. *Journal of Family Psychology, 31*(5), 629.

Baucom, D. H., & Epstein, N. (1990). *Cognitive-behavioral marital therapy*. Brunner/Mazel.

Baucom, D. H., Snyder, D. K., & Gordon, K. C. (2011). *Helping couples get past the affair: A clinician's guide*. Guilford Press.

Blais, R. K. (2020). Lower sexual satisfaction and function mediate the association of assault military sexual trauma and relationship satisfaction in partnered female service members/veterans. *Family Process, 59*(2), 586–596. https://doi.org/10.1111/famp.12449

Blow, A. J., Curtis, A. F., Wittenborn, A. K., & Gorman, L. (2015). Relationship problems and military related PTSD: The case for using emotionally focused therapy for couples. *Contemporary Family Therapy, 37*(3), 261–270. https://doi.org/10.1007/s10591-015-9345-7

Burns, J. W., Gerhart, J., Post, K. M., Smith, D. A., Porter, L. S., Buvanendran, A., Fras, A. M., & Keefe, F. J. (2018). Spouse criticism/hostility toward partners with chronic pain: The role of spouse attributions for patient control over pain behaviors. *The Journal of Pain, 19*(11), 1308–1317. https://doi.org/10.1016/j.jpain.2018.05.007

Burns, J. W., Post, K. M., Smith, D. A., Porter, L. S., Buvanendran, A., Fras, A. M., & Keefe, F. J. (2019). Spouse and patient beliefs and perceptions about chronic pain: Effects on couple interactions and patient pain behavior. *The Journal of Pain, 20*(10), 1176–1186. https://doi.org/10.1016/j.jpain.2019.04.001

Campbell, D. J., & Nobel, O. B.-Y. (2009). Occupational stressors in military service: A review and framework. *Military Psychology, 21*(sup2), S47–S67. https://doi.org/10.1080/08995600903249149

Christensen, A., Atkins, D. C., Berns, S., Wheeler, J., Baucom, D. H., & Simpson, L. E. (2004). Traditional versus integrative behavioral couple therapy for significantly and chronically distressed married couples. *Journal of Consulting and Clinical Psychology, 72*(2), 176–191. https://doi.org/10.1037/0022-006x.72.2.176

Christensen, A., Atkins, D. C., Baucom, B., & Yi, J. (2010). Marital status and satisfaction five years following a randomized clinical trial comparing traditional versus integrative behavioral couple therapy. *Journal of Consulting and Clinical Psychology, 78*(2), 225–235. https://doi.org/10.1037/a0018132

Christensen, A., & Glynn, S. (2019). Integrative behavioral couple therapy. In *APA handbook of contemporary family psychology: Family therapy and training, Vol. 3* (pp. 275–290). American Psychological Association. https://doi.org/10.1037/0000101-017

Christensen, A., Doss, B. D., & Jacobson, N. S. (2020). *Integrative behavioral couple therapy: A therapist's guide to creating acceptance and change*. WW Norton & Company.

Connolly, S. L., Stolzmann, K. L., Heyworth, L., Weaver, K. R., Bauer, M. S., & Miller, C. J. (2020). Rapid increase in telemental health within the department of veterans affairs during the COVID-19 pandemic. *Telemedicine and e-Health, 27*(4), 454–458. https://doi.org/10.1089/tmj.2020.0233

Coughlin, S. S. (2021). Racism and discrimination in the military and the health of US service members. *Military Medicine, 186*(5–6), 147–147.

Dattilio, F. M. (2010). *Cognitive-behavioral therapy with couples and families: A comprehensive guide for clinicians.* The Guilford Press.

Doss, B. D., Roddy, M. K., Wiebe, S. A., & Johnson, S. M. (2022). A review of the research during 2010–2019 on evidence-based treatments for couple relationship distress. *Journal of Marital and Family Therapy, 48*(1), 283–306. https://doi.org/10.1111/jmft.12552

Epstein, N. B., Dattilio, F. M., & Baucom, D. H. (2016). Cognitive-behavior couple therapy. In *Handbook of family therapy.* (pp. 361–386). Routledge/Taylor & Francis Group.

Fadden, G. (1991). Depression in marriage. S. R. H. Beach, E. E. Sandeen, and K. D. O'Leary. Treatment manuals for practitioners. Guilford Press, 1990. *Stress Medicine, 7*(3), 194–194. https://doi.org/10.1002/smi.2460070319

Gill, C. J., Sander, A. M., Robins, N., Mazzei, D., & Struchen, M. A. (2011). Exploring experiences of intimacy from the viewpoint of individuals with traumatic brain injury and their partners. *The Journal of Head Trauma Rehabilitation, 26*(1), 56–68.

Gilmore, A. K., Brignone, E., Painter, J. M., Lehavot, K., Fargo, J., Suo, Y., Simpson, T., Carter, M. E., Blais, R. K., & Gundlapalli, A. V. (2016). Military sexual trauma and co-occurring posttraumatic stress disorder, depressive disorders, and substance use disorders among returning Afghanistan and Iraq veterans. *Women's Health Issues: Official Publication of the Jacobs Institute of Women's Health, 26*(5), 546–554. https://doi.org/10.1016/j.whi.2016.07.001

Goldberg, S. B., Livingston, W. S., Blais, R. K., Brignone, E., Suo, Y., Lehavot, K., Simpson, T. L., Fargo, J., & Gundlapalli, A. V. (2019). A positive screen for military sexual trauma is associated with greater risk for substance use disorders in women veterans. *Psychology of Addictive Behaviors, 33*(5), 477–483. https://doi.org/10.1037/adb0000486

Gordon, K. C., Baucom, D. H., & Snyder, D. K. (2004). An integrative intervention for promoting recovery from extramarital affairs. *Journal of Marital and Family Therapy, 30*(2), 213–231. https://doi.org/10.1111/j.1752-0606.2004.tb01235.x

Hinrichs, K. L., & Christie, K. M. (2019). Focus on the family: A case example of end-of-life care for an older LGBT veteran. *Clinical Gerontologist, 42*(2), 204–211.

Interian, A., Kline, A., Janal, M., Glynn, S., & Losonczy, M. (2014). Multiple deployments and combat trauma: Do homefront stressors increase the risk for posttraumatic stress symptoms? *Journal of Traumatic Stress, 27*(1), 90–97.

Jacobson, N. S., & Christensen, A. (1996). *Acceptance and change in couple therapy: A therapist's guide to transforming relationships.* WW Norton.

Jarnecke, A. M., Ridings, L. E., Teves, J. B., Petty, K., Bhatia, V., & Libet, J. (2020). The path to couples therapy: A descriptive analysis on a veteran sample. *Couple and Family Psychology, 9*(2), 73–89. https://doi.org/10.1037/cfp0000135

Johnson, S. M. (2004). *The practice of emotionally focused couple therapy: Creating connection* (2nd ed.). Routledge.

Kalai, C., & Eldridge, K. (2021). Integrative behavioral couple therapy for intercultural couples: Helping couples navigate cultural differences. *Contemporary Family Therapy, 43*(3), 259–275. https://doi.org/10.1007/s10591-020-09560-8

Kelly, S., & Iwamasa, G. Y. (2005). Enhancing behavioral couple therapy: Addressing the therapeutic alliance, hope, and diversity. *Cognitive and Behavioral Practice, 12*(1), 102–112. https://doi.org/10.1016/S1077-7229(05)80045-8

Klostermann, K., Mignone, T., Kelley, M. L., Musson, S., & Bohall, G. (2012). Intimate partner violence in the military: Treatment considerations. *Aggression and Violent Behavior, 17*(1), 53–58. https://doi.org/10.1016/j.avb.2011.09.004

Knobloch, L. K., Basinger, E. D., Wehrman, E. C., Ebata, A. T., & McGlaughlin, P. C. (2016). Communication of military couples during deployment and reunion: Changes, challenges, benefits, and advice. *Journal of Family Communication, 16*(2), 160–179. https://doi.org/10.1080/15267431.2016.1146723

LaTaillade, J. J. (2006). Considerations for treatment of African American couple relationships. *Journal of Cognitive Psychotherapy, 20*(4), 341–358.

Le, Y., Rothman, K., Christensen, A., & Doss, B. D. (2021). Integrating the online ourrelationship program into a stepped-care model of couple therapy. *Journal of Family Therapy, 43*(2), 215–231. https://doi.org/10.1111/1467-6427.12321

Liebman, R. E., Whitfield, K. M., Sijercic, I., Ennis, N., & Monson, C. M. (2020). Harnessing the healing power of relationships in trauma recovery: A systematic review of cognitive-behavioral conjoint therapy for PTSD. *Current Treatment Options in Psychiatry, 7*(3), 203–220. https://doi.org/10.1007/s40501-020-00211-1

Linehan, M. (2014). *DBT Skills training manual*. Guilford Publications.

Linhof, A. Y., & Allan, R. (2019). A narrative expansion of emotionally focused therapy with intercultural couples. *The Family Journal, 27*(1), 44–49. https://doi.org/10.1177/1066480718809426

Makin-Byrd, K., Gifford, E., McCutcheon, S., & Glynn, S. (2011). Family and couples treatment for newly returning veterans. *Professional Psychology: Research and Practice, 42*(1), 47–55. https://doi.org/10.1037/a0022292

Marmar, C. R., Schlenger, W., Henn-Haase, C., Qian, M., Purchia, E., Li, M., Corry, N., Williams, C. S., Ho, C.-L., & Horesh, D. (2015). Course of posttraumatic stress disorder 40 years after the Vietnam War: Findings from the National Vietnam Veterans Longitudinal Study. *JAMA Psychiatry, 72*(9), 875–881.

McCrady, B., & Epstein, E. E. (2009). *Overcoming alcohol problems*. Oxford University Press.

McCrady, B., Wilson, A., Muñoz, R., Fink, B., Fokas, K., & Borders, A. (2016). Alcoholfocused behavioral couple therapy. *Family Process, 55*(3), 443–459. https://doi.org/10.1111/famp.12231

McFarlane, W. R. (2002). *Multifamily groups in the treatment of severe psychiatric disorders*. Guilford Press.

Meis, L. A., Griffin, J. M., Greer, N., Jensen, A. C., Macdonald, R., Carlyle, M., Rutks, I., & Wilt, T. J. (2013). Couple and family involvement in adult mental health treatment: A systematic review. *Clinical Psychology Review, 33*(2), 275–286. https://doi.org/10.1016/j.cpr.2012.12.003

Monson, C. M., Taft, C. T., & Fredman, S. J. (2009). Military-related PTSD and intimate relationships: From description to theory-driven research and intervention development. *Clinical Psychology Review, 29*(8), 707–714. https://doi.org/10.1016/j.cpr.2009.09.002

Monson, C. M., & Fredman, S. J. (2012). *Cognitive-behavioral conjoint therapy for posttraumatic stress disorder: Therapist's manual*. Guilford Press.

Mueser, K. T., & Glynn, S. M. (1999). *Behavioral family therapy for psychiatric disorders* (2nd ed.). New Harbinger.

Nightingale, M., Awosan, C. I., & Stavrianopoulos, K. (2019). Emotionally focused therapy: A culturally sensitive approach for African American heterosexual couples. *Journal of Family Psychotherapy, 30*(3), 221–244. https://doi.org/10.1080/08975353.2019.1666497

O'Farrell, T. J., & Fals-Stewart, W. (2006). *Behavioral couples therapy for alcoholism and drug abuse*. Guilford Press.

O'Farrell, T. J., & Schein, A. Z. (2011). Behavioral couples therapy for alcoholism and drug abuse. *Journal of Family Psychotherapy, 22*(3), 193–215. https://doi.org/10.1080/08975353.2011.602615

Olenick, M., Flowers, M., & Diaz, V. J. (2015). US veterans and their unique issues: Enhancing health care professional awareness. *Advances in Medical Education and Practice, 6*, 635–639. https://doi.org/10.2147/AMEP.S89479

O'Neill, A. S., Mohr, C. D., Bodner, T. E., & Hammer, L. B. (2020). Perceived partner responsiveness, pain, and sleep: A dyadic study of military-connected couples. *Health Psychology, 39*(12), 1089–1099. https://doi.org/10.1037/hea0001035

Owen, J. E., Jaworski, B. K., Taylor, K., Simon, E., Cuellar, J., Ramsey, K. M., Steinmetz, S., & Chang, A. (2020). *Couples coach*. (Version 1.0) https://mobile.va.gov/app/couples-coach

Parcell, E. S., & Maguire, K. C. (2014). Turning points and trajectories in military deployment. *Journal of Family Communication, 14*(2), 129–148. https://doi.org/10.1080/15267431.2013.864293

Pentel, K. Z., Baucom, D. H., Weber, D. M., Wojda, A. K., & Carrino, E. A. (2021). Cognitive-behavioral couple therapy for same-sex female couples: A pilot study. *Family Process, 60*(4), 1083–1097. https://doi.org/10.1111/famp.12696

Ponsford, J. (2003). Sexual changes associated with traumatic brain injury. *Neuropsychological Rehabilitation, 13*(1–2), 275–289.

Powers, M. B., Vedel, E., & Emmelkamp, P. M. G. (2008). Behavioral couples therapy (BCT) for alcohol and drug use disorders: A meta-analysis. *Clinical Psychology Review, 28*(6), 952–962. https://doi.org/10.1016/j.cpr.2008.02.002

Pugh, M. J., Swan, A. A., Carlson, K. F., Jaramillo, C. A., Eapen, B. C., Dillahunt-Aspillaga, C., Amuan, M. E., Delgado, R. E., McConnell, K., & Finley, E. P. (2018). Traumatic brain injury severity, comorbidity, social support, family functioning, and community reintegration among veterans of the Afghanistan and Iraq wars. *Archives of Physical Medicine and Rehabilitation, 99*(2), S40–S49.

Rastogi, M., & Thomas, V. (2009). *Multicultural couple therapy*. https://doi.org/10.4135/9781452275000

Redmond, S., Wilcox, S., Campbell, S., Kim, A., Finney, K., Barr, K., & Hassan, A. (2015). A brief introduction to the military workplace culture. *Work, 50*(1), 9–20.

Sayers, S. L. (2011). Family reintegration difficulties and couples therapy for military veterans and their spouses. *Cognitive and Behavioral Practice, 18*(1), 108–119.

Schumm, J. A., Monson, C. M., O'Farrell, T. J., Gustin, N. G., & Chard, K. M. (2015). Couple treatment for alcohol use disorder and posttraumatic stress disorder: Pilot results from U.S. military veterans and their partners. *Journal of Traumatic Stress, 28*(3), 247–252. https://doi.org/10.1002/jts.22007

Schuyler, A. C., Klemmer, C., Mamey, M. R., Schrager, S. M., Goldbach, J. T., Holloway, I. W., & Castro, C. A. (2020). Experiences of sexual harassment, stalking, and sexual assault during military service among LGBT and non-LGBT service members. *Journal of Traumatic Stress, 33*(3), 257–266.

Sherman, M. D. (2006). Updates and five-year evaluation of the SAFE program: A family psychoeducational program for serious mental illness. *Community Mental Health Journal, 42*(2), 213–219.

Snyder, D. K., & Whisman, M. A. (2004). Treating distressed couples with coexisting mental and physical disorders: Directions for clinical training and practice. *Journal of Marital and Family Therapy, 30*(1), 1–12. https://doi.org/10.1111/j.1752-0606.2004.tb01218.x

Snyder, D. K., Baucom, D. H., & Gordon, K. C. (2007). *Getting past the affair: A program to help you cope, heal, and move on–Together or apart*. Guilford Press.

Stevens, L. F., Lapis, Y., Tang, X., Sander, A. M., Dreer, L. E., Hammond, F. M., Kreutzer, J. S., O'Neil-Pirozzi, T. M., & Nakase-Richardson, R. (2017). Relationship stability after traumatic brain injury among veterans and service members: A VA TBI model systems study. *The Journal of Head Trauma Rehabilitation, 32*(4), 234.

Taft, C. T., Creech, S. K., Gallagher, M. W., Macdonald, A., Murphy, C. M., & Monson, C. M. (2016a). Strength at home couples program to prevent military partner violence: A randomized controlled trial. *Journal of Consulting and Clinical Psychology, 84*(11), 935–945. https://doi.org/10.1037/ccp0000129

Taft, C. T., Macdonald, A., Creech, S. K., Monson, C. M., & Murphy, C. M. (2016b). A randomized controlled clinical trial of the strength at home men's program for partner violence in military veterans. *Journal of Clinical Psychiatry, 77*(9), 1168–1175. https://doi.org/10.4088/JCP.15m10020

Taft, C. T., Murphy, C. M., & Creech, S. K. (2016c). *Trauma-informed treatment and prevention of intimate partner violence*. American Psychological Association.

Tanielian, T., Trail, T. E., & Corry, N. (2018). Designing and implementing strategic research studies to support military families. In L. Hughes-Kirchubel, S. Wadsworth, & D. Riggs (Eds.), *A battle plan for supporting military families. Risk and resilience in military and veteran families*. Springer. https://doi.org/10.1007/978-3-319-68984-5_18

Turchik, J. A., & Wilson, S. M. (2010). Sexual assault in the US military: A review of the literature and recommendations for the future. *Aggression and Violent Behavior, 15*(4), 267–277.

Vanderploeg, R. D., Curtiss, G., Duchnick, J. J., & Luis, C. A. (2003). Demographic, medical, and psychiatric factors in work and marital status after mild head injury. *The Journal of Head Trauma Rehabilitation, 18*(2), 148–163.

Weisman, O., Zagoory-Sharon, O., Schneiderman, I., Gordon, I., & Feldman, R. (2013). Plasma oxytocin distributions in a large cohort of women and men and their gender-specific associations with anxiety. *Psychoneuroendocrinology, 38*(5), 694–701. https://doi.org/10.1016/j.psyneuen.2012.08.011

Whisman, M. A., & Robustelli, B. L. (2016). Intimate relationship functioning and psychopathology. In *The Oxford handbook of relationship science and couple interventions* (pp. 69–82). Oxford University Press.

Whisman, M. A., Salinger, J. M., Gilmour, A. L., Steele, B. A., & Snyder, D. K. (2020). Love and war: Prospective associations between relationship distress and incidence of psychiatric disorders in active-duty Army personnel. *Journal of Abnormal Psychology 130*(1), 3–8.

Wilson, L. C. (2016). The prevalence of military sexual trauma: A meta-analysis. *Trauma, Violence, & Abuse, 19*(5), 584–597. https://doi.org/10.1177/1524838016683459

Woodall, K. A., Richardson, S. M., Pflieger, J. C., Hawkins, S. A., & Stander, V. A. (2020). Influence of work and life stressors on marital quality among dual and nondual military couples. *Journal of Family Issues, 41*(11), 2045–2064. https://doi.org/10.1177/0192513X20903377

Family Therapy with Active-Duty Service Members and Veterans

10

Angela L. Lamson, Florence J. Lewis, Natalie M. Richardson, and Krysttel C. Stryczek

Systemic Therapies for Diverse Service Members, Veterans, and Their Families

The military is the largest employer in the United States (U.S.), with more than 3.5 million personnel currently serving in the Department of Defense (DoD) active duty, National Guard, and Reserves (DoD, 2021). Alongside the active duty population, it is estimated that there are currently over 22 million veterans (as defined by the U.S Department of Veterans Affairs; https://www.va.gov/health-care/eligibility/) in the United States (U.S. Census Bureau, 2012). Couple these figures with the number of partners and dependents or children of current or former service members, and the needs for military and veteran populations grows exponentially. To give some perspective, approximately 52% of all military personnel are married and about 42% of those in a reserve component are married. Of all current veterans, about 65% of men and 49% of women identify as married (Department of Veterans Affairs, 2019).

DOI: 10.4324/9781003185949-10

Whether partnered or not, there are almost 1 million dependent children in active duty families and 664,000 dependent children in National Guard and Reserve families (DoD, 2021). Behind each of these statistics is a face that is situated within multiple relationships and whose health and wellbeing are determined—at least in part—by their likelihood to sustain a career with the military or maintain healthy lives and relationships as veteran families. These relationships are embedded in a web of local, state, and federal military or veteran systems.

Systems at their core are complex and reflected in each military, veteran, and family decision or dynamic. A change in one (e.g., service member or veteran) influences a change in all others around them (e.g., unit, command, family, country; von Bertalanffy, 1968) and simply adding one element (e.g., a change of station) to the next (e.g., a new marriage) does not capture the complexity of the culminated decisions or dynamics.

A unique culture accompanies military service: language, roles, duties, and a sense of belonging that reflects a complex system at work. However, the trend toward solidarity and uniformity can create an oversight or omission in the intricacies of the service member's (and their family's) social locations (e.g., race, ethnicity, nation of origin, sexual orientation, gender identity, faith, age) and interactions within their daily life. The histories that coincide with marginalized social locations are often silenced. As such, these service members are exposed to discrimination and further marginalization. With so much diversity in the armed forces, it is surprising how little research exists on relational support or interventions that are intentionally designed for ethnoracial or ethnocultural service member and veteran couples and families.

This chapter is devoted to the recognition of ethnoracial and ethnocultural identities of service members, veterans, and their families (SMVF). Particularly, systemic treatments indicated for ethnoracial and ethnocultural SMVF couples and families will be described. The length constraints on this chapter will not allow for every potential diagnosis or presenting concern to be addressed, nor can we recognize every evidence-based treatment for SMVF. Our aim is to attend to the treatments that have promising results for diverse social locations in contrast to interventionists who merely collected diverse demographics but did not test for racial, ethnic, sexual orientation, or other differences and intricacies.

Diversity among Active-Duty Service Members and Veterans

Historically, the U.S. military has had a long history of various types of social diversity that include differences in gender (e.g., Bell & Crow, 2017; Dunwoody

& Sandberg, 2015; Wales, 2020), race (e.g. Mullenbach, 2013; Rohall et al., 2017; Stone, 2013), and immigration status (Van Wagenen, 2015). When the draft (i.e. involuntary military service) ended in 1973 (Vergun, 2020), there was a distinct increase in the shifts to promote social diversity to increase recruit levels (Rohall et al., 2017). However, the U.S. military values order, homogeneity, and discipline throughout the ranks; these values make recognizing and attending to diversity and minorities complex. Those who identify as a minority (in relation to a person of majority, by power or prevalence) in one or many social diversities (i.e., intersectionality; Crenshaw, 1989) must constantly navigate the intersection of policies, legislation, and laws made on the national level as well as global conflicts (e.g., Black Lives Matter, same-sex marriage, travel bans) that directly influence the lives of service members and their families (Rohall et al., 2017). These larger system shifts are not uncommon discussions in couple and family therapy.

The increasing social diversity in the U.S. Armed Forces has spanned decades (e.g. Alt & Alt, 2002; Bell & Crow, 2017; Farrell, 2019; Gamble, 2020; Mullenbach, 2013; Van Wagenen, 2015). An understanding of the history of diversity and inclusion in the military can be incredibly useful for family therapists to incorporate into their joining, assessment, and treatment of military clients. Much of what makes family therapy unique is the incorporation of contextual factors, like interpersonal and societal relationships, in treating behavioral and mental health concerns. Although there are various types of social diversities, the groups discussed most frequently include gender minorities, race and/or ethnic minorities, sexual minorities, and those with immigrant, or non–U.S. citizen status. A brief introduction of these social diversities is described next, followed by tested and indicated treatments for family therapy interventions with socially diverse active duty and veteran couples and families. This chapter concludes with a series of innovative designs that are currently under trial with service members, veterans, and their families (SMVF).

Gender Minorities

The role of women in U.S. military service has grown substantially since 2013, following a policy change allowing women to serve in combat when the 1994 Direct Combat Exclusion Rule was lifted (Laurence, 2017; Pellerin, 2015). Shifts in recognizing the potential roles for women in the military date back to the Armed Services Integration Act of 1948, which was a pivotal piece of legislation that formally allowed women to serve in the military. Before this act was passed, women were only authorized to serve in nurse-related positions that didn't include rank or benefits (Laurence, 2017).

Women account for an estimated 16.9% of those who are active duty, while males comprise the remaining 83.1% (1.1 million personnel; Department of Defense Office of the Deputy Assistant Secretary of & Defense for Military Community and Family Policy, 2017). Furthermore, women comprise 19.6% of Reserves and Guard (DoD, 2016). Among active duty women, there is a 4.2 to 1 ratio for women who are enlisted compared to women who are officers, in contrast with men who have a 4.8 to 1 ratio (Department of Defense Office of the Deputy Assistant Secretary of & Defense for Military Community and Family Policy, 2017). Comparatively, women are 19% of the overall officer corp.

With increasing numbers of women serving in the U.S. military, the number of women veterans enrolled in VA health care has tripled from 159,810 to 439,791 in fiscal years 2000 to 2015, a rate of growth exceeding that of male veterans. Additionally, women's utilization of VA health care has more than doubled within the same timeframe (Frayne et al., 2018). Although White women comprise the majority of the women veteran population, women veterans are more racially and ethnically diverse than the male veteran population, with 42% of women veterans belonging to a racial or ethnic minority group. Diversity among women veterans continuously increased between fiscal years 2000 to 2015 among African American/Black (24%–30%), and Hispanic/Latina (3%–7%) groups. American Indian/Alaskan Native, Asian, Native Hawaiian/Pacific Islander, and multi-race women veterans maintained 1% over the same period.

A 2017 article by Lacks et al. (2017) punctuated the inequities not just in the prevalence of women in the military but in recognizing their unique needs as service members. This research described 49 articles that had been published on the biological, psychological, social/relational, and spiritual health of active duty women. While women in service also experience musculoskeletal injuries, traumatic brain injuries, and deployment stress (as are often researched with servicemen), 27 of the 49 articles on women service members were publications related to pregnancy. Most of the publications around women's social health and relationships pertained to military sexual assault and harassment, not the challenges associated with being a deployable parent or concerning needed social support.

Approximately 63% of women veterans receive VA service-connected disability for injuries or illnesses incurred or exacerbated by military service, and 38% of these women represent a rating of 50% or higher level of disability (Frayne et al., 2018). The increasing proportion of women veterans of reproductive age yields increasing demand for reproductive health services and ongoing gender-specific care across women's lifespans. The Veterans Health Administration policies and initiatives have focused on increasing women veterans' access to care and improving the quality of gender-sensitive services as part of a commitment to gender equity in providing veteran health care, including gender-sensitive mental health and reproductive health care, to meet the unique needs and preferences of women veterans (Marshall et al., 2021; Veterans Health Administration, 2018). While challenges and barriers to access persist, efforts to increase women veterans' access to equitable VA health care continue, and women veterans' increasing use of VA services indicates a degree of improvement in closing the gaps in women's care.

Family life experiences can be especially challenging for women service members, particularly if they are single parents or without supportive extended families. Of those married in the military, men are more likely to be married compared to women (85%–15%), and many military women who are married (20%) are married to military men (DoD, 2021; Laurence, 2017). Being a dual military couple, where both partners serve at the same time, presents its own strengths and challenges; for example, Lacks et al. (2015) found that as dual military wives' rank increased, dual military husbands' marital satisfaction decreased. Dual military couples may be most in need of additional social support, such as family therapy, and yet face the greatest time restraints to receive such services. Dual military couples are underrepresented in the research, but what is known is that the majority of dual military couples are enlisted service members of lower rank are more likely to be part of an ethnic or racial minority group, are younger, are married for a shorter period of time, and have fewer children (Anderson et al. 2011; Office of the Deputy Under Secretary of Defense, 2009).

A new layer of gender diversity that the U.S. Armed Forces are currently navigating is supporting transgender service members. On June 30, 2016, the U.S. secretary of defense (at the time) declared that transgender service members were permitted to openly serve (DoD, 2016; Rosenstein, 2017), a ban that had been in place since 1960. A restriction was placed back into action from April 12, 2019 to January 25, 2021, that individuals could not enlist if they had "medically transitioned" and that those who were already serving could only do so under their biological sex. It is difficult to determine how many transgender service members are currently serving in the military because not all seek to undergo gender affirmation surgeries or openly report their identity. RAND Cooperation estimated that there are approximately 2,450 transgender military personnel who are active duty (Schaefer et al., 2016).

Overall, per the U.S. forces leadership, there are three main concerns that are considered when openly transgender people serve in the military that may worry leaders on the impact of mission readiness or the ability of transgender service members to do their job: (1) the risks to mental health, (2) impact of hormone replacement therapy on overall health, and (3) the need or risk associated with surgical procedures (Rosenstein, 2017). More is needed to learn how these concerns influence relational health and extend into the treatment provided in family therapy.

As service members are now provided with the medical support for gender affirmation treatments (DoD, 2016), these same supports are being extended, partially, to the dependents/family of service members as well who seek gender affirmation treatments. TRICARE, the health care insurance program for soldiers, retirees, and their families, states that hormone therapy and psychological counseling are fully covered for those who qualify for "gender dysphoria" even though gender affirmation-related surgeries may need additional support proving that they are "medically necessary" in order to ensure insurance coverage (Tricare, 2020).

The VA's increasing efforts to support gender health equity also extend to improving the quality and accessibility of services for transgender and intersex veterans (Mattocks et al., 2014). While the number of transgender veterans and their needs for VA services are uncertain, the growing presence of transgender veterans using VA services and efforts to provide affirming care are promising (Mattocks et al., 2014). Current VA policies on transgender care (Veterans Health Administration Directive 1341) include provisions for medically necessary care, including hormone therapy, specialized mental health care, preoperative evaluation, and postoperative and long-term care associated with gender-affirming surgery. However, the VA cannot currently perform or fund gender-affirming surgery. As these policies continue to develop to assist transgender service members and veterans, a combination of presenting concerns involved in the gender-affirming and gender-confirming processes may arise in family therapy.

Sexual Minorities

The end of 1993s "Don't Ask, Don't Tell" Policy in 2010 permitted gay and lesbian service members to openly serve in the U.S. military (Slack, 2012; Smith & De Angelis, 2017). It is estimated that 5.8% of active duty service members identify as lesbian, gay, or bisexual (LGB; 3.9% of men identify as gay or bisexual and 16.1% of women identify as lesbian or bisexual; RAND, 2015). The exact number of LGB veterans is not known; it is estimated that 3% of all LGB Americans are U.S. Veterans (Lamson et al., 2018).

Currently, same-sex marriage is legal, and benefits can be provided to spouses (e.g., health care, causality notification, and housing). Gay and lesbian service members and their spouses have had numerous obstacles to face through military regulations as well as federal and state laws, beyond what may be experienced in the approval or dismissal from their own family or colleagues. These multilayered systemic experiences have multilayered systemic outcomes for the service member, spouse, and children.

The next step for supporting same-sex couples is related to alternative family planning options (e.g., adoption, in vitro fertilization [IVF], etc.) that may not be fully covered by insurance or reimbursed by the military (Smith & De Angelis, 2017). Although infertility treatments, procedures, and services (e.g., infertility counseling, genetic testing, surgeries, medications) are covered as part of VA health-care benefits, access to IVF or other assisted reproductive technology services is limited to veterans with service-connected conditions associated with infertility (e.g., genital injuries, polytrauma, side effects of chronic medical conditions; VHA Directive 1332(2). The VA maintains a policy to support LGB veterans, in order to ensure LGB veterans receive affirming and clinically appropriate, equitable care (VHA Directive 1340: Health Care for Veterans who Identify as Lesbian, Gay or Bisexual) and mandates a specialized program to attend to health disparities affecting LGB, transgender and intersex veterans (VHA Directive 1340; VHA Directive 1341). Other common issues that may be part of LGB affirming care include attending to higher rates of PTSD and increased likelihood of suicidal ideation (Blosnich et al., 2021; Matarazzo et al., 2014).

Racial and Ethnic Minorities

Among those who serve, relatively one third, approximately 400,000 service members have reported identifying as a racial minority (i.e., Black or African American, Asian, American Indian or Alaska Native, Native Hawaiian or other Pacific Islander, multi-racial, or other/unknown), which is a higher representation than the U.S. general population (i.e., 68.7% of active duty are White whereas the U.S. general population is 76.3% White). Ethnically, 16.7% of personnel are reported to identify as Hispanic[1] (Department of Defense Office of the Deputy Assistant Secretary of & Defense for Military Community and Family Policy, 2017), which matches the prevalence of Hispanics in the U.S. general population. Further, approximately 15% of male veterans identify as non-White and non-Hispanic while 25% of female veterans identify as non-White and non-Hispanic. About 7% of Hispanic veterans are men and about 9.5% who identify as women (National Center for Veterans Analysis and Statistics, 2019).

Some challenges throughout service are unique to respective racial and/or ethnic groups. For example, African American and Black-identifying service members continue to endure racial tensions from white service members, worsened by the lack of diversity education or inability to attend to racial tension or discrimination from military leaders, particularly in how to manage a diverse force, discrimination, and racism (Han, 2017). An issue often faced by Asian Americans who serve, is societal discrimination within the U.S. that adds a level of stress for Asian American soldiers as they navigate both military and civilian worlds (Sohoni, 2017). Additionally, there is a trend that Hispanic women are enlisting at a higher rate compared to Hispanic men (De Angelis, 2017), which may bring concerns related to social identity, intersectionality (i.e., gender, race, ethnicity, etc.), and family life into the therapy room. All these societal and larger system stressors may contribute to presenting problems that are addressed in family therapy.

Over 9 million veterans used Veterans Affairs (VA) benefits and services in fiscal year 2017 (National Center for Veterans Analysis and Statistics, 2018). Although the average veterans enrolled in VA health care are White and non-Hispanic (73%), a 2017 survey of veteran enrollees reported a trend of racial and ethnic variation by age group (Huang et al., 2018). Veterans over the age of 65 identified as White and non-Hispanic (82.7%); however, younger enrollees were more racially and ethnically diverse. For example, veterans under age 45 were more likely to identify as Hispanic or Latino (12%). Black non-Hispanic veterans were more likely to compose the middle-aged (45–64) group (20%). Asian veterans were most represented in the under-45 age group (2.9%), as well as veterans identifying as multi-racial (3.3%). American Indian/Alaskan Native and Native Hawaiian Veteran data were not reported for the under-45 age group, but their highest groups were reported in the 45–64 age group (1.2% and 0.5%).

Immigrant/Foreign-born Service Members

Throughout the history of the U.S. Armed Forces, non–U.S. citizens have been heavily relied upon for service (Sohoni, 2017; Ford, 2001). Immigrant, or foreign-born, service members have served in the U.S. military for hundreds of years and in some of America's first wars like the Mexican-American War (Van Wagenen, 2015) and World War 1 (Ford, 2001). It is estimated that there are approximately 45,000 personnel who are currently serving in the U.S.

military and 700,000 foreign-born veterans, with roughly 5,000 legal permeant residents enlisting yearly (FWD.US, 2020; U.S. Department of Defense, n.d.; U.S. Citizenship and Immigration Services, 2021; U.S. Department of Homeland Security, 2020). As of 2018, the two main countries of origin are Mexico and the Philippines (Zong & Batalova, 2019).

Foreign-born service members have many unique challenges they must face in contrast to their counterparts, including having to manage the negative U.S. sentiment toward the presence of immigrants and risks of deportation for self or family members (during or post-service; Rodriguez & Manley, 2020). For foreign-born service members, the adaption to the U.S. military includes (1) adjusting to the culture of the military that includes its own language, social norms, and expectations, (2) navigating U.S. culture, which may be different from that of their country of origin, and (3) learning the English language, if the service member is not English dominant, in both the context of the U.S. military culture and civilian culture. This significant adjustment along with working to complete the naturalization process may be among the topics of discussion during family therapy.

Having an awareness of SMVF demographics and the ways in which service members and veterans are socially diverse can only enhance family therapists' awareness of social location and intersectionality when considering and implementing indicated treatments. Each of the characteristics described are at-risk groups with higher rates of health and mental health conditions, generally higher utilizers of services, and present with stressors and challenges that have implications for relational/family wellbeing and vulnerability for relational/family stress (Mattocks et al., 2014). A service member or veteran can identify with more than one of these identities. With the literature already being limited regarding the impacts and appropriate/efficacious treatments based on each individual characteristic, we really do not know much about the impacts or treatments for those who identify with multiple characteristics. The following section describes some of the SMVF interventions based on what we do know about social diversity and intersectionality through the design via sampling and/or analysis of outcomes.

Service Members and Family/Couple Therapy Interventions

Military families face many systemic strengths and challenges just as civilian families do. However, the rules, traditions, context, and culture of the military often create unique circumstances for these families (Fenell, 2016) and influence their ability to access appropriate services. One strength for service members (including the National Guard and Reservists) and their beneficiaries is the Military Health System (MHS). The MHS is an intricate web of health care led by the Office of the Assistant Secretary of Defense for Health Affairs within the DoD, and includes public health, health care delivery, and medical education for service members and serves over 10 million beneficiaries (MHS, 2017). Some additional advantages to military service include the opportunity for social and economic mobility that may not be as accessible to all in civilian life (Han, 2017). There are benefits like health-care coverage and housing that are afforded to racial and/or ethnic minority service members and their families that are often not as accessible or equitably available to minority civilians. Furthermore, service members, as well as their families, have access to numerous support systems that are often much more difficult to navigate in civilian life (e.g., financial and legal services, employment support for civilian partners, education benefits, and relational support including services for children with special needs, parenting programs, and family therapy).

There are also some challenges that are much more frequent or military-specific for service members and their families. Moving, particularly moving frequently, is often one of life's greatest stressors, but for military families, who typically move an average of once every three years, the effects can be intensified (Burrell et al., 2006). And yet, relocation or moving is only one of the many stressors that affect military couples and families. Work stress, deployment, financial issues, adjustment to new locations, isolation, and separation from support systems are just some of the top stressors often experienced by military families (Pianin, 2015). Additionally, approximately 33% of active-duty service members report experiencing marital or relationship distress as one of the top stressors endured during their time in the military (Pianin, 2015). Given that most military personnel are married and or have children (Department of Defense [DoD], 2021), it is imperative that clinicians better understand the systemic challenges often experienced by those in uniform. Clinical services and relational supports may need to be adapted to better serve our military families and couples during active duty.

The lifestyle associated with military culture is common for couples and families to discuss as part of family therapy services; adapting to such challenges are often difficult and experienced differently by each family member (Fenell, 2016). Specifically, adjustment challenges related to frequent relocations and family separation during training, deployment, or the permanent change of station (PCS) for the service member are faced by many active-duty couples and families. Constant worry or fear from partners and children related to the service member's safety, as well as potential changes related to biopsychosocial and/or spiritual wounds (e.g., traumatic brain injury, posttraumatic stress, moral injury) associated with military service or wartime experience also influence relationship functioning, connection, and intimacy for many military couples and families (Johnson et al., 2007; McFarlane, 2009; Sammons & Batten, 2008).

Members and families of the National Guard and Reserves face their own unique challenges. Oftentimes, these families may not live in or near communities with mental health services or family support (Sullivan & Harrison, 2011). These families often feel less prepared for deployments and relocations compared to active duty (Sullivan & Harrison, 2011). Additionally, there is typically a disconnect between what services are available to them as members of the Guard or Reserves, leaving many families to feel largely estranged from the support systems in place for active duty and VA–connected veterans. In response to the needs of service members and their families, numerous support programs as well as couple and family therapy interventions have been created. Select programs and interventions that incorporate findings with socially diverse couples and families are described in the following.

Support Programs for Military Couples and Families

Each military branch offers couple and family programs to enrich relationships and family connection during active service. However, little is known about the effectiveness of such programs and supports for addressing the unique experiences among socially diverse populations within the armed forces, including ability, racial and ethnic minority groups, LGBTQIA+ couples and families, or dual military couples.

For example, the Army promotes the Strong Bonds Program, a program that works to build relationship resiliency through chaplain-led weekend retreats for families and couples facing deployment. The Marine Corps offers the Prevention and Relationship Enhancement Program (PREP) for active duty and reserve couples. Based on 20 years of research, PREP is a research-informed approach to educating couples (premarital and marital) on how to communicate effectively, work as a team to solve problems, manage conflicts without damaging closeness, and preserve and enhance commitment and friendship. The *Chaplains Religious Enrichment Development Operations* within the Navy offers marriage enrichment retreats that provide opportunities for couples to learn about handling conflict, growing their marriage, building intimacy, communication, and understanding each other. Further, the Air

Force Chaplain Corps offers the MarriageCare program to promote healthy communication, forgiveness, and other relational skills to couples and families on Air Force installations. While many of these programs are supported by the DoD and available to all active-duty personnel and their partners/families, few of these programs and interventions have been studied with emphasis on ethnoracial or ethnocultural factors that influence the lives of socially diverse military couples and minority service member families. The following section highlights effective family and couple therapy interventions and/or programs with active-duty service members and their families in the context of ethnoracial and ethnocultural diversity.

One example of a program for families includes the Exceptional Family Member Program (EFMP). This is a program supported by the DoD and offered by each branch of the military that provides services and support for families with special health-care or educational needs (Huebner, 2019). EFMP has provided comprehensive support for family members by taking an all-inclusive approach to coordinate the military and civilian community, education, medical, housing, and personnel services to help service members and their families with unique needs (MilitaryOneSource, 2021a). Any active-duty family member with a chronic medical condition or special education need is eligible to be enrolled in the EFMP.

Interventions with Military Couples and Families

Interventions intentionally designed and analyzed with ethnoracial and ethnocultural service member couples and families in mind are limited. The following are examples of psychoeducation and couple or family treatments that have offered outcomes with minority service member couples and families.

The Families Over Coming Under Stress program (FOCUS, 2017) is one of the first trauma-informed, skill-based interventions that has been designed specifically for military families (Saltzman et al., 2007, 2011). The aim of the program is to teach practical skills to help families and couples overcome everyday obstacles related to military life and combat stress injuries (Beardslee et al., 2013); the program works to enhance communication, problem-solving, emotional regulation, goal setting, and managing trauma and stress reminders for both service members and their families. FOCUS was designed to enhance individual functioning in parents and children, as well as functioning across relationship dyads (Beardslee et al., 2013; Saltzman et al., 2011). According to the founders of the program, the FOCUS family resilience-enhancing program "is designed for culturally diverse, single and dual parent families contending with challenges encountered during pre-deployment, deployment, reintegration, and long-term post-deployment" (Saltzman et al., 2011).

The FOCUS interventions are tailored to fit the unique needs of the family and family members, including service members, partners and spouses, and children. The FOCUS development team adapted the intervention's core activities and methods to attend to the emerging needs of other special military populations, including families of service members with physical or psychological injuries (i.e., traumatic brain injury, posttraumatic stress; Beardslee et al., 2013; Cozza et al., 2013), families with young children, couples, and National Guard and Reservist families (Beardslee et al., 2013). To allow for even more access, the program has expanded to include online resources and teleconference training through their virtual networks, known as TeleFOCUS (www.focusproject.org/telefocus) and FOCUS World (www.focusworld.org).

Building Strong and Ready Families (BSRF) emphasizes the importance of marriage education among married U.S. Army couples. Stanley et al. (2005) found that couples with significant stress in their relationships reported positive impacts from the education intervention and significant improvements in relationship functioning. The authors explored group differences based on gender and racial background; of the males who completed both pre– and post–BSRF data, 44% were White, 20% African American, 11% Hispanic/Latino, 1% Asian, 1% Native American, and 11% identified as "Other." For females, 40% reported their race as White, 19% African American, 18% Hispanic/Latino, 2% Asian, and 10% "Other." No significant gender or racial group differences were found in ratings of BSRF components. In fact, these positive effects held for both men and women, couples of diverse ethnic and racial backgrounds, and couples with lower incomes compared with those from higher incomes, suggesting that BSRF may be a helpful resource for teaching marriage education to diverse samples in nontraditional contexts.

LGBTQIA+ COUPLES

Historically, active-duty military service members who identify as LGBTQIA+ have experienced further stressors and barriers to care related to additional stigma and lack of social support (Blount et al., 2017). Prior federal regulations excluded sexual minorities from openly serving in the military, thereby limiting the available mental health services for same-sex couples. After the repeal of the U.S. policy known as "Don't Ask, Don't Tell" in 2010, gay and lesbian service members have increased opportunities to obtain behavioral health care. One therapeutic intervention that has been found to be available to sexual minority military couples is cognitive-behavioral conjoint therapy (CBCT), which effectively addresses co-occurring posttraumatic stress disorder (PTSD) and relationship dysfunction (Blount et al., 2017). Female partners shared concerns about being accepted as a gay couple by their families and the greater military community, which impacted the service member's PTSD maladaptive beliefs and ability to connect with others (Blount et al., 2017). Overall, outcomes revealed high satisfaction with CBCT for military-related posttraumatic stress symptoms and expressed appreciation for the opportunity to participate in treatment as a couple (Blount et al., 2017).

LOWER-INCOME COUPLES

One way to improve access to services and support for military personnel is through internet-based and online programs; these services have grown tremendously throughout the COVID-19 pandemic. OurRelationship and ePREP programs, when conducted online, were found to significantly improve relationship satisfaction, conflict resolution, emotional support, and breakup potential among military couples (Salivar et al., 2020). Online interventions may not only reduce access barriers for service members and their partners/families, but they may also be a more appropriate platform for those with unique barriers to access (e.g., time limitations, financial stress, living in rural communities, vulnerable populations, etc.; Hull & Mahan, 2017; Shore et al., 2018).

ETHNORACIAL AND ETHNOCULTURAL COUPLES

Expressive writing has been found to benefit an individual's biopsychosocial health (e.g., Frattaroli, 2006; Sloan et al., 2005), and expressive writing specifically about one's relationship has been linked to "longer-lived relationships" (Slatcher & Pennebaker, 2006), reductions in anger, and decreased marital distress after infidelity in couples (Snyder et al., 2004). Military couples have also been found to benefit from brief, expressive writing interventions. Baddeley and Pennebaker (2011) conducted a randomized controlled trial with 102 active-duty couples who had experienced at least one deployment that explored the impact of expressive writing on marital satisfaction. Participants from the study had been married for an average of 7.5 years ($SD = 5.6$ years), with 66% of participants identifying as White, 17% as Latino, and 14% as Black. The researchers found that when soldiers write about emotional topics, their marital satisfaction increases (Baddeley & Pennebaker, 2011). For those couples whose service member was above the median in combat exposure, they experienced greater marital satisfaction at one month if the soldier wrote about emotional topics. While this intervention has been explored with somewhat racially diverse military samples, little is known about potential ethnoracial/ethnocultural differences for expressive writing interventions.

An abbreviated, intensive, multi-couple group version of cognitive behavioral couples therapy for PTSD (AIM-CBCT for PTSD) has been found to be effective for active-duty couples when delivered over a single weekend (Fredman et al., 2020). Among a group of 24 heterosexual couples who participated in the weekend group retreat, nonmilitary partners reported significant reductions in their partners' PTSD symptoms and endorsed overall improvements in their own depressive systems and relationship satisfaction at three months following the retreat (Fredman et al., 2020). While differences among racial and ethnic groups were not explored in this study, the sample included various individuals for different ethnoracial groups, including approximately 31% African American participants, 4% Asian-American participants, and approximately 23% who identified as "other" in relation to race. Therefore, an abbreviated, intensive, multi-couple group format may be an efficient strategy for improving patient, partner, and relational wellbeing in military couples with PTSD (Fredman et al., 2020).

An additional brief intervention for attending to relationship health that has been found to be effective for military couples has been the Marriage Checkup (Cordova, 2009). Specifically, the Marriage Checkup has been a helpful assessment tool for attending to relational health in integrated behavioral health care settings (i.e., primary care clinics; Cigrang et al., 2016; Cordova et al., 2017). Cordova and colleagues included 30 heterosexual couples in one study to explore relationship strengths, identify relationship health concerns, and provide feedback on how couples could improve their relationship health using the Marriage Checkup intervention. Participants were scheduled for three 30-minute appointments: the first appointment assessed relationship strengths, the second identified relationship health concerns, and the third appointment provided feedback (Cordova et al., 2017). Of the participants, 17% were Latino, 14% were Black, 11% were Asian, 5% were multiracial, and 12% declined to report their ethnicity. After treatment, participating couples reported improvements in their overall marital relationship health based on measures of relationship satisfaction and intimacy (Cordova et al., 2017). During other annual checkups, such as physical and dental health exams, integrated behavioral health care professionals can use the Marriage Checkup to briefly assess and intervene with couple-related stressors using a specific protocol that can be easily adapted for fast-paced military primary care settings (Cordova et al., 2017).

While these examples may not include all services and supports for attending to relational health for military couples and families, it does highlight the limited emphasis on issues of diversity in systemic interventions. Unfortunately, racial, ethnic, gender, and sexual minorities, among others, are grossly underrepresented in existing literature exploring couple and family therapy interventions. Therefore, less is known about the clinical effectiveness of interventions for ethnoracial/ethnocultural differences among service members. Much work is needed to improve the support and services to manage the unique challenges and stressors faced by our service members in uniform from socially diverse groups, without such attention these concerns may continue into the lives of our veterans.

Veterans and Family/Couple Programs and Therapy Interventions

The VA's mission is to provide equitable veteran-centered care, improve access to health-care services, and deliver services that honor veterans' treatment and appointment preferences (National Academies of Sciences, Engineering, and Medicine, 2018). This mission demands improving our understanding of the unique needs of veterans among underrepresented groups to develop new treatments and services, or adapt existing ones, to better serve minority veterans.

Veterans who utilize VA health-care services present with significantly higher health needs compared to other veterans and an increased need for specialty services for PTSD and substance use disorders (SUDs) among other mental health conditions (Meffert et al., 2019; Tsai et al., 2014a). For example, the use of mental health and SUD services increased almost five times among women veterans between the fiscal years 2000 to 2015 (Frayne et al., 2018). Alcohol use disorders are the most prevalent substance use problem among men and women veterans (Carr et al., 2021; Teeters et al., 2017), followed by tobacco use, and SUDs commonly co-occur with mental health conditions such as PTSD, depression, anxiety, and adjustment disorders (Teeters et al., 2017). One study reported that Black veterans were less likely to screen positive for alcohol use disorder compared to White and Hispanic veterans, but more likely than White veterans to have a mood or anxiety disorder. Hispanic veterans were more likely to have current mood or anxiety disorders (depression, PTSD) compared to White veterans, and reported poorer functioning and quality of life compared to White and Black veterans (Carr et al., 2021).

Studies of veteran mental health treatment preferences have found that veterans have an interest in and preference for couples and family interventions over individual mental health treatment (Batten et al., 2009; Khaylis et al., 2011; Thompson-Hollands et al., 2021). Veterans and their family members have also expressed a desire for programs focused on information, practical skills, support, and gaining a better perspective on veterans' experiences to facilitate post-deployment readjustment and reintegration into civilian life (Fischer et al., 2015) as well as support for parenting-related issues (Fischer et al., 2015; Sherman et al., 2016).

Research conducted with combat veterans and their families supports the importance of intimate relationships and interventions that can systemically address family dynamics and challenges associated with a variety of military prevalent concerns such as PTSD and SUDs (Monson et al., 2009; Sherman et al. 2005). Couple and family relationships are often adversely influenced by any negative or traumatizing experiences related to the veteran's military experiences and may in turn contribute to the development or exacerbation of mental health symptoms in their partner (Trump et al., 2015) or children (Ridings et al., 2019). Relational distress in turn may exacerbate a veteran's existing mental health difficulties (Creech et al., 2019), demonstrating a cyclical effect of stress on the family system. Intimate relationship satisfaction, however, may also mediate veterans' utilization of mental health care (McGinn et al., 2017).

Parenting challenges are also commonly observed by clinicians and recognized as a potential area for engaging veterans in mental health treatment (Creech et al., 2019). While there is clear evidence presenting a need for intervention to alleviate mental health symptoms with veterans and their family system, as well as veterans' preferences for these interventions, research on the use and effectiveness of systemic interventions with veterans either as a standalone relationship/family service or as an alternative, or adjunct, treatment for comorbid conditions is infinitesimal. In fact, much of the existing research primarily focuses on couple and family treatments for veterans' PTSD and some SUDs.

Rarely are the systemic interventions designed to consider the unique intersectional needs of ethnoracial and ethnocultural veterans and their families. The National Center for Veteran Analysis and Statistics via the U.S. Veterans Eligibility Trends and Statistics (2017) reported that Native Hawaiian/Pacific Islander, Black, and Hispanic veterans have a higher utilization rate of VA benefits compared to other racial groups, while American Indian/Alaskan Native and veterans of other races are the least likely to utilize VA benefits. Studies of racial and ethnic differences in mental health care utilization show similar rates across demographics, with some differences among types of treatments accessed that may be attributed to personal preferences (Koo et al., 2015; Spoont et al., 2009). Overall utilization trends may reflect a range of continuous VA access improvement efforts (Spoont et al., 2009). Though some of the available studies described below include ethnoculturally mixed veteran samples (e.g., LGBTQIA+, ethnic and racial minorities veterans), improving the inclusion of socially diverse couples and families in therapy are necessary to better inform culturally attuned couples and family interventions. In the following, some examples of effective interventions with diverse samples and ethnoracial or ethnocultural outcomes are described.

Veteran Couples Interventions

Couples' therapies that have been researched typically fall into one of three categories: (1) couples therapy attending to relationship distress, (2) disorder-specific couples therapy, or (3) as an adjunct therapy for the treatment of presenting issues. Studies of couples therapy interventions have documented promising results in supporting the effectiveness of couples' interventions for veterans. For many veterans, usual couples therapy treatment has been found to be effective in reducing psychological and relational distress over the long term (Nowlan et al., 2017). One study found that the positive impact of couples therapy on veterans' relationships across various factors, including demographic (e.g., race), psychological (i.e., depression, anxiety, substance use), and relationship characteristics (e.g., initial relationship satisfaction) (Doss et al., 2011). However, African American participants exhibited significantly more change in relationship satisfaction compared to White participants. Doss et al.'s (2015) outcome study with couples therapy among a racially/ethnic heterogeneous sample of partnered veterans (White, non-Hispanic 70% men and 68% women; African American 22% men and 19% women; White Hispanic 6% men and 10% women; and Asian American 2% men and 4% women) found improved communication, emotional closeness, and psychological distress mediated the treatment effect of couples therapy on relationship satisfaction. Although couples' demographic characteristics were not found to moderate the mechanism of change in couples therapy or relationship satisfaction, there were some key results associated with racial/ethnic differences predicting relationship satisfaction. For example, compared to White, non-Hispanic partners, African American men and women's emotional closeness and women's communication predicted relationship satisfaction.

Couple interventions have shown successful results in improving PTSD, SUD, and major depressive disorder (MDD) symptoms (Kugler et al., 2019). The Veterans Affairs and Department of Defense (VA/DoD) clinical practice guidelines for PTSD (2017), SUDs (2015), and MDD (2016) discuss recommendations for couples therapy intervention as a form of treatment for these specific disorders. The strongest recommendation for couples therapy (Department of Veterans Affairs, 2015) supports the use of behavioral couples therapy (BCT) as an effective, first-line alternative intervention for male or female veterans with alcohol SUDs, with empirical support that BCT is at least as effective as usual treatment and improves marital satisfaction (Fals-Stewart et al., 2006; Kugler et al., 2019; O'Farrell et al., 2017; Rotunda et al., 2008; Schumm et al. 2014, 2015). However, BCT effectiveness for other SUDs is unknown.

Although studies are limited, VA/DoD Clinical Practice Guidelines for major depressive disorder (2016) suggests offering couples-focused therapy as monotherapy or in combination with pharmacotherapy in cases of mild to moderate MDD and significant relationship distress. The workgroup discusses the risks and benefits of utilizing couples therapy over individual treatment when preferred by the veteran.

However, in contrast to guidelines for SUDs and MDD, the VA/DoD clinical practice guidelines for PTSD (2017) conclude there is limited evidence to recommend for or against trauma-focused or non-trauma-focused couples therapy as a first-line treatment for PTSD, although therapy may be considered when treating PTSD symptoms in veteran relationships. PTSD-specific couples' interventions with promising, but limited, support include cognitive behavioral conjoint therapy (CBCT) for PTSD, a disorder-specific couples therapy intervention, found to improve PTSD symptoms and relationship satisfaction (Fredman et al., 2011; Kugler et al. 2019; Monson et al., 2004, 2008, 2012; Schumm et al., 2013), and structured approach therapy (Sautter et al., 2014). Existing studies of couples therapy for PTSD provide evidence for improved PTSD symptoms in veterans and improved relationship satisfaction (Kugler et al., 2019). However, couples' treatment may not be suitable or as effective in cases of severe or complex PTSD (Sherman et al., 2006).

Other couples therapy interventions studied in the veteran population, though not specifically discussed in the VA/DoD practice guidelines, include integrative behavioral couples therapy (IBCT) (Erbes et al., 2008; Fischer et al., 2018), critical interaction therapy (Johnson et al., 1995), structured approach therapy for PTSD (Kugler et al., 2019; Sautter et al., 2009, 2014, 2015), mindfulness-based cognitive behavioral conjoint therapy (MB-CBCT; Kugler et al., 2019; Luedtke et al., 2015), and emotion focused couples therapy (EFCT; Batten et al., 2018; Blow et al., 2015; Kugler et al., 2019; Weissman et al., 2018).

Finally, Warrior to Soulmate (Stolldorf et al., 2018) has been adopted by VA health-care facilities nationwide. This structured community-based program based on Practical Application of Intimate Relationship Skills (PAIRS) curriculum is focused on teaching effective communication and conflict resolutions skills and has been found to improve marital relationship and satisfaction and increase intimacy between partners. Another relationally-focused retreat model, Veteran Couples Integrative Intensive Retreat (VCIIR; Monk et al., 2016, 2017) aimed to reduce the impact of PTSD and was also found to improve relationship functioning and significantly decrease trauma symptoms for both the veteran and support persons. The VCIIR has included very diverse samples, including 40% who identified as Hispanic or Latino, 5% who identified as Native American (Monk et al., 2016), 35.5% who identified as African American, and 2.6% who identified as Asian (Monk et al., 2017).

Veteran Family Interventions

Like couples therapy interventions, studies with family-based interventions aimed to address family system dynamics as an adjunct to veterans' treatment(s) for PTSD have presented promising results. Veteran retention in mental health treatment is a concern. Of the veterans who enter mental health treatment for PTSD, only a fraction complete an adequate number of sessions to experience treatment effects (Seal et al., 2010; McGinn et al., 2017). Engaging family members to support veterans in their initiation and ongoing participation in mental health treatment is another avenue for improving veterans' mental health and stress on the family system. For example, Thompson-Hollands et al. (2021) study piloted a brief family intervention (BFI) to reduce veteran dropout rates for veterans with PTSD beginning cognitive processing therapy or prolonged exposure therapies. The study intervention included a two-session protocol focused on psychoeducation and skill-building aimed to enhance the family members' understanding of trauma-focused treatment in order to alleviate their concerns for harm and to reduce family behaviors that may undermine the veterans' treatment (i.e., symptom accommodation). Veteran treatment dropout was substantially reduced compared to controls, though not statistically significant. Researchers observed a slight reduction in accommodating behaviors among family members in the intervention group compared to controls. In this study, veterans' race and ethnic demographics included 70% White, 15% Black, and 15% Hispanic. However, this study's demographic sample was notable in that, most veterans identified as males partnered with cohabitating female spouses or female partners, but one veteran identified as transgender. The authors noted a limitation of the small sample size of the study and could not extrapolate any results regarding diverse dyads.

One exemplar effort in providing a culturally attuned family intervention was created with Asian American and Pacific Islander veterans, a growing demographic that possess many protective factors (e.g., higher levels of education and health compared to other minority veterans, less likely to smoke than White veterans, more likely to have private insurance; Whealin et al., 2017). Whealin et al.'s (2017) cultural adaptation of an existing cognitive-behavioral psychoeducational intervention, "Koa," was constructed for rural Pacific Island veterans and their family members. Map of the adaptation process (MAP) was used to develop the intervention integrating Pacific Islander values, beliefs, and traditions, including those relevant to interpersonal relationships, spirituality, and holistic mental health. The intervention included an assessment of the veteran and family member dyad, an exploration of their relationship and the meaning of family, psychoeducation on PTSD and depression (e.g., the influence of PTSD or MDD on relationships), and skills for managing PTSD symptoms (e.g., anger and conflict management, assertive communication, stress management, wellness).

Whealin's pilot intervention outcomes reported positive reception and acceptability of the intervention by participants, statistically significant improvement in post-intervention relationship quality (dyadic adjustment scale, relationship satisfaction), including improved relationship cohesion and satisfaction, and significant improvement in family caregiving burden. With considerable negative impacts of PTSD on relationships and family functioning, this pilot intervention demonstrated that family-focused treatment can help veterans and family members develop more supportive relationships in the context of PTSD, and potentially alleviate family member distress or burden. The findings from this pilot project are especially influential in the context of another study that found that few Asian American veterans accessed mental health services despite an expressed need or desire (Tsai et al., 2014b).

Innovations in Interventions for Diversity, Equity, and Inclusion with SMVF

Through accountability for a national charge toward ethnoracial and ethnocultural awareness, sensitivity, and humility, numerous clinical research teams have been working to improve their interventions to better attend to socially diverse SMVF through their designs, implementation, and evaluation of outcomes. One exemplar is a team that has conducted a pilot randomized control trial entitled Safe Actions for Families to Encourage Recovery (SAFER; Goodman, 2021), which is focused on engaging families in veteran suicide prevention efforts. This team's pilot study was conducted with a sample of 35% Hispanic veterans and 49% Black/African American veterans. The intervention includes manualized 90-minute individual sessions with the veteran as well as four family-based treatment sessions.

Eye movement desensitization and reprocessing (EMDR; Shapiro, 2018) also continues to grow as an individual and relational therapy for trauma, accepted by the DoD and VA, as an effective form of treatment for service members and veterans (Brickell et al., 2015). Further, EMDR has been implemented with racially diverse and LGBT individuals, couples, and families (Nickerson, 2017). Future endeavors can work to strengthen the effectiveness of EMDR by implementing and evaluating ethnoracial and ethnocultural service members and veteran couples and families who engage in this trauma-focused treatment.

In addition to these research initiatives, the Department of Defense and Veterans Affairs have taken strides to strategically address diversity and inclusion for SMVF through numerous current and anticipated actions (MilitaryOneSource, 2021b). Some of these actions include taking stronger protections against discrimination; training to detect bias; removing photographs and references to race, ethnicity, and gender from personnel files that may influence promotions; and diversifying senior-level positions.

While confidential nonmedical counseling has been a long-standing option for service members and their families through their installations (i.e., with Military Family Life Counseling programs), more recently numerous SMVFs have reached out for support through the Military Crisis Line or Veteran Crisis Line. These options all help to reduce stigma and maximize accessible and equitable care for socially diverse SMVF while aiming to reduce a most concerning public health epidemic (i.e., service member and veteran suicide). Through initiatives that are both within the DoD and VA, along with intentional efforts by clinical researchers, efforts can be made to overcome some of the current challenges to delivering systemic therapies and better attending to the gaps in SMVF ethnoracial and ethnocultural intervention research.

Challenges to Delivering Systemic Therapies

There are several factors that couple and family therapists must consider when treating service members, veterans, and their families. For example, the severity of symptoms or comorbidities (e.g., PTSD along with SUDs) may preclude the delivery of couples and family interventions as an initial treatment option. However, family therapists in integrated care contexts (i.e., where physical and mental health care are provided simultaneously; Lamson et al., 2018) are trained to conduct assessments on the risks and benefits of delivering couple or family therapy and the appropriateness of indicated interventions in tandem with the veterans' other health-care treatment needs and preferences.

Family therapists' systemic training also prepares them to be aware of instances in which couples therapy may be contraindicated (e.g., in couples with a partner experiencing severe PTSD symptoms) whereby the prevalence of domestic violence may increase due to a veteran's experience of PTSD while attending to relational distress via couples therapy (Sherman et al. 2005, 2006; Teten et al., 2009). Little is known about treatment effectiveness under these conditions since couples presenting with these issues are commonly referred out for individual treatment and generally excluded from studies on couples and family interventions (Nowlan et al., 2017; Sherman et al., 2006). However, one study has found a significant decrease in intimate partner violence (IPV) following couples' treatment (Nowlan et al., 2017) and raises questions for further exploration of factors predicting improvement in the setting of IPV among veterans, such as improvement in veteran's mental health (Monson et al., 2009).

Engagement and retention in couples therapy is another challenge to navigate in the delivery of services. One study (Jarnecke et al., 2020) found that although most veterans attempted to improve their relationship (via individual therapy, book, friend, clergy member, etc.) before initiating couples' treatment, researchers estimated couples waited 4–7 years before pursuing couples therapy for relational issues. Further, premature termination in couples therapy among veterans is estimated to occur at 50–80% (Doss et al., 2011, 2015; Norona et al., 2021). Norona et al.'s (2021) study of treatment engagement and dropout among veterans reported a notable demographically diverse sample, including transgender men and women (.6% each) and racial/ethnic minorities (13% Asian, 13% Black/African American, 10.2% Hispanic/Latino, 5.1% Native Hawaiian/Pacific Islander, 1.1% biracial, and .6% American Indian/Native American). Analyses revealed no significant differences between groups regarding treatment engagement and dropout based on demographic factors, including gender identity and race/ethnicity.

Understanding risk factors for premature or early dropout in couples therapy is critical to improving assessment and intervention outcomes of couples. For example, Fischer et al. (2018) found that more severe symptoms among non-veteran partners were associated with higher dropout rates; no other demographics or treatment delivery factors were found to be related to dropout. Findings reported by Sherman et al. (2008) also reported partner factors that may present barriers to treatment, such as their own hopelessness about the veterans' potential to improve and logistical challenges such as scheduling and childcare. Furthermore, few family therapists have attended to reasons that ethnoracial and ethnocultural clients may not return for services (e.g., lack of representation in therapists' office space via paintings or magazines in the lobby, lack of representation in therapists' documentation via the use of binary language or with lack of attention to linguistic considerations, lack of attention to social diversity when joining). These findings highlight the need to attend to both partners' factors as well as ethnoracial and ethnocultural factors that may contribute to engagement and retention in couples therapy.

Research Limitations/Gaps

While few studies have evaluated the application of couple and family clinical interventions or examined their effectiveness among ethnoracial and ethnocultural service members, veterans, and their families, the existing evidence is growing. Future studies should compare the effectiveness of these modalities with that of individual treatment (VA/DoD, 2015, 2016, 2017) and begin to replicate studies that have been shown to be effective with majority samples (i.e., White) to attend more specifically to socially diverse samples. An alternative would be to expand on novel research that has been conducted with ethnoracial veterans via a race-related stressors group (Loo et al., 2007) by implementing this model with veterans and their partners or as part of family-based group therapies. Evidence for the application of interventions to demographically underrepresented and historically marginalized veterans with families is demonstrably limited.

The average veteran enrolled in VA health-care services most commonly identifies as White, married, male, and with at least one dependent (Huang et al., 2018). This demographic was reflected through most of the studies mentioned throughout this chapter; samples included were commonly White, heterosexual couples, and married couples or couples in long-term relationships. Many of the samples' ethnoracial demographics were grouped together (further marginalizing the unique differences within and between socially diverse couples) and most did not report whether dyads included interracial or ethnically mixed couples.

Veterans Affairs mental health care access is an ongoing challenge and focus of congressional mandates (e.g., Choice Act, MISSION Act; Department of Veterans Affairs, 2018; Huang et al., 2018; VA MISSION Act of 2018) and VA initiatives nationally (e.g., MyVA Access, also known as ChooseVA) (Huang et al., 2018; National Academies of Sciences, Engineering, and Medicine, 2018) in response to veterans' reports of barriers to accessing mental health services (Bovin et al., 2019; National Academies of Sciences, Engineering, and Medicine, 2018). The degree that access, or demand for, couples and family services is being met particularly for ethnoracial and ethnocultural couples and families is largely unknown and warrants national attention.

Conclusion: Implications for Research and Practice

Further study of couples and family intervention for underrepresented and historically marginalized service members, veterans, and their families is necessary to improve our understanding of the unique needs of these populations as well as to develop culturally adapted and efficacious interventions. Also, differentiation between clinical significance and statistical significance should be defined in future studies to aid in the translation of outcome measurements to clinical practice. Demonstrated need and SMVF's desire for couple/family treatment options warrant further study in the design and implementation of couple/family interventions as well as indicated protocols and interventions that enhance retention in treatment.

Acknowledgement

This material is the result of work supported with resources and the use of facilities at the VA Northeast Ohio Healthcare System, Cleveland, OH.

Disclaimer

The views expressed in this article are those of the authors and do not necessarily reflect the position or policy of the U.S. Department of Veterans Affairs or the United States government.

Note

1 The term "Hispanic" is used because this is how U.S. military literature labels this population. Terms like "Latino", "Latina", and/or "Latinx" may be more appropriate when describing this population.

References

Alt, W. E., & Alt, B. L. (2002). *Black soliders, white wars: Black warriors from antiquity to the present*. Westport: Praeger Publishers.

Anderson, J. R., Johnson, M. D., Goff, B. N., Cline, L. E., Lyon, S. E., & Gurss, H. (2011). Factors that differentiated distressed and nondistressed marriages in Army soldiers. *Marriage & Family Review, 47*, 459–473. https://doi.org/10.1080/01494929.2011.619301

Baddeley, J. L., & Pennebaker, J. W. (2011). A postdeployment expressive writing intervention for military couples: A randomized controlled trial. *Journal of Traumatic Stress, 24*(5), 581–585. https://doi.org/10.1002/jts.20679

Batten, S. V., Drapalski, A. L., Decker, M. L., DeViva, J. C., Morris, L. J., & Mann, M. A. (2009). Veteran interest in family involvement in PTSD treatment. *Psychological Services, 6*(3), 184–189. https://doi.org/10.1037/a0015392

Batten, S. V., Rheem, K. D., Wiebe, S. A., Pasillas, R. M., Potts, W., Barone, M., Brown, C. H., & Dixon, L. B. (2018). The effectiveness of emotionally focused couples therapy with veterans with PTSD: A pilot study. *Journal of Couple & Relationship Therapy, 17*(1), 25–41. https://doi.org/10.1080/15332691.2017.1285261

Bell, J., & Crow, T. (2017). *It's my country too: Women's military stories from the American Revolution to Afghanistan*. Lincoln, Nebraska, USA: University of Nebraska Press.

Beardslee, W. R., Klosinski, L. E., Saltzman, W., Mogil, C., Pangelinan, S., McKnight, C. P., & Lester, P. (2013). Dissemination of family-centered prevention for military and veteran families: Adaptations and adoption within community and military systems of care. *Clinical Child and Family Psychology Review, 16*, 394–409. https://doi.org/10.1007/s10567-013-0154-y

von Bertalanffy, L. (1968). *General system theory: Foundations, development, applications*. NewYork: George Braziller, revised edition 1976: ISBN 0-8076-0453-4

Blosnich, J. R., Hilgeman, M. M., Cypel, Y. S., Akhtar, F. Z., Fried, D., Ishii, E. K., Schneiderman, A., & Davey, V. J. (2021). Potentially traumatic events and health among lesbian, gay, bisexual and heterosexual Vietnam veterans: Results from the Vietnam Era Health Retrospective Observational study. *Psychological Trauma: Theory, Research, Practice, and Policy. Advance Online Publication.* https://doi.org/10.1037/tra0001025

Blount, T. H., Peterson, A. L., & Monson, C. M. (2017). A case study of cognitive-behavioral conjoint therapy for combat-related PTSD in a same-sex military couple. *Cognitive and Behavioral Practice, 24*(3), 319–328. https://doi.org/10.1016/j.cbpra.2016.05.004

Blow, A. J., Curtis, A. F., Wittenborn, A. K., & Gorman, L. (2015). Relationship problems and military related PTSD: The case for using emotionally focused therapy for couples. *Contemporary Family Therapy, 37*(3), 261–270. https://doi.org/10.1007/s10591-015-9345-7

Bovin, M. J., Miller, C. J., Koenig, C. J., Lipschitz, J. M., Zamora, K. A., Wright, P. B., Pyne, J. M., & Burgess, J. F., Jr. (2019). Veterans' experiences initiating VA-based mental health care. *Psychological Services, 16*(4), 612–620. https://doi.org/10.1037/ser0000233

Brickell, M., Russell, M. C., & Smith, R. B. (2015). The effectiveness of evidence-based treatments in treatment of active military personnel and their families. *Journal of EMDR Practice and Research, 9*(4), 198–208.

Burrell, L. M., Adams, G. A., Durand, D. B., & Castro, C. A. (2006). The impact of military lifestyle demands on well-being, Army, and family outcomes. *Armed Forces and Society, 33*(1), 43–58. https://doi.org/10.1177/0002764206288804

Carr, M. M., Potenza, M. N., Serowik, K. L., & Pietrzak, R. H. (2021). Race, ethnicity, and clinical features of alcohol use disorder among US military veterans: Results from the national health and resilience in veterans study. *The American Journal on Addictions, 30*(1), 26–33. https://doi.org/10.1111/ajad.13067

Cordova, J. V. (2009). *The marriage checkup: A scientific program for sustaining and strengthening marital health.* New York: Jason Aronson.

Cigrang, Jeffrey A., Cordova, James V., Gray, Tatiana D., Najera, Elizabeth, Hawrilenko, Matt, Pinkley, Crystal, Nielsen, Matthew, Tatum, JoLyn, & Redd, Kristen. (2016). The Marriage Checkup: Adapting and Implementing a Brief Relationship Intervention for Military Couples. *Cognitive and Beharioral Practice, 23*(4), 561–570.

Cordova, J. V., Cigrang, J. A., Gray, T. D., Najera, E., Havrilenko, M., Pinkley, C., Nielsen, M., Tatum, J., & Redd, K. (2017). Addressing relationship health needs in primary care: Adapting the marriage checkup for use in medical settings with military couples. *Journal of Clinical Psychology in Medical Settings, 24,* 259–269. https://doi.org/10.1007/s10880-017-9517-8

Cozza, S. J., Holmes, A. K., & Van Ost, S. L. (2013). Family-centered care for military and veteran families affected by combat injury. *Clinical Child and Family Psychology Review, 16*(3), 311–321. https://doi.org/10.1007/s10567-013-0141-3

Creech, S. K., Brown, E. K., Saenz, J. J., Kelley, J. W., Fenstermacher, S. R., Glynn, S. M., & McCutcheon, S. J. (2019). Addressing parent–child functioning problems in veterans with posttraumatic stress disorder: Veterans affairs provider practices and perspectives. *Couple and Family Psychology: Research and Practice, 8*(2), 105–120. https://doi.org/10.1037/cfp0000122

Crenshaw, K. (1989). Demarginalizing the intersection of race and sex: Black feminist critique of antidiscrimination doctrine, feminist theory and antiracist politics. *University of Chicago Legal Forum, 1*(8), 139–168.

De Angelis, K. (2017). Rising Minority: Hispanics in the US Military. In D. E. Rohall, M. G. Ender, & M. D. Matthews, *Inclusion in the American Military: A Force for Diversity.* Lanham: Maryland.

Department of Defense [DoD] (n.d.). *Military accessions vital to national interest (MAVNI) Recruitment pilot program.* https://dod.defense.gov/news/mavni-fact-sheet.pdf

Department of Defense [DoD]. (2016). *Secretary of defense ash carter announces policy for transgender service members.* https://www.defense.gov/Newsroom/Releases/Release/Article/821675/secretary-of-defense-ash-carter-announces-policy-for-transgender-service-members/

Department of Defense [DoD] (2021). *2020 Demographics Profile of the Military Community.* (n.d.). Retrieved October 2, 2022, from https://download.militaryonesource.mil/12038/MOS/Reports/2020-demographics-report.pdf

Department of Defense, Office of the Deputy Assistant Secretary of Defense for Military Community and Family Policy. (2017). *2017 Demographics: Profile of the Military Community.* Military One Source, Department of Defense. download.militaryonesource.mil/12038/MOS/Reports/2017-demographics-report.pdf

Department of Veterans Affairs. (2018, May). Expanded access to non-VA care through the veterans choice program. Final rule. *Federal Register, 83*(92), 21893–21897.

Department of Veterans Affairs. (2019). *Profile of veterans: 2017.* https://www.va.gov/vetdata/docs/SpecialReports/Profile_of_Veterans_2017.pdf

Department of Veterans Affairs & Department of Defense. (2015). *VA/DoD Clinical Practice Guideline for the Management of Substance Use Disorders, Version 3.0*. https://www.healthquality.va.gov/

Department of Veterans Affairs & Department of Defense. (2016). *VA/DoD Clinical Practice Guideline for the Management of Major Depressive Disorder, Version 3.0*. https://www.healthquality.va.gov/

Department of Veterans Affairs & Department of Defense. (2017). *VA/DoD clinical practice guideline for management of post-traumatic stress disorder and acute stress disorder, Version 3.0*. Washington, DC: Author. https://www.healthquality.va.gov/

Doss, B. D., Hsueh, A. C., & Carhart, K. (2011). Premature termination in couple therapy with veterans: Definitions and prediction of long-term outcomes. *Journal of Family Psychology, 25*(5), 770–774. https://doi.org/10.1037/a0025239

Doss, B. D., Mitchell, A., Georgia, E. J., Biesen, J. N., & Rowe, L. S. (2015). Improvements in closeness, communication, and psychological distress mediate effects of couple therapy for veterans. *Journal of Consulting and Clinical Psychology, 83*(2), 405–415. https://doi.org/10.1037/a0038541

Dunwoody, A., & Sandberg, S. (2015). *A higher standard: Leadership strategies from America's First Female four-star general*. Boston: Da Capo Press.

Erbes, C. R., Polusny, M. A., MacDermid, S., & Compton, J. S. (2008). Couple therapy with combat veterans and their partners. *Journal of Clinical Psychology, 64*(8), 972–983. https://doi.org/10.1002/jclp.20521

Fals-Stewart, W., Birchler, G. R., & Kelley, M. L. (2006). Learning sobriety together: A randomized clinical trial examining behavioral couples therapy with alcoholic female patients. *Journal of Consulting and Clinical Psychology, 74*(3), 579–591. https://doi.org/10.1037/0022-006X.74.3.579

Farrell, M. C. (2019). *Standing up against hate: How black women in the Army Helped Change the course of WWII*. New York: Abrams Books for Young Readers.

Fenell, D. (2016). Military couples and families. In J. Carlson & S. B. Dermer (Ed.), *The SAGE encyclopedia of marriage, family, and couples counseling*. SAGE Publications.

Fischer, E. P., Sherman, M. D., McSweeney, J. C., Pyne, J. M., Owen, R. R., & Dixon, L. B. (2015). Perspectives of family and veterans on family programs to support reintegration of returning veterans with posttraumatic stress disorder. *Psychological Services, 12*(3), 187–198. https://doi.org/10.1037/ser0000033

Fischer, M. S., Bhatia, V., Baddeley, J. L., Al-Jabari, R., & Libet, J. (2018). Couple therapy with veterans: Early improvements and predictors of early dropout. *Family Process, 57*(2), 525–538. https://doi.org/10.1111/famp.12308

FOCUS. (2017). *TeleFOCUS: FOCUS family resilience training is available at a distance*. https://www.focusproject.org/telefocus

Ford, D. N. G. (2001). *Americans All!: Foreign-born soldiers in World War I*. College Station: Texas A&M University Press.

Frattaroli, J. (2006). Experimental disclosure and its moderators: A meta-analysis. *Psychological Bulletin, 132*(6), 823–865. https://doi.org/10.1037/0033-2909.132.6.823

Frayne, S. M., Phibbs, C. S., Saecho, F., Friedman, S. A., Shaw, J. G., Romodan, Y., Berg, E., Lee, J., Ananth, L., Iqbal, S., Hayes, P. M., & Haskell, S. (2018). *Sourcebook: Women Veterans in the Veterans Health Administration. Volume 4: Longitudinal Trends in Sociodemographics, Utilization, Health Profile, and Geographic Distribution*. Washington, DC: Women's Health Evaluation Initiative, Women's Health Services, Veterans Health Administration, Department of Veterans Affairs.

Fredman, S. J., Monson, C. M., & Adair, K. C. (2011). Implementing cognitive-behavioral conjoint therapy for PTSD with the newest generation of veterans and their partners. *Cognitive and Behavioral Practice, 18*(1), 120–130. https://doi.org/10.1016/j.cbpra.2009.06.007

Fredman, S. J., Macdonald, A., Monson, C. M., Dondanville, K. A., Blount, T. H., Hall-Clark, B. N., Fina, B. A., Mintz, J., Litz, B. T., Young-McCaughan, S., Hancock, A. K., Rhoades, G. K., Yarvis, J. S., Resick, P. A., Roache, J. D., Le, Y., Wachen, J. S., Niles, B. L., McGeary, C. A., Keane, T. M., & Peterson, A. L. (2020). Intensive, multi-couple group therapy for PTSD: A nonrandomized pilot study with military and veteran dyads. *Behavior Therapy, 51*(5), 700–714. https://doi.org/10.1016/j.beth.2019.10.003

FWD.US. (2020, January 6). *Immigrants in the Military: 5 Things to Know*. FWD.Us. https://www.fwd.us/news/immigrants-in-the-military/

Gamble, D. R. (2020). Toward a racially inclusive military. *U.S. Army War College, 50*(3), 57.

Goodman, M. (2021). New directions in safety planning and lethal means safety for at-risk, suicidal veterans. *SPRINT Cyberseminar*. June 2, 2021.

Han, J. (2017). *African-Americans in the US military*. In D. E. Rohall, M. G. Ender & M. D. Matthews (Eds.), *Inclusion in the American Military: A force for diversity* (pp. 19–36). Landham: Lexington Books.

Huang, G., Muz, B., Kim, S., & Gasper, J. (2018, April). *2017 Survey of Veteran Enrollees' Health and Use of Healthcare: Data Findings Report*. https://www.va.gov/healthpolicyplanning/soe2017/va_enrollees_report_data_findings_report2.pdf

Huebner, C. R. (2019). Health and mental health needs of children in US military families. *Pediatrics, 143*(1), 1–13. https://doi.org/10.1542/peds.2018-3258

Hull, T. D., & Mahan, K. (2017). A study of asynchronous mobile-enabled sms text psychotherapy. *Telemedicine Journal and e-Health, 23*(3), 240–247. https://doi.org/10.1089/tmj.2016.0114

Jarnecke, A. M., Ridings, L. E., Teves, J. B., Petty, K., Bhatia, V., & Libet, J. (2020). The path to couples therapy: A descriptive analysis on a veteran sample. *Couple and Family Psychology: Research and Practice, 9*(2), 73–89. https://doi.org/10.1037/cfp0000135

Johnson, D. R., Feldman, S., & Lubin, H. (1995). Critical interaction therapy: Couples therapy in combat-related posttraumatic stress disorder. *Family Process, 34*(4), 401–412. https://doi.org/10.1111/j.1545-5300.1995.00401.x

Johnson, S. J., Sherman, M. D., Hoffman, J. S., James Johnson, P. L., Lochman, J. E., Magee, T. N., & Riggs, D. (2007). *The psychological needs of US Military Service Members and their families: A preliminary report*. Washington, DC: American Psychological Association.

Khaylis, A., Polusny, M. A., Erbes, C. R., Gewirtz, A., & Rath, M. (2011). Posttraumatic stress, family adjustment, and treatment preferences among National Guard soldiers deployed to OEF/OIF. *Military Medicine, 176*, 126–131. https://doi.org/10.7205/MILMED-D-10-00094

Koo, K. H., Madden, E., & Maguen, S. (2015). Race-ethnicity and gender differences in VA health care service utilization among U.S. veterans of recent conflicts. *Psychiatric Services, 66*(5), 507–513. https://doi.org/10.1176/appi.ps.201300498

Kugler, J., Andresen, F. J., Bean, R. C., & Blais, R. K. (2019). Couple-based interventions for PTSD among military veterans: An empirical review. *Journal of Clinical Psychology, 75*(10), 1737–1755. https://doi.org/10.1002/jclp.22822

Lacks, M., Lamson, A. L., Lewis, M., & White, M. (2015). Reporting for double duty: A dyadic perspective on the biopsychosocial health of dual military couples. *Contemporary Family Therapy, 37*(3), 302–315. http://doi.org/10.1007/s10591-015-9341-y

Lacks, M. H., Lamson, A. L., Rappleyea, D. L., Russoniello, C. V., & Littleton, H. L. (2017). A systematic review of the biopsychosocial-spiritual health of active duty women. *Military Psychology, 29*(6), 570–580. https://doi.org/10.1037/mil0000176

Lamson, A., Lacks, M., Cobb, E., & Seamon. G. (2018). Medical family therapy in military and veteran health systems. In T. Mendenhall, A. Lamson, J. Hodgson, & M. Baird (Eds.), *Clinical methods in medical family therapy* (pp. 537–582). New York: Springer.

Laurence, J. H. (2017). Women and the US Military. In D. E. Rohall, M. G. Ender, & M. D. Matthews, *Inclusion in the American Military: A Force for Diversity*. Lanham: Maryland.

Loo, C. M., Ueda, S. S., & Morton, R.K. (2007). Group treatment for race-related stresses among minority Vietnam veterans. *Transcultural Psychiatry, 44*(1), 115–135. https://doi.org/10.1177/1363461507074980

Luedtke, B., Davis, L., & Monson, C. (2015). Mindfulness-based cognitive-behavioral conjoint therapy for posttraumatic stress disorder: A case study. *Journal of Contemporary Psychotherapy, 45*(4), 1–8. https://doi.org/10.1007/s10879-015-9298-z

Marshall, V., Stryczek, K. C., Haverhals, L., Young, J., Au, D. H., Ho, P. M., Kaboli, P. J., Kirsh, S., & Sayre, G. (2021). The focus they deserve: Improving women veterans' health care access. *Women's Health Issues: Official Publication of the Jacobs Institute of Women's Health, 31*(4), 399–407. https://doi.org/10.1016/j.whi.2020.12.011

Matarazzo, B. B., Barnes, S. M., Pease, J. L., Russell, L. M., Hanson, J. E., Soberay, K. A., & Gutierrez, P. M. (2014). Suicide risk among lesbian, gay, bisexual, and transgender military personnel and veterans: What does the literature tell us?. *Suicide & Life-threatening Behavior, 44*(2), 200–217. https://doi.org/10.1111/sltb.12073

Mattocks, K. M., Kauth, M. R., Sandfort, T., Matza, A. R., Sullivan, J. C., & Shipherd, J. C. (2014). Understanding health-care needs of sexual and gender minority veterans: How targeted research and policy can improve health. *LGBT Health, 1*(1), 50–57. https://doi.org/10.1089/lgbt.2013.0003

McFarlane, A. C. (2009). Military deployment: The impact on children and family adjustment and the need for care. *Current Opinion in Psychiatry, 22*(4), 369–373. https://doi.org/10.1097/YCO.0b013e32832c9064

McGinn, M. M., Hoerster, K. D., Stryczek, K. C., Malte, C. A., & Jakupcak, M. (2017). Relationship satisfaction, PTSD symptom severity, and mental healthcare utilization among OEF/OIF veterans. *Journal of Family Psychology, 31*(1), 111–116. https://doi.org/10.1037/fam0000224

Meffert, B. N., Morabito, D. M., Sawicki, D. A., Hausman, C., Southwick, S. M., Pietrzak, R. H., & Heinz, A. J. (2019). U.S. veterans who do and do not utilize Veterans Affairs health care services: Demographic, military, medical, and psychosocial characteristics. *The Primary Care Companion for CNS Disorders, 21*(1), 18m02350. https://doi.org/10.4088/PCC.18m02350

Military Health System. (2017). *About the Military Health System*. https://www.health.mil/About-MHS

MilitaryOneSource (2021a). *EFMP: Resources, Options, Consultations (ROC): The Essentials*. Retrieved from https://www.militaryonesource.mil/family-relationships/special-needs/exceptional-family-member/exceptional-family-member-program-the-essentials/

MilitaryOneSource (2021b). *How the Military Supports Diversity and Inclusion*. https://www.militaryonesource.mil/military-life-cycle/friends-extended-family/military-diversity-and-inclusion/

Monk, J. K., Ogolsky, B. G., & Bruner, V. (2016). Veteran couples integrative intensive retreat model: An intervention for military veterans and their relational partners. *Journal of Couple & Relationship Therapy, 15*(2), 158–176. https://doi.org/10.1080/15332691.2015.1089803

Monk, J. K., Oseland, L. M., Goff, B. S. N., Ogolsky, B. G., & Summers, K. (2017). Integrative intensive retreats for veteran couples and families: A pilot study assessing change in relationship adjustment, posttraumatic growth, and trauma symptoms. *Journal of Marital and Family Therapy, 43*(3), 448–462. https://doi.org/10.1111/jmft.12230

Monson, C. M., Schnurr, P. P., Stevens, S. P., & Guthrie, K. A. (2004). Cognitive-behavioral couple's treatment for posttraumatic stress disorder: Initial findings. *Journal of Traumatic Stress, 17*(4), 341–344. https://doi.org/10.1023/B:JOTS.0000038483.69570.5b

Monson, C. M., Fredman, S. J., & Adair, K. C. (2008). Cognitive-behavioral conjoint therapy for posttraumatic stress disorder: Application to Operation Enduring and Iraqi Freedom veterans. *Journal of Clinical Psychology, 64*(8), 958–971. https://doi.org/10.1002/jclp.20511

Monson, C. M., Taft, S. T., & Fredman, S. J. (2009). Military-related PTSD and intimate relationships: From description to theory-driven research and intervention development. *Clinical Psychology Review, 29*(8), 707–714. https://doi.org/10.1016/j.cpr.2009.09.002

Monson, C. M., Fredman, S. J., Macdonald, A., Pukay-Martin, N. D., Resick, P. A., & Schnurr, P. P. (2012). Effect of cognitive-behavioral couple therapy for PTSD: A randomized controlled trial. *JAMA: Journal of the American Medical Association, 308*(7), 700–709. https://doi.org/10.1001/jama.2012.9307

Mullenbach, C. (2013). *Double victory: How African American Women Broke Race and gender barriers to help win World War II*. Chicago: Chicago Review Press.

National Academies of Sciences, Engineering, and Medicine (2018). *Evaluation of the Department of Veterans Affairs Mental Health Services*. Washington, DC: The National Academies Press. https://doi.org/10.17226/24915

National Center for Veterans Analysis and Statistics, *Veteran Population, Population Tables: Race/Ethnicity* [2019; Data Set]. https://www.va.gov/vetdata/veteran_population.asp

Nickerson, M. (2017). *Cultural competence and healing culturally based trauma with EMDR therapy: Innovative strategies and protocols*. New York: Springer Publishing Company.

Norona, J. C., Borsari, B., Armstrong, K., & Shonkwiler, S. (2021). Veterans' treatment engagement and dropout from couple and family therapy in a Veterans Affairs Health Care System. *Military Behavioral Health, 9*(2), 223–237. https://doi.org/10.1080/21635781.2020.1864526

Nowlan, K. M., Georgia, E. J., & Doss, B. D. (2017). Long-term effectiveness of treatment-as-usual couple therapy for military veterans. *Behavior Therapy, 48*(6), 847–859. https://doi.org/10.1016/j.beth.2017.05.007

O'Farrell, T. J., Schumm, J. A., Murphy, M. M., & Muchowski, P. M. (2017). A randomized clinical trial of behavioral couples therapy versus individually-based treatment for drug-abusing women. *Journal of Consulting and Clinical Psychology, 85*(4), 309–322. https://doi.org/10.1037/ccp0000185

Pellerin, C. (2015). *Carter opens all military occupations, positions to women*. U.S. Department of Defense. https://www.defense.gov/Explore/News/Article/Article/632536/carter-opens-all-military-occupations-positions-to-women/

Pianin, E. (2015). *Top 5 Problems Facing U.S. Military Families*. Retrieved from https://finance.yahoo.com/news/top-5-problems-facing-u-203500587.html

RAND (2015). *2015 Health Related Behaviors Survey Sexual Orientation, Transgender Identity, and Health Among U.S. Active-Duty Service Members.* https://doi.org/10.7249/RB9955.6

Ridings, L. E., Moreland, A. D., & Petty, K. H. (2019). Implementing trauma-focused CBT for children of veterans in the VA: Providing comprehensive services to veterans and their families. *Psychological Services, 16*(1), 75–84. https://doi.org/10.1037/ser0000278

Rodriguez, D. X., & Manley, E. (2020). How we fail US foreign-born veterans: A scoping study of the literature. *Journal of Veterans Studies, 6*(3), 1–9. https://doi.org/10.21061/jvs.v6i3.186

Rohall, David E., Ender, Morton G., & Matthews, Michael D. (2017). *Inclusion in the American Military: A Force for Diversity.* Lanham, Maryland: Lexington Books.

Rosenstein, Judith E. (2017). The Integration of Trans People into the Military. In D. E. Rohall, M. G. Ender, & M. D. Matthews, *Inclusion in the American Military: A Force for Diversity.* Lanham: Maryland.

Rotunda, R. J., O'Farrell, T. J., Murphy, M., & Babey, S. H. (2008). Behavioral couples therapy for comorbid substance use disorders and combat-related posttraumatic stress disorder among male veterans: An initial evaluation. *Addictive Behaviors, 33*(1), 180–187. https://doi.org/10.1016/j.addbeh.2007.06.001

Salivar, E. G., Knopp, K., Roddy, M. K., Morland, L. A., & Doss, B. D. (2020). Effectiveness of online OurRelationship and ePREP programs for low-income military couples. *Journal of Consulting and Clinical Psychology, 88*(10), 899–906. https://doi.org/10.1037/ccp0000606

Saltzman, W. R., Lester, P., Beardslee, W., & Pynoos, R. (2007). *FOCUS for military families: Individual family resiliency training manual* (1st ed.). UCLA: Unpublished Manual.

Saltzman, W. R., Lester, P., Beardslee, W., Layne, C. M., Woodward, K., & Nash, W. P. (2011). Mechanisms of risk and resilience in military families: Theoretical and empirical basis of a family-focused resilience enhancement program. *Clinical Child and Family Psychology Review, 14,* 213–230. https://doi.org/10.1007/s10567-011-0096-1

Sammons, M. T., & Batten, S. V. (2008). Psychological services for returning veterans and their families: Evolving conceptualizations of the sequelae of war-zone experiences. *Journal of Clinical Psychology, 64*(8), 921–927. https://doi.org/10.1002/jclp.20519

Sautter, F. J., Glynn, S. M., Thompson, K. E., Franklin, L., & Han, X. (2009). A couple-based approach to the reduction of PTSD avoidance symptoms: Preliminary findings. *Journal of Marital and Family Therapy, 35*(3), 343–349. https://doi.org/10.1111/j.1752-0606.2009.00125.x

Sautter, F. J., Glynn, S. M., Arseneau, J. R., Cretu, J. B., & Yufik, T. (2014). Structured approach therapy for PTSD in returning veterans and their partners: Pilot findings. *Psychological Trauma: Theory, Research, Practice, and Policy, 6*(Suppl 1), S66–S72. https://doi.org/10.1037/a0036762

Sautter, F. J., Glynn, S. M., Cretu, J. B., Senturk, D., & Vaught, A. S. (2015). Efficacy of structured approach therapy in reducing PTSD in returning veterans: A randomized clinical trial. *Psychological Services, 12*(3), 199–212. https://doi.org/10.1037/ser0000032

Schaefer, A. G., Iyengar Plumb, R., Kadiyala, S., Kavanagh, J., Engel, C. C., Williams, K. M., & Kress, A. M. (2016). *Assessing the Implications of Allowing Transgender Personnel to Serve Openly.* https://www.rand.org/pubs/research_reports/RR1530.html

Schumm, J. A., Fredman, S. J., Monson, C. M., & Chard, K. M. (2013). Cognitive-behavioral conjoint therapy for PTSD: Initial findings for operations Enduring and Iraqi Freedom male combat veterans and their partners. *American Journal of Family Therapy, 41*(4), 277–287. https://doi.org/10.1080/01926187.2012.701592

Schumm, J. A., O'Farrell, T. J., Kahler, C. W., Murphy, M. M., & Muchowski, P. (2014). A randomized clinical trial of behavioral couples therapy versus individually based treatment for women with alcohol dependence. *Journal of Consulting and Clinical Psychology, 82*(6), 993–1004. https://doi.org/10.1037/a0037497

Schumm, J. A., Monson, C. M., O'Farrell, T. J., Gustin, N. G., & Chard, K. M. (2015). Couple treatment for alcohol use disorder and posttraumatic stress disorder: Pilot results from U.S. military veterans and their partners. *Journal of Traumatic Stress, 28*(3), 247–252. https://doi.org/10.1002/jts.22007

Seal, K. H., Maguen, S., Cohen, B., Gima, K. S., Metzler, T. J., Ren, L., Bertenthal, D., & Marmar, C. R. (2010). VA mental health services utilization in Iraq and Afghanistan veterans in the first year of receiving new mental health diagnoses. *Journal of Traumatic Stress, 23*(1), 5–16. https://doi.org/10.1002/jts.20493

Shapiro, F. (2018). *Eye movement desensitization and reprocessing (EMDR) therapy: Basic principles, protocols, and procedures* (3rd ed.). New York: The Guilford Press.

Sherman, M. D., Zanotti, D. K., & Jones, D. E. (2005). Key elements in couples therapy with veterans with combat-related posttraumatic stress disorder. *Professional Psychology: Research and Practice, 36*(6), 626–633. https://doi.org/10.1037/0735-7028.36.6.626

Sherman, M. D., Sautter, F., Jackson, M. H., Lyons, J. A., & Han, X. (2006). Domestic violence in veterans with posttraumatic stress disorder who seek couples therapy. *Journal of Marital and Family Therapy, 32*(4), 479–490. https://doi.org/10.1111/j.1752-0606.2006.tb01622.x

Sherman, M. D., Blevins, D., Kirchner, J., Ridener, L., & Jackson, T. (2008). Key factors involved in engaging significant others in the treatment of Vietnam veterans with PTSD. *Professional Psychology: Research and Practice, 39*(4), 443–450. https://doi.org/10.1037/0735-7028.39.4.443

Sherman, M. D., Gress Smith, J. L., Straits-Troster, K., Larsen, J. L., & Gewirtz, A. (2016). Veterans' perceptions of the impact of PTSD on their parenting and children. *Psychological Services, 13*(4), 401–410. https://doi.org/10.1037/ser0000101

Shore, J. H., Yellowlees, P., Caudill, R., Johnston, B., Turvey, C., Mishkind, M., Krupinski, E., Myers, K., Shore, P., Kaftarian, E., & Hilty, D. (2018). Best practices in videoconferencing-based telemental health. *Telemedicine and e-Health, 24*(11), 827–832. https://doi.org/10.1089/tmj.2018.0237

Slack, M. (2012, September 20). *From the archives: The end of don't ask, don't tell.* https://obamawhitehouse.archives.gov/blog/2012/09/20/archives-end-dont-ask-dont-tell

Slatcher, R. B., & Pennebaker, J. W. (2006). How do I love thee? Let me count the words: The social effects of expressive writing. *Psychological Science, 17*(8), 660–664. https://doi.org/10.1111/j.1467-9280.2006.01762.x

Sloan, D., Marx, B., & Epstein, E. (2005). Further examination of the exposure model underlying the efficacy of written emotional disclosure. *Journal of Consulting and Clinical Psychology, 73*(3), 549–554. https://doi.org/10.1037/0022-006X.73.3.549

Smith, David G., & De Angelis, Karin (2017). Lesbian and Gay Service Members and Their Families. In D. E. Rohall, M. G. Ender, & M. D. Matthews, *Inclusion in the American Military: A Force for Diversity.* Lanham: Maryland.

Spoont, M. R., Hodges, J., Murdoch, M., & Nugent, S. (2009). Race and ethnicity as factors in mental health service use among veterans with PTSD. *Journal of Traumatic Stress, 22*(6), 648–653.

Snyder, D. K., Gordon, K. C., & Baucom, D. H., (2004). Treating affair couples: Extending the written disclosure paradigm to relationship trauma. *Clinical Psychology: Science and Practice, 11*(2), 155–159. https://doi.org/10.1093/clipsy/bph066

Sohoni, Deenesh. (2017). Fighting to Belong: Asian-American Military Service and American Citizenship. In D. E. Rohall, M. G. Ender, & M. D. Matthews, *Inclusion in the American Military: A Force for Diversity*. Lanham: Maryland.

Stanley, S. M., Allen, E. S., Markman, H. J., Saiz, C. C., Bloomstrom, G., Thomas, R., Schumm, W. R., & Bailey, A. E. (2005). Dissemination and evaluation of marriage education in the Army. *Family Process, 44*(2), 187–201. https://doi.org/10.1111/j.1545-5300.2005.00053.x

Stolldorf, D. P., Fortune-Britt, A. G., Nieuwsma, J. A., Gierisch, J. M., Datta, S. K., Angel, C., Millspaugh, D. D., & Jackson, G. L. (2018). Measuring sustainability of a grassroots program in a large integrated health care delivery system: The Warrior to Soul Mate Program. *Journal of Military, Veteran and Family Health, 4*(2), 81–90. https://doi.org/10.3138/jmvfh.2017-0007

Stone, T. L. (2013). *Courage has no color, the true story of the triple nickles: America's first black paratroopers*. Somerville: Candlewick Press.

Sullivan, M., & Harrison, C. (2011). *Strengthening Resources and Supports for National Guard and Couples and Families*. Retrieved from https://www.brainline.org/article/strengthening-resources-and-supports-national-guard-and-couples-and-families

Teeters, J. B., Lancaster, C. L., Brown, D. G., & Back, S. E. (2017). Substance use disorders in military veterans: Prevalence and treatment challenges. *Substance Abuse and Rehabilitation, 8*, 69–77. https://doi.org/10.2147/SAR.S116720

Teten, A. L., Sherman, M. D., & Han, X. (2009). Violence between therapy-seeking veterans and their partners: Prevalence and characteristics of nonviolent, mutually violent, and one-sided violent couples. *Journal of Interpersonal Violence, 24*(1), 111–127. https://doi.org/10.1177/0886260508315782

Thompson-Hollands, J., Lee, D. J., & Sloan, D. M. (2021). The use of a brief family intervention to reduce dropout among veterans in individual trauma-focused treatment: A randomized controlled trial. *Journal of Traumatic Stress*. Advance online publication. https://doi.org/10.1002/jts.22680

Tricare. (2020). *Gender Dysphoria Services | TRICARE*. https://www.tricare.mil/CoveredServices/IsItCovered/GenderDysphoriaServices

Trump, L. J., Lamson, A. L., Lewis, M., & Muse, A. (2015). His and hers: The interface of military couples' biological, psychological, and relational health. *Contemporary Family Therapy, 37*(3), 316–328. http://doi.org/10.1007/s10591-015-9344-8

Tsai, J., Desai, M. U., Cheng, A. W., & Chang, J. (2014a). The effects of race and other socioeconomic factors on health service use among American military veterans. *The Psychiatric Quarterly, 85*(1), 35–47. https://doi.org/10.1007/s11126-013-9268-0

Tsai, J., Whealin, J. M., & Pietrzak, R. H. (2014b). Asian American and Pacific Islander military veterans in the United States: Health service use and perceived barriers to mental health services. *American Journal of Public Health, 104*(Suppl 4), S538–S547. https://doi.org/10.2105/AJPH.2014.302124

U.S. Citizenship and Immigration Services. (2021, March 3). *Military Naturalization Statistics | USCIS*. https://www.uscis.gov/military/military-naturalization-statistics

U.S. Department of Homeland Security. (2020, September 24). *Table 20. Petitions for Naturalization Filed, Persons Naturalized, and Petitions for Naturalization Denied: Fiscal Years 1907 to 2019*. https://www.dhs.gov/immigration-statistics/yearbook/2019/table20

VA Maintaining Internal Systems and Strengthening Integrated Outside Networks Act of 2018 or VA MISSION Act of 2018, 115th Cong., S. 2372 (2017–2018). https://www.congress.gov/bill/115th-congress/senate-bill/2372

Van Wagenen, M. S. (2015). Devotion to the adopted country: U.S. immigrant volunteers in the Mexican war. *Journal of American Ethnic History*, 34(3), 105–107.

Vergun, D. (2020, April 7). *First Peacetime Draft Enacted Just Before World War II*. https://www.defense.gov/Explore/Features/Story/Article/2140942/first-peacetime-draft-enacted-just-before-world-war-ii/

Veterans Health Administration. (n.d.). *Health Care Services for Women Veterans, VHA Handbook 1330.01(2)*. Washington, DC: U.S. Department of Veterans Affairs. Amended July 24, 2018.

Wales, S. (2020). *Braided in Fire: Black GIs and Tuscan Villagers on the Gothic Line 1944*. USA: Knox Press.

Weissman, N., Batten, S. V., Rheem, K. D., Wiebe, S. A., Pasillas, R. M., Potts, W., & Dixon, L. B. (2018). The effectiveness of emotionally focused couples therapy with veterans with PTSD: A pilot study. *Journal of Couple and Relationship Therapy*, 17(1), 25–41. https://doi.org/10.1080/15332691.2017.12852

Whealin, J. M., Yoneda, A. C., Nelson, D., Hilmes, T. S., Kawasaki, M. M., & Yan, O. H. (2017). A culturally adapted family intervention for rural Pacific Island veterans with PTSD. *Psychological Services*, 14(3), 295–306. https://doi.org/10.1037/ser0000186

Zong, J., & Batalova, J. (2019, May 13). Immigrant veterans in the United States. *Migrationpolicy.Org*. https://www.migrationpolicy.org/article/immigrant-veterans-united-states-2018

Treating Depression and Persistent Depressive Disorders in Active-Duty Service Members and Veterans

Alan L. Peterson, Chelsea J. Sterne, Anthony A. Cesare, and Brittany Hall-Clark

Similarities and Differences in Civilian, Military, and Veteran Populations

Although there are many similarities related to the treatment of depression and persistent depressive disorders between civilian, military, and veteran populations, there are also some noteworthy differences. One difference is that treatments that work for civilian populations may or may not work for military and veteran populations. Similarly, treatments that work for veteran populations may or may not work for active-duty military populations. For example, the primary evidence-based treatment for obstructive sleep apnea is

DOI: 10.4324/9781003185949-11

the use of continuous positive airway pressure (CPAP). Although CPAP may be a treatment option for civilian and veteran populations, active-duty military personnel who require CPAP to manage their sleep apnea are subject to discharge from active duty through a medical board. Similarly, one evidence-based approach for chronic pain management is the use of an implantable spinal cord stimulator; however, the use of such a device is incompatible with continued active-duty service. Similarly, trauma-focused cognitive behavioral treatments for posttraumatic stress disorder (PTSD) initially tested in civilian populations are less effective in military and veteran populations. However, military-specific adaptations to PTSD treatments can improve treatment outcomes (Peterson et al., 2021). Throughout this chapter, we have considered the potential similarities and differences between civilian, military, and veteran populations related to the treatment of depression and persistent depressive disorders.

Etiology and Epidemiology of Depression in Active-Duty Service Members and Veterans

Active-duty service members and veterans are susceptible to a unique set of environmental factors that put them at a particularly elevated risk for the development of depression. Significant life stressors have been identified as one of the strongest predictors of depression onset. Beyond civilian-related stressors, military members are also exposed to unique experiences such as deployment, combat, and combat training that can be significantly stress-inducing (Inoue et al., 2021). This exposure combined with extended separation from family members, the financial burden of deployment, and exposure to others in danger puts military members and veterans at much greater risk for the onset and maintenance of depression. Veterans are at increased risk as well. Separation from service can drastically change a service member's available support system, resulting in lasting feelings of isolation and emotional distress. Many of these veterans also experience a change in their available health care, resulting in more limited avenues by which to receive adequate diagnosis and treatment for their potential mental health symptoms.

Depression is one of the most common mental health conditions in the military, leading to increased health-care utilization, decreased life satisfaction, and increased susceptibility to common comorbid psychiatric disorders such as posttraumatic stress disorder and generalized anxiety disorder (Trivedi et al., 2015). Estimates of prevalence rates of depression within the military vary based on study perimeters, measurement tools, and time period. One meta-analysis estimated the prevalence rates of depression to range from 12% among currently deployed active-duty members, 13% among previously deployed service members, and 5.7% among those who have never deployed (Gadermann et al., 2014). A recent study found 9.6% of veterans surveyed between 2005 and 2016 met criteria for depression, 37% of whom had never sought treatment for their symptoms (Liu et al., 2019).

Ethnocultural Issues Related to Treating Depression in Military and Veteran Populations

Ethnocultural differences in the prevalence of depression have been reported. Studies have consistently found that White service members tend to endorse higher rates of depression and suicide (Liu et al., 2019; Tanielian & Jaycox, 2008). Liu et al. (2019) reported that Whites have consistently endorsed higher levels of depression relative to Blacks and Hispanics. They also found ethnoracial differences in use of psychotropics. Whites were twice as likely as Hispanics to be on antidepressants, which may reflect ethnocultural preferences in pharmacological treatment.

In addition, stigma, access to care, and cultural attitudes toward mental health care are ethnocultural factors that have been investigated in the treatment of depression (Chu et al., 2021; Tanielian & Jaycox, 2008). Chu et al. (2021) found that Asian American veterans who perceived stigma were less likely to utilize mental health services relative to Black, White, and other race veterans. Among those who did not perceive stigma, there were no racial differences observed.

One study found veterans of color with health-care coverage during the past year initiated treatment more rapidly for depression compared to veterans without health coverage (Goldberg et al., 2020). Thus, findings suggest that health-care coverage provided by the military and VA can reduce health disparities. Other factors that may reduce disparities in active-duty and veteran populations may be universal mental health screening.

Treatment Settings

Most active-duty military personnel receive their mental health care through local military treatment facilities (MTFs). The availability of evidence-based treatments for depression and persistent depressive disorders varies widely at individual MTFs. In some cases, if behavioral health providers are not available at an MTF, active duty are referred to local civilian behavioral health providers who are approved by TRICARE, the military's medical insurance program.

For veterans who are qualified and seek care at a VA MTF, the policies, procedures, and available treatments for depression and persistent depressive disorder are quite similar to those available at military MTFs. The VA treatment settings include medical centers, outpatient behavioral health clinics within the VA health care system, and community-based outpatient clinics. Similar to military treatment settings, if behavioral health providers are not available at a VA MTF, veterans can be referred to local civilian behavioral health providers through the recently approved Veterans Choice Program.

Evidence-Based Treatments for Depression in Civilians

Current evidence-based treatments for depression include pharmacological, psychotherapy, medical devices (e.g., transcranial magnetic stimulation), and combined treatment approaches (American Psychological Association [APA], 2019). The vast majority of this research was with civilian populations, including over 700 clinical trials of psychotherapy treatments (Plessen et al., 2022) and more than 500 clinical trials of pharmaceutical interventions (Cuijpers et al., 2020). How well the results of these studies generalized to military and veteran populations is unclear.

Evidence-Based Treatments for Depression in Active-Duty Service Members and Veterans

Behavioral health providers who treat depression in military and veteran populations should be familiar with the historical, cultural, and ethical considerations that are unique in these populations (Moore & Barnett, 2013). For active-duty military, there are requirements to maintain fitness for duty. Historically, the specific details of these guidelines have (1) varied across military branches, (2) been adjusted during time of military operational conflicts, and (3) been dependent on the treatment setting (e.g., in garrison versus deployed locations). As compared to research with civilian populations, there is a dearth of clinical trials with active-duty and veteran populations (Department of Veterans Affairs/Department of Defense, 2016; Hundt et al., 2014). A thorough review of the literature identified 10 clinical trials for depression and persistent depressive disorders in active-duty and veteran populations.

These clinical trials included pharmacological (1), psychotherapy (5), medical devices (2), and combination treatments (2).

Pharmacological Treatments

Surprisingly, only one pharmacological randomized clinical trial (RCT) has been conducted with active-duty military or veteran populations. The large RCT was limited to veterans ($N = 1522$) and was called the VA Augmentation and Switching Treatments for Improving Depression Outcomes (VAST-D) trial (Mohamed et al., 2017; see Table 11.1). VAST-D was a multisite RCT at 35 VA MTFs including veterans who were diagnosed with moderate to severe depression and experienced resistance to previous antidepressant treatment. In this three-armed RCT, veterans were randomized to (1) be switched from their current antidepressant to another antidepressant (bupropion), (2) have their current antidepressant augmented with bupropion, or (3) have their current antidepressant augmented with a common antipsychotic medication (aripiprazole). At the conclusion of a 12-week treatment phase it was determined the group augmented with aripiprazole had significantly increased remission rates (29%) over the group that switched to bupropion (22%). However, the overall effect size was small and the adverse events were greater with the aripiprazole treatment. As a result, further analysis including cost-effectiveness is needed to understand the net utility of this approach for veterans.

Psychotherapy Treatments

Five clinical trials were identified (see Table 11.1) that evaluated psychotherapy treatments for depression in military and veteran populations (Bedford et al., 2018; Egede et al., 2015; Luxton et al., 2016; Peterson & Halstead, 1998; Pfeiffer et al., 2020). Interestingly, all but one focused on the employment of technology as their method for delivering treatment. The two RCTs that showed the most significant response and remission rates were the ones in which the treatment was computer based, either as a problem-solving intervention (Bedford et al., 2018) or a peer-supported CBT (Pfeiffer et al., 2020). In the trial completed by Bedford et al. there was a 69% overall improvement over the control group on posttreatment assessment scores. In the other computer-based RCT completed by Pfeiffer and colleagues, both response and remission rates were significantly higher than the control group at sustained

Table 11.1 Summary of Clinical Trials of Treating Depression in Active Duty Military and Veteran Populations

Reference Citation	Participants	Inclusion Criteria/Baseline Assessment	Research Design	Treatment Intervention	Primary Outcome Measures	Results
Bedford et al., 2018	N = 24 100% veterans 79% males 21% females 71% White, non-Hispanic 29% Hispanic	> 4 PHQ-9	2-armed RCT of computer-guided PST for depression, PTSD, and insomnia or minimal contact control group	6 weekly PST treatment sessions	PHQ-9	PST resulted 69% improvement over control group on PHQ-9 scores.
Egede et al., 2015	N = 241 100% veterans 98% males 2% females 60% White 40% Black	>25 BDI >20 GDS	RCT of behavioral activation delivered in person or via telehealth	8 weekly 60-minute sessions of behavioral activation	GDS BDI	Response rates for telehealth (22%) vs. in person (20%) on the GDS were not significantly different. Response rates for telehealth (24%) vs. in person (23%) on the BDI were not significantly different.
Engel et al., 2016	N = 666 100% AD 81% males 19% females 48% White, non-Hispanic 34% Other, non-Hispanic 18% Hispanic	65% classified as depressed at baseline on the PHQ-9	2-armed RCT of Centrally Assisted Collaborative Telecare (CACT) for PTSD and depression (n = 332) or usual care (n = 334)	CACT patients received 12 months of stepped psychosocial and pharmacologic treatment with nurse telecare management of caseloads, symptoms, and treatment	SCL-20	CACT resulted in greater reductions in SCL-20 depression scores (56% vs. 31%) and significantly more participants had 50% improvement at 12 months (30% vs 59%).

(Continued)

Table 11.1 (Continued)

Reference Citation	Participants	Inclusion Criteria/Baseline Assessment	Research Design	Treatment Intervention	Primary Outcome Measures	Results
Lande et al., 2011	$N = 40$ 100% AD 65% males 35% females No racial/ethnic data	57 Baseline Zung Score	2-armed nonrandomized clinical trial	Participants were alternatively assigned to receive light therapy at 10,000 lux or 50 lux for 90 minutes, 5 day a week over 3 weeks	Zung	20 participants completed treatment and posttreatment measures were significantly reduced, but these changes dissipated 1 week later.
Luxton et al., 2016	$N = 120$ 75% AD 25% veteran 82% male 18% female 68% White 15% Black 3% Asian 10% Hispanic 1% Native American 3% Other	100% met SCID depression criteria	2-armed noninferiority RCT of behavioral activation delivered via telehealth or in-person	Weekly 60-minute treatment sessions for 8 weeks	BDI-II	Posttreatment analyses showed BDI-II reductions of 18 points for in-office and 13 points for telehealth. Noninferiority analyses not supported.

Mohamed et al., 2017	N = 1522 100% veterans 85% male 15% female 69% White* 26% Black* 10% Hispanic* 9% Other* *Participants could choose more than one race/ethnic group	>11 QIDS	Multisite RCT of antidepressant switching to bupropion, augmentation with bupropion, and augmentation with aripiprazole in treatment resistant patients	3-armed RCT	QIDS	Remission rates at 12 weeks were 29% with augmented aripiprazole, 27% with augmented bupropion, and 22% with switched bupropion. Response rates on the QIDS at 12 weeks were 74% with augmented aripiprazole, 66% with augmented bupropion, and 62% with switched bupropion.
Peterson & Halstead, 1998	N = 138 57% AD or veterans 43% spouses 32% males 68% females No racial/ethnic data	Met DSM-IV depressive disorder criteria	Clinical replication series	6-session, 12-hour group cognitive behavioral therapy for depression	BDI	BDI scores decreased for 84% of participants. Average BDI reduction was 38%. 43% of the participants had > 50% reduction in BDI score.

(*Continued*)

Table 11.1 (Continued)

Reference Citation	Participants	Inclusion Criteria/Baseline Assessment	Research Design	Treatment Intervention	Primary Outcome Measures	Results
Pfeiffer et al., 2020	N = 330 100% veterans 80% male 20% female 71% White 21% Black 9% Other 3% Hispanic	Met depression diagnosis criteria an QIDS	2-armed RCT of peer-supported, computer-based CBT versus usual care	3 months of peer-supported, computer-based CBT	QIDS	Response rate was 20% for CBT 6% for usual care at 3 months and (25% vs 16%) at 6 months. Remission rate was 14% for CBT 6% for usual care at 3 months and (22% vs 11%) at 6 months.
Ruskin et al., 2004	N = 119 100% veterans 88% male 12% female 61% White 36% Black 3% Asian or Hispanic	>16 HDRS	2-armed RCT of telehealth versus in-person treatment	Both groups received 8 sessions of medication management, psychoeducation, and support counseling	HDRS	Response rates were 49% for telehealth and 43% for in-person on the HDRS. Remission rates were 39% for telehealth and 35% for in-person on the HDRS.
Yesavage et al., 2018	N = 164 100% veterans 80% males 20% females 77% White 23% Non-White/Other	>20 HRSD	2-armed RCT of active or sham rTMS	Active and sham rTMS groups received up to 30 sessions.	HRSD	Overall 39% collectively achieved remission rates. No significant difference between groups in remission rates.

Notes: AD = Active Duty Military; BA = Behavioral Activation; BDI = Beck Depression Inventory; BDI-II = Beck Depression Inventory 2nd edition; PST = Problem Solving Therapy; GDS = Geriatric Depression Scale; HRSD = Hamilton Rating Scale for Depression; PHQ-9 = 9-item Patient Health Questionnaire; CBT = Cognitive Behavioral Therapy; QIDS = Quick Inventory of Depressive Symptomatology; RCT =Randomized Clinical Trial; rTMS = Repetitive Transcranial Magnetic Stimulation; SCID = Structured Clinical Interview; SCL-20 = Symptom Checklist Depression-20 Items; Zung = Zung Self Rating Depression Scale.

lengths of three and six months. Out of the four RCTs where technology was used in delivering treatment, two of them involved the use of a telecommunication device with video streaming capabilities. Behavioral activation was evaluated in two clinical trials (Egede et al., 2015; Luxton et al., 2016). However, only the Luxton et al. RCT showed a significant reduction in posttreatment measures of depression. One clinical trial ($N = 138$) evaluated the use of group cognitive behavioral therapy for depression in military veterans treated in a military MTF (Peterson & Halstead, 1998). The results indicated that there was an average reduction of 38% in depression measures at the posttreatment period, and 43% of the participants had greater than a 50% reduction in depression.

Combination Treatment

Of the 10 clinical trials that examined depression treatment in military and veteran populations, two used a combination of pharmacological and psychotherapy interventions (Engel et al., 2016; Ruskin et al., 2004; see Table 11.1). Both studies incorporated the use of telehealth to deliver treatment. The largest RCT to evaluate the treatment of depression and PTSD in active-duty military personnel ($N = 666$) was the Stepped Enhancement of PTSD Services Using Primary Care (STEPS-UP) study. At the baseline assessment, 65% (433/666) were classified as depressed. This two-armed trial evaluated the use of a centrally assisted collaborative telecare (CACT) method as compared to treatment as usual (Engel et al., 2016). The CACT intervention involved a combination of CBT for depression and medication management by a nurse and with supervision by a primary care provider. The CBT was delivered through telehealth and web-based systems. The control group received the same CBT and pharmacological therapy interventions, but through a usual care integration of screening by nurse case manager and follow up by clinical provider. The results revealed that CACT intervention resulted in greater reductions in depression scores (56%) as compared to treatment as usual (31%) and significantly more CACT participants (30%) had a 50% or greater reduction in depression improvement at 12 months as compared to usual care (21%).

Another study evaluated the treatment of depression in veterans ($N = 119$) using a combined treatment of psychotropic medications, psychoeducation, and brief supportive counseling (Ruskin et al., 2004). Participants were randomized to receive the combined treatment through telehealth or in person. The results showed reductions in depression measures for both telehealth (49%) and in-person (43%) treatments as well as remission rates (telehealth

= 39%; in-person = 35%), but there were not significant differences between treatment groups. These results provide strong support for telehealth treatment of depression, which has been particularly important since the start of the COVID-19 pandemic.

Medical Devices

A double-blind sham-controlled study evaluated the use of repetitive transcranial magnetic stimulation (rTMS) for the veterans ($N = 164$) with depression (Yesavage et al., 2018). The results indicated that 39% of veterans experienced clinically significant reductions in depression symptoms, but there were not significant differences between groups. A nonrandomized ($N = 40$) study evaluated two levels of light therapy (10,000 lux or 50 lux) in active-duty military personnel for 90 minutes daily, five days per week for three weeks. Twenty participants (50%) completed treatment and reported a temporary reduction in depression symptoms, but these reductions dissipated one week later (Lande et al., 2011).

Ethnocultural Considerations in Randomized Clinical Trials

Overall, there has been little direct attention to ethnocultural factors in clinical trials focused on the treatment of depression in military service members and veterans. Nine of the 10 clinical trials reported race/ethnicity as a demographic variable and had fairly diverse samples, ranging from 48% to 86% White. However, only 20% reported race/ethnicity when examining treatment outcomes (Pfeiffer et al., 2020; Ruskin et al., 2004). Only one study reported examining a race by treatment interaction, and it did not find a significant difference (Egede et al., 2015).

The distribution of people of color varied widely depending on the study. In summary, Hispanic participants represented in six studies was 3–29% (Engel et al., 2016; Luxton et al., 2016; Mohamed et al., 2017; Pfeiffer et al., 2020; Ruskin et al., 2004). Black participants were represented in five studies, ranging from 15% to 40% of samples (Egede et al., 2015; Luxton et al., 2016; Mohamed et al., 2017; Pfeiffer et al., 2020; Ruskin et al., 2004). Asians were represented in one study, at 3% of the sample (Luxton et al., 2016). Native Americans were only specifically reported in one study at 1% of the sample size (Luxton et al., 2016). One study reported a combination of Hispanic or Asian participants that comprised 3% of the sample (Ruskin et al., 2004).

There was variability in how race/ethnicity were classified, and which racial/ethnic groups were part of the "other" category: Non-Hispanic other were 34% of one study (Engel et al., 2016); Non-White/other was reported to be 23% of another study (Yesavage et al., 2018) and Other ranged from 3% to 9% in three more studies (Luxton et al., 2016; Mohamed et al., 2017; Pfeiffer et al., 2020). The variability in demographic reporting race and ethnicity suggests that the field could benefit from greater consistency in language and racial/ethnic categorization and use of APA inclusive language.

Current Research Gaps in Evidence-Based Treatments for Military and Veteran Populations

This chapter highlights the significant dearth in clinical trials research in treating depression and persistent depressive disorders in active-duty military and veteran populations. The modest effect sizes in these trials suggest that tailoring interventions to address military and veteran cultural, occupational, and operational factors may be a key in improving outcomes. The inclusion of culturally specific strengths and stressors such as unit cohesion, stigma, military and ethnocultural identities, and racial discrimination could also enhance understanding of ethnocultural aspects of depression treatment.

References

American Psychological Association [APA]. (2019). APA clinical practice guideline for the treatment of depression across three age cohorts. *American Psychological Association*. https://www.apa.org/depression-guideline/guideline.pdf

Bedford, L. A., Dietch, J. R., Taylor, D. J., Boals, A., & Zayfert, C. (2018). Computer-guided problem-solving treatment for depression, PTSD, and insomnia symptoms in student veterans: A pilot randomized controlled trial. *Behavior Therapy, 49*(5), 756–767. https://doi.org/10.1016/j.beth.2017.11.010

Chu, K. M., Garcia, S. M. S., Koka, H., Wynn, G. H., & Kao, T.-C. (2021). Mental health care utilization and stigma in the military: Comparison of Asian Americans to other racial groups. *Ethnicity & Health, 26*(2), 235–250. https://doi.org/10.1080/13557858.2018.1494823

Cuijpers, P., Stringaris, A., & Wolpert, M. (2020). Treatment outcomes for depression: Challenges and opportunities. *The Lancet Psychiatry, 7*(11), 925–927. https://doi.org/10.1016/S2215-0366(20)30036-5

Department of Veterans Affairs/Department of Defense. (2016). VA/DoD clinical practice guideline for the management of major depressive disorder. Version 3.0. VA website. Retrieved March 1, 2022 from https://www.healthquality.va.gov/guidelines/MH/mdd/

Egede, L. E., Acierno, R., Knapp, R. G., Lejuez, C., Hernandez-Tejada, M., Payne, E. H., & Frueh, B. C. (2015). Psychotherapy for depression in older veterans via telemedicine: A randomised, open-label, non-inferiority trial. *The Lancet Psychiatry*, 2(8), 693–701. https://doi.org/10.1016/s2215-0366(15)00122-4

Engel, C. C., Jaycox, L. H., Freed, M. C., Bray, R. M., Brambilla, D., Zatzick, D., Litz, B., Tanielian, T., Novak, L. A., Lane, M. E., Belsher, B. E., Olmsted, K. L., Evatt, D. P., Vandermaas-Peeler, R., Unützer, J., & Katon, W. J. (2016). Centrally assisted collaborative telecare for posttraumatic stress disorder and depression among military personnel attending primary care: A randomized clinical trial. *JAMA Internal Medicine*, 176(7), 948–956. https://doi.org/10.1001/jamainternmed.2016.2402

Gadermann, A. M., Engel, C. C., Naifeh, J. A., Nock, M. K., Petukhova, M., Santiago, P. N., Benjamin, W., Zaslavsky, A. M., & Kessler, R. C. (2014). Prevalence of DSM-IV major depression among U.S. military personnel: Meta-analysis and simulation. *Military Medicine*, 177, 47–59. https://doi.org/10.7205/milmed-d-12-00103

Goldberg, S. B., Fortney, J. C., Chen, J. A., Young, B. A., Lehavot, K., & Simpson, T. L. (2020). Military service and military health care coverage are associated with reduced racial disparities in time to mental health treatment initiation. *Administration and Policy in Mental Health and Mental Health Services Research*. https://doi.org/10.1007/s10488-020-01017-2

Hundt, N. E., Barrera, T. L., Robinson, A., & Cully, J. A. (2014). A systematic review of cognitive behavioral therapy for depression in Veterans. *Military Medicine*, 179(9), 942–949. https://doi.org/10.7205/MILMED-D-14-00128

Inoue, C., Shawler, E., Jordan, C. H., & Jackson, C. A. (2021). Veteran and military mental health issues. In *StatPearls*. StatPearls Publishing.

Lande, R. G., Williams, L. B., Gragnani, C., & Albert Tsai. (2011). Effectiveness of light therapy for depression among active duty service members: A nonrandomized controlled pilot trial. *Complementary Therapies in Medicine*, 19(3), 161–163. https://doi.org/10.1016/j.ctim.2011.04.003

Liu, Y., Collins, C., Wang, K., Xie, X., & Bie, R. (2019). The prevalence and trend of depression among veterans in the United States. *Journal of Affective Disorders*, 245(15), 724–727. https://doi.org/10.1016/j.jad.2018.11.031

Luxton, D. D., Pruitt, L. D., Wagner, A., Smolenski, D. J., Jenkins-Guarnieri, M. A., & Gahm, G. (2016). Home-based telebehavioral health for U.S. military personnel and veterans with depression: A randomized controlled trial. *Journal of Consulting and Clinical Psychology*, 84(11), 923–934. https://doi.org/10.1037/ccp0000135

Mohamed, S., Johnson, G. R., Chen, P., Hicks, P. B., Davis, L. L., Yoon, J., Gleason, T. C., Vertrees, J. E., Weingart, K., Tal, I., Scrymgeour, A., Lawrence, D. D., Planeta, B., Thase, M. E., Huang, G. D., Zisook, S., the VAST-D Investigators, Rao, S. D., Pilkinton, P. D., Wilcox, J. A., ... Little, J. T. (2017). Effect of antidepressant switching vs augmentation on remission among patients with major depressive disorder unresponsive to antidepressant treatment: The VAST-D randomized clinical trial. *JAMA*, 318(2), 132–145. https://doi.org/10.1001/jama.2017.8036

Moore, B. A., & Barnett, J. E. (2013). *Military psychologists' desk reference* (1st ed.). Oxford University Press.

Peterson, A. L., & Halstead, T. S. (1998). Group cognitive behavioral treatment for depression in a community setting: A clinical replication series. *Behavior Therapy*, 29, 3–18. https://doi.org/10.1016/S0005-7894(98)80015-4

Peterson, A. L., Niles, B. L., Young-McCaughan, S., & Keane, T. M. (2021). Assessment and treatment of combat-related posttraumatic stress disorder: Results from STRONG STAR and the Consortium to Alleviate PTSD. In N. Gorbunov (Ed.), *Military medicine*. In Tech Open. https://doi.org/10.5772/intechopen.96323

Pfeiffer, P. N., Pope, B., Houck, M., Benn-Burton, W., Zivin, K., Ganoczy, D., Kim, H. M., Walters, H., Emerson, L., Nelson, C. B., Abraham, K. M., & Valenstein, M. (2020). Effectiveness of peer-supported computer-based CBT for depression among veterans in primary care. *Psychiatric Services*, 71(3), 256–262. https://doi.org/10.1176/appi.ps.201900283

Plessen, C. Y., Karyotaki, E., & Cuijpers, P. (2022). Exploring the efficacy of psychological treatments for depression: A multiverse meta-analysis protocol. *BMJ Open*, 12(1), e050197. https://doi.org/10.1136/bmjopen-2021-050197

Ruskin, P. E., Silver-Aylaian, M., Kling, M. A., Reed, S. A., Bradham, D. D., Hebel, J. R., Barrett, D., Knowles, F., & Hauser, P. (2004). Treatment outcomes in depression: Comparison of remote treatment through telepsychiatry to in-person treatment. *American Journal of Psychiatry*, 161(8), 1471–1476. https://doi.org/10.1176/appi.ajp.161.8.1471

Tanielian, T. L., Jaycox, L., & Rand Corporation. (2008). *Invisible wounds of war: Psychological and cognitive injuries, their consequences, and services to assist recovery*. Santa Monica, CA: RAND.

Trivedi, R. B., Post, E. P., Sun, H., Pomeranz, A., Saxon, A. J., Piette, J. D., Maynard, C., Arnow, B., Curtis, I., Fihn, S. D., & Nelson, K. (2015). Prevalence, comorbidity, and prognosis of mental health among US veterans. *American Journal of Public Health*, 105(12), 2564–2569. https://doi.org/10.2105/AJPH.2015.302836

Yesavage, J. A., Fairchild, J. K., Mi, Z., Biswas, K., Davis-Karim, A., Phibbs, C. S., Forman, S. D., Thase, M., Williams, L. M., Etkin, A., O'Hara, R., Georgette, G., Beale, T., Huang, G. D., Noda, A., & George, M. S. (2018). Effect of repetitive transcranial magnetic stimulation on treatment-resistant major depression in US veterans: A randomized clinical trial. *JAMA Psychiatry*, 75(9), 884–893. https://doi.org/10.1001/jamapsychiatry.2018.1483

12 Obsessive-Compulsive Disorder and Related Disorders in Active-Duty Service Members and Veterans

Nathaniel Van Kirk, Rose Luehrs, and Elizabeth McIngvale

Introduction

Obsessive compulsive disorder (OCD) is a heterogeneous diagnosis afflicting approximately 2.3% of the population (Ruscio et al., 2010). While the symptoms of OCD can manifest in a multitude of ways, OCD is characterized by the presence of obsessions and compulsions (also called rituals) that are considered time consuming or cause significant distress. Currently, obsessions are defined as thoughts, images, urges, or feelings that are considered unwanted and intrusive in nature, resulting in significant distress (American Psychiatric Association [APA], 2013). Generally speaking, the first emotional response that comes to mind when talking about OCD is the feeling of anxiety/fear one may experience in response to obsessions. However, as a clinician it is important to recognize that the presence of obsessions may result in more than just anxiety alone, as feelings of disgust, obsessional guilt/shame (e.g., Stewart & Shapiro, 2011), or incompleteness/uneasiness (typically termed "not just right" OCD symptoms) are common. In an attempt to prevent a feared outcome or neutralize the unwanted obsessional thought/feeling, individuals may feel driven to engage in repetitive behaviors or mental acts, also known as compulsions or rituals (APA, 2013). While compulsions can take almost any form (and in many instances may start out as seemingly functional behaviors), their application becomes rigid and highly excessive in nature, eliminating the functionality of the underlying behavior. Importantly, how compulsions serve to prevent the feared outcome is not always immediately obvious (or may seem to violate the laws of physics)—what is most important to understand is how the individual with OCD experiences the link between their obsessions and compulsions. In many instances, individuals with OCD may recognize that their compulsions are not truly effective in preventing the feared outcome or rationally linked to neutralizing the obsessions. This would be classified as having "good insight," or the ability to see one's symptoms as excessive or irrational. However, insight exists on a continuum and can range from "good" to "poor," where an individual believes the obsessions are "probably true" (APA, 2013, p. 237). In some instances, an individual may also present with absent insight or delusional quality to their obsessional beliefs. Convinced their obsessional fears are true, the beliefs are held even in the presence of significant contrary evidence. Clinically, individuals with OCD may present with variable insight that fluctuates along the insight continuum based on the intensity of their distress or between symptom types.

The OCD Cycle

When left untreated, OCD tends to intensify over time due to the self-reinforcing nature of the OCD cycle. The heterogeneous nature of obsessions can lead to a wide variety of triggers that may be interspersed throughout daily life. When confronted with these triggers, the increase in distress around the associated obsessions amplify an individual's urge to ritualize in an attempt to reduce/neutralize unwanted thoughts or feelings and prevent the obsessional feared consequence from occurring. Unfortunately, the ongoing cycle of utilizing compulsions to combat the distress caused by seemingly never-ending obsessional fears results in a self-reinforcing cycle that maintains/intensifies OCD symptoms if left untreated. While compulsions may provide short-term relief, the act of ritualizing reinforces the belief that the obsession is

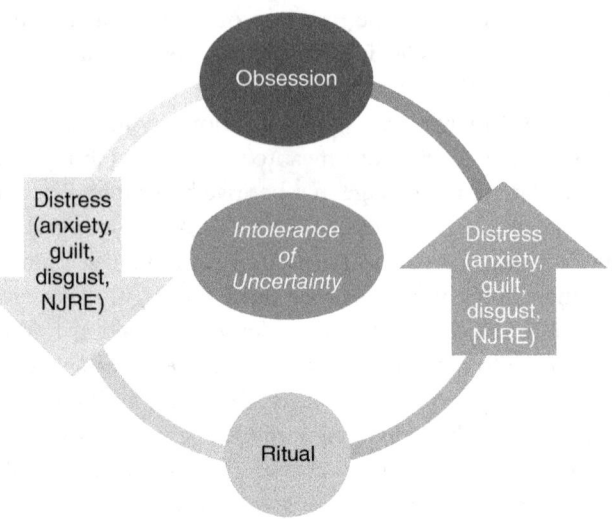

Figure 12.1 OCD Cycle.
Adapted from "OCD and its spectrum disorders: What is it really?" by N. Van Kirk (2017). Presentation at the Behavioral Health Partial Program practicum seminar at McLean Hospital, Belmont, MA, United States.

dangerous and that the compulsions are necessary for anxiety/distress reduction (see Figure 12.1). It is important to note that while the compulsions may initially achieve the desired outcome (i.e., rapid reduction in distress), the rigidity and extent to which one engages in these behaviors quickly becomes less adaptive, with many individuals reporting it becomes increasingly difficult to "complete" the compulsion and achieve the desired reduction in distress. In order to truly understand the OCD cycle, it is necessary to acknowledge the role *uncertainty* plays in OCD. Recent findings have highlighted the role of intolerance of uncertainty as a core element of this cycle (e.g., Grayson, 2010; Obsessive Compulsive Cognitions Working Group, 1997). In comparison to other anxiety disorders, OCD beliefs focus on a perceived need to gain 100% certainty around the obsession/feared outcome (even if that outcome is that the fear will come true), resulting in the continual increase in ritualistic behaviors as one seeks absolute certainty.

OCD in Active Duty and Veteran Populations

There has been limited evaluation of OCD within active-duty military populations, however emerging evidence with veterans and individuals who have experienced high rates of trauma suggest OCD's prevalence rate may be even higher in military personnel compared to the general population. Recent studies have demonstrated great variability in OCD's prevalence rates within the Veteran's Health Administration (VHA), with estimates varying from .04% to 28% (McIngvale et al., 2019). Overall, rates of OCD diagnosis appear to be higher amongst veterans who are actively seeking psychiatric care/have other psychiatric comorbidities compared to the general community (Barrera et al., 2019). In their review, McIngvale et al. (2019) demonstrated that the method of assessment had a large impact on the prevalence estimates across studies, along with the specific setting in which the evaluation took place. Even when utilizing a structured clinical interview to assess for OCD symptoms, prevalence rates ranged from 1% to 10.8% (McIngvale et al., 2019); however they were generally higher than studies utilizing VHA record reviews, which may suggest OCD is under-recognized in military settings (Barrera et al., 2019). Similarly, prevalence rates appear to be lower in active-duty personnel compared to veterans. The exact reason for this variability is unknown and may be influenced by hesitancy to report symptoms while on active duty or under-recognition/misdiagnosis of OCD symptoms when not using validated screening measures for OCD or structured clinical interviews. However, given the high rates of trauma exposure in military personnel, it is important to note that stressful life events have been found to be associated with OCD onset, with more severe and frequent stressful life events observed within the six months before symptom onset (McKeon et al., 1984). Further, 54% of individuals with OCD report having experienced at least one traumatic life event, with these experiences being associated with increased OCD symptom severity (Cromer et al., 2007). Thus, careful evaluation and appropriate screening for OCD is important when working with individuals on active duty who are seeking psychiatric care.

Considerations in Diagnosis and Clinical Assessment

Empirically Based Assessment Practices and Scale Selection

OCD is often both misunderstood and misdiagnosed, thus the use of standardized and validated assessment measures is crucial when evaluating/screening for OCD symptoms. Validated measures can aid in the identification and conceptualization of an individual's OCD symptoms, along with tracking symptom severity across treatment through routine outcome monitoring. Given the high comorbidity rates with other anxiety disorders, screening for

OCD symptoms is recommended as part of standard practice when working with anxiety disorders in general. In addition, given the link between OCD and traumatic experiences, clinicians may want to assess for OCD symptoms (along with PTSD symptoms) when working with active-duty personnel and veterans—especially if they disclose experiencing intrusive/distressing thoughts and/or images or repetitive behaviors aimed at reducing distress. The average time from onset of symptoms to effective treatment is 17 years (Jenike, 2004), making it critical that validated clinical assessments are used to properly identify OCD symptoms from the outset in an effort to reduce this gap.

Multiple validated OCD-specific screening and symptom severity measures exist to aid in the identification and routine outcome monitoring of OCD symptoms. Currently, the Yale-Brown Obsessive Compulsive Scale (YBOCS; Goodman et al., 1989a, 1989b) and Dimensional Obsessive Compulsive Scale (DOCS; Abramowitz et al., 2010) are among the most prevalent OCD severity measures. The YBOCS is a widely used, validated measure that has relatively low assessment burden and high clinical utility (Goodman et al., 1989a, 1989b). The YBOCS has both clinician-administered and self-report versions. The symptom severity scale includes 10 items, five focused on obsessions and five focused on compulsions. Total scores range from 0 to 40, representing severity categories of subclinical, mild, moderate, severe, and extreme symptoms. The YBOCS has an accompanying symptom checklist that categorizes common examples of obsessions and compulsions. The checklist should be used to identify and better understand past/present OCD symptoms and can be used in a clinical interview to facilitate a functional analysis of an individual's symptoms. More recently an updated version, the YBOCS-II (Storch et al., 2010), has been published, updating the symptom checklist and severity scale (which remains a 10-item measure of obsessions and compulsions). YBOCS-II scoring is now based on a 50-point scale. A recent study found a recommended cutoff score of 13 or higher as indicating a potential OCD diagnosis (Castro-Rodrigues et al., 2018).

The DOCS is a 20-item self-report measure of OCD severity that evaluates severity within four primary domains of OCD symptoms (Abramowitz et al., 2010). The DOCS can be particularly helpful as part of a routine screening for potential OCD symptoms during admission (to be followed up by a more in-depth functional analysis) and ongoing symptom monitoring across OCD treatment. Given the previously described variability in OCD diagnostic rates in veteran samples, utilizing structured/semi-structured clinical interviews to follow up on initial self-report OCD symptom screenings is incredibly important to confirm the OCD diagnosis prior to treatment planning. In addition to the variability by assessment method/setting described by McIngvale et al.

(2019), data suggests OCD symptoms may be misidentified as high as 38.9% of the time, with PTSD, psychosis, and generalized anxiety disorder being among the most common misdiagnoses (Glazier et al., 2013). Given this, it is incredibly important for treatment planning to confirm the symptoms being reported are not better accounted for by other clinical disorders or influenced by comorbid symptoms.

Differential Diagnosis Challenges and Considerations

Given the heterogeneity of OCD symptoms and overlap with other anxiety/trauma-related disorders, clinicians should keep in mind a few core elements of OCD during the assessment process. Specifically, the assessor should ensure the thoughts/images/urges are unwanted and intrusive in nature, causing distress and not bringing pleasure or joy. Similarly, clinicians should assess the functional relationship between the identified obsessions and reported compulsions, ensuring the compulsions are aimed at alleviating distress/attempting to prevent the identified obsessional fears from occurring (i.e., not completed in order to prevent re-experiencing of a traumatic event as in PTSD or repetitive actions one is unable to disengage from such as behavioral perseveration in certain traumatic brain injury presentations or tic disorders). Diagnostic evaluations should also include screening for other obsessive compulsive spectrum disorders due to their high comorbidity rates with OCD, including body dysmorphic disorder (BDD), body focused repetitive behaviors (BFRBs; i.e., trichotillomania and excoriation disorder), and hoarding disorder. Unfortunately, there has been limited evaluation of these disorders in active-duty military and veterans.

Clinical Presentation and Comorbidity

Another challenge that may influence OCD prevalence rates is the notoriously heterogeneous nature of the disorder. Studies of OCD symptom presentations have generally identified four main dimensions of OCD symptoms. These include fears associated with (1) contamination/germs, (2) being responsible for harm, injury, and/or bad luck, (3) unacceptable/taboo thoughts, and (4) symmetry, order, and not-just-right experiences (Abramowitz et al., 2010). Within these categories, there is wide variability in the type of behaviors/mental acts that may be employed as compulsions. Some of these may also look like symptoms of other disorders, such as the presence of checking compulsions which may look similar to safety behaviors present in PTSD or a preoccupation with order, symmetry, and perfectionism that may resemble behavioral patterns that are part of military procedure/life. Regardless of the presentation, the underlying OCD cycle and the focus on attempting to achieve 100% certainty through ritualistic behaviors remains the same, reinforcing the importance of a comprehensive functional analysis of these behaviors in order to select the appropriate treatment approach.

OCD also commonly co-occurs with other psychiatric diagnoses, with studies of clinical samples finding OCD comorbidity rates around 48% for clinical disorders and 36% for characterological disorders (Denys et al., 2004). Epidemiological studies have indicated lifetime comorbidity rates as high as 90%, with a diagnosis of another anxiety disorder being the most common group of comorbidities (Ruscio et al., 2010). While there has been limited evaluation of comorbidity within an active duty/military population, findings from the VHA found OCD prevalence is generally higher within individuals who have already been diagnosed with another psychiatric condition, ranging from 4.2% to 5% (McIngvale et al., 2019). Importantly, a study by Ecker et al. (2019) found that 36% of veterans who had an OCD diagnosis also met criteria for a comorbid substance use disorder.

Ethnoracial and Ethnocultural Considerations

When assessing and treating OCD in active-duty and veteran individuals it is crucial to consider racial, ethnic, and cultural factors that may impact symptom presentation, willingness to seek services and engage in treatment, and treatment response. It is widely known that the stigma associated with mental illness prevents many active-duty service members and veterans from reporting symptoms and seeking treatment (Greene-Shortridge et al., 2007). In fact, one study on military members found that career worry, which refers to consequences impacting one's career, was the most important factor when evaluating willingness to seek treatment (Brown & Bruce, 2016). Unfortunately, there is a dearth of literature addressing the influence of culture and intersectionality of an individual's identities on OCD in the active-duty and veteran population. However, research has shown there are cross-cultural, racial, and ethnic differences in the presentation of OCD. These considerations should be considered when approaching OCD assessment and treatment in active-duty service members and veterans due to the intersectionality of their identities. Notably, research has found that those who are marginalized experience greater OCD severity across symptoms of contamination, harm-related obsessions and symmetry (Wadsworth, Potluri, Schreck, & Hernandez-Vallant, 2020). The literature points to several important differences in OCD symptoms across racial and ethnic groups, which are outlined below.

OCD in Black and African Americans

Individuals who identify as Black and/or African American experience OCD symptoms surrounding contamination two times more often than European Americans with OCD (Williams et al., 2020). The same is true of animal-related obsessions when comparing Black and African American individuals with OCD to their European counterparts. Williams et al. (2012) offer an explanation for increased concern around animals in this population being that animals were historically used to hunt slaves. Further, daily discrimination experienced by members of the Black and African American community has been identified as a risk factor for increased contamination symptoms and increased experience of intrusive/unacceptable thoughts (Williams et al., 2020). Due to fears of discrimination and of validating racial stereotypes, Black and African American adults are less likely to report sexual obsessions and harm-related obsessions (Williams et al., 2020). The high rate of diagnostic comorbidity in Black and African American adults with OCD (e.g., Williams et al., 2020) suggests that professionals working with active-duty service members and veterans who identify in this way should thoroughly assess all psychological symptoms before confirming diagnoses and making treatment recommendations.

OCD in Asian Americans

There is a need for more research on OCD in Asian Americans. Given that one study highlighted an increased risk of suicide in Asian Americans with OCD (Gupta, Avasthi, Grover, & Singh, 2014), it is important to appropriately assess risk and attend to unique factors that may be exacerbating symptoms in this population. Other research has found that the presence of a stronger ethnic identity in Asian Americans leads to more severe OCD symptoms when compared to the role of comparatively lower ethnic identity in White participants (Ching & Williams, 2019). Clinically, it appears that perfectionism and tolerating uncertainty are more closely associated with contamination symptoms in Asian Americans when compared to individuals from other ethnic and racial groups (Williams et al., 2020). Further, Asian Americans reported experiencing more severe harm-related obsessions; greater checking, ordering, and symmetry symptoms; and more neutralizing compulsions comparatively (Ching & Williams, 2019).

OCD in Latinx Populations

Due to the lack of research on OCD in the Latinx populations it is challenging to confidently compare symptom dimensions amongst Latinx subgroups, as well as comparing across other racial and ethnic groups (Wetterneck et al., 2012). Based on the handful of studies focused on individuals who identify as Latinx, findings suggest that symptom presentation does vary by Latinx subgroup, indicating an even greater need for more specific and focused research (Wetterneck et al., 2012). To date, the limited research that has been conducted with Latinx participants suggests individuals from Costa Rica experience somatic and contamination obsessions more often than Caucasian individuals (Chavira et al., 2008). Further, individuals who identify as Mexican reported experiencing a higher presence of contamination-related obsessions (Nicolini et al., 1997) while those who identify as Brazilian endorsed greater obsessions surrounding religion and harm/aggression-related fears (Fontenelle et al., 2007). OCD symptoms around religion and harm can be particularly life-interfering due to the commonly held values of collectivism, family, and religion or spirituality within Latinx communities. While these values may serve as protective factors, clinicians should thoroughly assess the impact of OCD on these domains of daily life (if the client identifies with these values) to determine whether these factors are functioning in a protective manner or if OCD symptoms are interfering with these domains of life.

Overall, there is significant work needed to better understand not only the relationship between ethnic, racial, and cultural identities and OCD, but also how these identities may intersect with the other identities an individual may hold. In addition to an individual's identity as a member of the military, there are other intersecting identities that need to be considered, including their ethnicity, race, social economic status, sexual orientation, gender identity, religion, disability status, national origin, and cultural heritage (Hays, 1996). The need to carefully evaluate this intersectionality of identities is also exceedingly true within active-duty military and veteran populations to better understand the impact on OCD symptom presentation, treatment, and the overarching influence on mental health stigma.

OCD Treatment

Exposure and response prevention (ERP; Foa et al., 2012) has been widely established as the front-line, empirically based treatment for OCD (Abramowitz, 2006). Meta-analytic studies have found ERP to have an average effect size of 1.41, indicating a large effect of ERP on OCD symptom reduction (Abramowitz, 1996). ERP focuses on breaking the OCD cycle through repeated and prolonged exposure to triggers/situations that elicit obsessional fears. The second element of ERP (and a core element of any successful OCD treatment approach) is the elimination of rituals/compulsions as a method of reducing distress/neutralizing the obsessional fear. This both promotes extinction of the conditioned distress response to the obsessions and reduces the individual's belief in the necessity of compulsions to manage/reduce distress (Abramowitz, 2006). In comparison to treatment for other anxiety disorders where there is less focus on elimination of safety behaviors and they may be more gradually reduced across time, ritual prevention is arguably the most important element of successful OCD treatment. Even with well-formulated exposure exercises and repeated exposure practice, if the individual with OCD continues to engage in ritualistic behaviors following the exposure exercises, the cycle will be maintained. The act of ritualizing will continue to reinforce the obsessions as something to be feared and acted upon.

Recent empirical advances have expanded on the initial habituation-focused model of ERP, demonstrating the role inhibitory learning processes may play in successful ERP. In comparison to habituation-based models of ERP, which focused on fear reduction within/across exposure practices, inhibitory learning theory suggests the exposure process results in new "inhibitory" associations that compete with (versus replace) previous fear learning, regardless of degree of fear reduction (see Craske et al., 2008, 2014; Mathes et al., 2015). Within this framework, cognitive therapy strategies may be integrated post-exposure, with the goal of highlighting differences between the individual's pre-exposure expectations and post-exposure experiences, fostering the inhibitory learning process.

Stand-alone cognitive therapy focused on modifying maladaptive beliefs that maintain OCD (such as beliefs about the need for certainty) has also found support as an effective treatment for OCD (see Wilhelm & Steketee, 2006; Wilhelm et al., 2005, 2015). However, it is important to note that the cognitive restructuring process has slight variations compared to other anxiety and trauma-related disorders. For example, less focus is given to probability estimation within OCD (Fletcher et al., 2020) as this could serve as a form of reassurance and as described earlier, OCD symptoms are based more on the perceived need for certainty around an obsession than relative risk/perception of safety. Thus, cognitive restructuring should be focused more on addressing underlying beliefs that maintain the OCD cycle, such as maladaptive beliefs about perfectionism, need for certainty, and incompleteness (which have been identified as mediators of OCD symptom change in cognitive therapy; Wilhelm et al., 2015). Cognitive therapy strategies are also commonly used to augment ERP, with combined CBT approaches showing a similarly large meta-analytic effect size on OCD symptoms reduction ($d = 1.39$; Eddy et al., 2004).

Wide use of acceptance and commitment therapy (ACT) and ACT-enhanced ERP have also gained attention and empirical support. Within the ACT framework, focus is given to utilizing exposure strategies to increase psychological flexibility and allows individuals to focus on approaching value driven/positive experiences instead of attempting to avoid distressing internal emotions (Twohig et al., 2010). ACT approaches have been found to result in clinically significant reductions in OCD symptoms (Twohig et al., 2010), and a randomized controlled trial comparing ERP and ACT+ERP found both approaches to be equally effective, with no significant differences between the interventions (Twohig et al., 2018).

Treatment Considerations for Military Personnel

As Barrera et al. (2019) suggested, the variability in prevalence rates for OCD within active-duty military and veterans, combined with the incredibly low diagnostic rates and late average age of OCD diagnosis in studies using VHA record reviews, may represent an under-recognition/misclassification of OCD symptoms in these populations. This is complicated by the similarity in symptoms between OCD and PTSD (i.e., presence of intrusive thoughts/images and safety behaviors). As a result, careful screening and assessment for OCD symptoms using validated measures and structured clinical interviews is incredibly important for early detection and differential diagnosis. Additionally, given the higher rates of OCD evidenced in veterans with comorbid psychiatric conditions, special attention should be paid to screening for OCD symptoms when working with individuals with other comorbid psychiatric conditions, especially substance use disorders.

Unfortunately, findings suggest that only 23% of providers within the VHA have received specialized training in treating OCD and related disorders, and less than half of providers indicated they would recommend ERP for individuals with OCD (Stanley et al., 2017). Due to this, seeking additional training and supervision in empirically based treatments for OCD are recommended for those working with active-duty military and veterans (see Table 12.1 for a list of training resources). Given that the average number of individual therapy sessions attended in the VHA following an OCD diagnosis was 3.9 (Barrera et al., 2019), it is important for providers to utilize validated treatment protocols, including cognitive therapy and motivational interviewing strategies to increase engagement and reduce potential treatment drop-out.

An additional area for special consideration when treating OCD in military populations is the integration of trauma-informed care practices into treatment. Trauma-informed care is a framework for delivering care that acknowledges the impact of trauma (regardless of the specific diagnosis being addressed) and focuses on recognizing and responding to the signs and symptoms of trauma while resisting re-traumatization (Substance Abuse and Mental Health Services Administration, 2014). While OCD treatment primarily focuses on learning to tolerate uncertainty around a feared consequence/outcome, it is important to carefully assess for the presence and impact of trauma when working in military populations (even if PTSD or another trauma-related disorder is not the explicit focus of the intervention), as relationships between trauma and OCD symptoms have been shown in the literature. For example, posttraumatic cognitions were found to moderate the relationship between hyper-responsibility and intolerance of uncertainty

Table 12.1 OCD Training Resources

International OCD Foundation (IOCDF)	Provides resources for clinicians, researchers, clients, & family members, as well as a find therapist function	Iocdf.org
International OCD Foundation (IOCDF)	Professional Trainings	https://iocdf.org/professionals/training-institute/
Behavior Therapy Training Institute (BTTI)	3-day ERP training course from the International OCD Foundation	https://iocdf.org/professionals/training-institute/btti/
U.S. Department of Veterans Affairs	OCD & Related Disorders MIRECC SharePoint	https://www.mirecc.va.gov/visn16/ocd-pulse-page.asp
MGH Psychiatry Academy	Provides training courses in ERP & CBT for OCD in adults & adolescents.	https://lms.mghcme.org/
Anxiety & Depression Association of America	OCD & Related Disorders Special Interest Group Peer Consultation Program	https://adaa.org/resources-professionals/membership/committees/SIGs/peer-consultation#OCD

belief domains and OCD symptom distress; as well as being directly related to greater presence and intensity of obsessions, ritualistic doubting, and mental neutralizing rituals (McKay et al., 2016). This is particularly relevant for active-duty military and veterans where the high rates of trauma may result in a greater degree of mental compulsions that are not as easily observed as more well-known behavioral compulsions. This not only increases the risk of misidentification of OCD symptoms as PTSD, but also suggests directly addressing posttraumatic cognitions, such as global beliefs around self-blame or more general negative alterations to mood, in addition to standard OCD treatment may be warranted. Addressing these posttraumatic cognitions may help prepare individuals for OCD–related exposures and build confidence in their ability to tolerate uncertainty around future feared consequences when past traumatic experiences have also been experienced.

In closing, ERP has been found to be a highly effective treatment method for OCD; however, it is vitally important that clients are willing to appropriately engage in the treatment process if they are to garner maximum benefit. Therefore, a thorough intake assessment and routine outcome monitoring of symptoms throughout the treatment process is important to fully understand the individual's clinical presentation and develop appropriate exposure exercises/identify relevant rituals to resist. Additionally, providing a clear description of the treatment rationale and underlying treatment mechanisms should be completed prior to starting exposure exercises. Making sure clients have a full understanding of what ERP entails and the difference between effective and ineffective exposure exercises is crucial for enhancing treatment willingness and engagement with the exposure exercises. As a result, it is recommended that clinicians seek additional training and/or supervision in OCD assessment and treatment or refer to trained clinicians.

References

Abramowitz, J. S. (1996). Variants of exposure and response prevention in the treatment of obsessive-compulsive disorder: A meta-analysis. *Behavior Therapy, 27*(4), 583–600.

Abramowitz, J. S. (2006). The psychological treatment of obsessive-compulsive disorder. *Canadian Journal of Psychiatry, 51*(7), 407–416. https://doi.org/10.1177/070674370605100702

Abramowitz, J. S., Deacon, B. J., Olatunji, B. O., Wheaton, M. G., Berman, N. C., Losardo, D., & Hale, L. R. (2010). Assessment of obsessive-compulsive symptom dimensions: Development and evaluation of the dimensional obsessive-compulsive scale. *Psychological Assessment, 22*(1), 180–198. https://doi.org/10.1037/a0018260

American Psychiatric Association. (2013). *Diagnostic and Statistical Manual of Mental Disorders* (5th ed.). Washington, DC: American Psychiatric Association Press.

Barrera, T. L., McIngvale, E., Lindsay, J. A., Walder, A. M., Kauth, M. R., Smith, T. L., & Stanley, M. A. (2019). Obsessive-compulsive disorder in the veterans health administration. *Psychological Services, 16*(4), 605–611. https://doi.org/10.1037/ser0000249

Brown, N. B., & Bruce, S. E. (2016). Stigma, career worry, and mental illness symptomatology factors influencing treatment-seeking for operation enduring freedom and Operation Iraqi Freedom soldiers and veterans. *Psychological Trauma: Theory, Research, Practice, and Policy, 8*, 276–283. https://doi.org/10.1037/tra0000082

Castro-Rodrigues, P., Camacho, M., Almeida, S., Marinho, M., Soares, C., Barahona-Corrêa, J. B., & Oliveira-Maia, A. J. (2018). Criterion validity of the Yale-Brown Obsessive-Compulsive Scale second edition for diagnosis of obsessive-compulsive disorder in adults. *Frontiers in Psychiatry, 9*, 431. https://doi.org/10.3389/fpsyt.2018.00431

Chavira, D. A., Garrido, H., Bagnarello, M., Azzam, A., Reus, V. I., & Mathews, C. A. (2008). A comparative study of obsessive-compulsive disorder in Costa Rica and the United States. *Depression and Anxiety, 25*, 609–619. https://doi.org/10.1002/da.20357

Ching, T. H. W., & Williams, M. T. (2019). The role of ethnic identity in OC symptom dimensions among Asian Americans. *Journal of Obsessive-Compulsive and Related Disorders, 21*, 112–120. https://doi.org/10.1016/j.jocrd.2019.03.005

Craske, M. G., Kircanski, K., Zelikowsky, M., Mystkowski, J., Chowdhury, N., & Baker, A. (2008). Optimizing inhibitory learning during exposure therapy. *Behaviour Research and Therapy, 46*, 5–27. https://doi.org/10.1016/j.brat.2007.10.003

Craske, M. G., Treanor, M., Conway, C. C., Zbozinek, T., & Vervliet, B. (2014). Maximizing exposure therapy: An inhibitory learning approach. *Behaviour Research and Therapy, 58*, 10–23. https://doi.org/10.1016/j.brat.2014.04.006

Cromer, K. R., Schmidt, N. B., & Murphy, D. L. (2007). An investigation of traumatic life events and obsessive-compulsive disorder. *Behaviour Research and Therapy, 45*(7), 1683–1691. https://doi.org/10.1016/j.brat.2006.08.018

Denys, D., Tenney, N., van Megen, H. J., de Geus, F., & Westenberg, H. G. (2004). Axis I and II comorbidity in a large sample of patients with obsessive–compulsive disorder. *Journal of Affective Disorders, 80*(2–3), 155–162. https://doi.org/10.1016/S0165-0327(03)00056-9

Ecker, A. H., Stanley, M. A., Smith, T. L., Teng, E. J., Fletcher, T. L., Van Kirk, N., & Lindsay, J. A. (2019). Co-occurrence of obsessive-compulsive disorder and substance use disorders among US veterans: Prevalence and mental health utilization. *Journal of Cognitive Psychotherapy, 33*(1), 23–32. https://doi.org/10.1891/0889-8391.33.1.23

Eddy, K. T., Dutra, L., Bradley, R., & Westen, D. (2004). A multidimensional meta-analysis of psychotherapy and pharmacotherapy for obsessive-compulsive disorder. *Clinical Psychology Review, 24*(8), 1011–1030. https://doi.org/10.1016/j.cpr.2004.08.004

Fletcher, T. L., Van Kirk, N., & Hundt, N. (2020). Obsessive-compulsive disorder and comorbid posttraumatic stress disorder. In *Advanced casebook of obsessive-compulsive and related disorders* (pp. 105–121). Academic Press. https://doi.org/10.1016/B978-0-12-816563-8.00007-3

Foa, E. B., Yadin, E., & Lichner, T. K. (2012). *Treatments that work. Exposure and response (ritual) prevention for obsessive-compulsive disorder: Therapist guide* (2nd ed.). New York: Oxford University Press.

Fontenelle, L. F., de Souza, W. F., de Menezes, G. B., Mendlowicz, M. V., Miotto, R. R., Falcao, R., Versiani, M., & Figueira, I. L. (2007). Sexual function and dysfunction in Brazilian patients with obsessive-compulslive disorder and social anxiety disorder. *Journal of Nervous and Mental Disease, 195*, 254–257. https://doi.org/10.1097/01.nmd.0000243823.94086.6f

Glazier, K., Calixte, R. M., Rothschild, R., & Pinto, A. (2013). High rates of OCD symptom misidentification by mental health professionals. *Annals of Clinical Psychiatry, 25*, 201–209.

Goodman, W. K., Price, L. H., Rasmussen, S. A., Mazure, C., Delgado, P., Heninger, G. R., & Charney, D. S.(1989b) The yale-brown obsessive compulsive scale: II. Validity. *Archives of General Psychiatry, 46*(11), 1012–1016. https://doi.org/10.1001/archpsyc.1989.01810110054008

Goodman, W. K., Price, L. H., Rasmussen, S. A., Mazure, C., Fleischmann, R. L., Hill, C. L., Heninger, G. R., & Charney, D. S. (1989a). The Yale-Brown Obsessive Compulsive scale I. Development, use, and reliability. *Archives of General Psychiatry, 46*(11), 1006–1011. https://doi.org/10.1001/archpsyc.1989.01810110048007

Grayson, J. B. (2010). OCD and intolerance of uncertainty: Treatment issues. *Journal of Cognitive Psychotherapy, 24*(1), 3. https://doi.org/10.1891/0889-8391.24.1.3

Greene-Shortridge, T. M., Britt, T. W., & Castro, C. A. (2007). The stigma of mental health problems in the military. *Military Medicine, 172*, 157–161. https://doi.org/10.7205/MILMED.172.2.157

Gupta, G., Avasthi, A., Grover, S., & Singh, S. M. (2014). Factors associated with suicidal ideations and suicidal attempts in patients with obsessive compulsive disorder. *Asian Journal of Psychiatry, 12*, 140–146.

Hays, P. A. (1996). Addressing the complexities of culture and gender in counseling. *Journal of Counseling & Development, 74*(4), 332–338. https://doi.org/10.1002/j.1556-6676.1996.tb01876.x

Jenike, M. A. (2004). Obsessive-compulsive disorder. *New England Journal of Medicine, 350*(3), 259–265. https://doi.org/10.1056/NEJMcp031002

Mathes, B. M., Van Kirk, N., & Elias, J. A. (2015). Review of psychotherapeutic approaches for OCD and related disorders. *Current Treatment Options in Psychiatry, 2*(3), 284–296. https://doi.org/10.1007/s40501-015-0052-7

McIngvale, E., Van Kirk, N., Amspoker, A. B., Stanley, M. A., & Fletcher, T. L. (2019). Prevalence and treatment of obsessive-compulsive disorder in veterans and active-duty service members: A systematic review. *Journal of Cognitive Psychotherapy: An International Quarterly, 33*, 1. https://doi.org/10.1891/0889-8391.33.1.11

McKay, D., Ojserkis, R., & Elhai, J. D. (2016). Shared cognitive features of posttraumatic cognitions and obsessive–compulsive symptoms. *Cognitive Therapy and Research, 40*(2), 173–178. https://doi.org/10.1007/s10608-015-9733-1

Mckeon, J., Roa, B., & Mann, A. (1984). Life events and personality traits in obsessive-compulsive neurosis. *British Journal of Psychiatry, 144*(2), 185–189. https://doi.org/10.1192/bjp.144.2.185

Nicolini, H., Benilde, O., & Giuffra, L. (1997). Age of onset, gender and severity in obsessive-compulsive disorder: A study on a Mexican population. *Salud Mental, 20*, 1–4.

Obsessive Compulsive Cognitions Working Group. (1997). Cognitive assessment of obsessive-compulsive disorder. *Behaviour Research and Therapy, 35*(7), 667–681. https://doi.org/10.1016/S0005-7967(97)00017-X

Ruscio, A. M., Stein, D. J., Chui, W. T., & Kessler, R. C. (2010). The epidemiology of obsessive-compulsive disorder in the national comorbidity survey replication. *Molecular Psychiatry, 15*, 53–63. https://doi.org/10.1038/mp.2008.94

Stanley, M. A., McIngvale, E., Barrera, T. L., Amspoker, A. B., Lindsay, J. A., Kauth, M. R., & Teng, E. (2017). VHA providers' knowledge and perceptions about the diagnosis and treatment of obsessive-compulsive disorder and related symptoms. *Journal of Obsessive-Compulsive and Related Disorders, 12,* 58–63. https://doi.org/10.1016/j.jocrd.2016.12.004

Stewart, S. E., & Shapiro, L. (2011). Pathological guilt: A persistent yet overlooked treatment factor in obsessive-compulsive disorder. *Annals of Clinical Psychiatry, 23*(1), 63–70.

Storch, E. A., Rasmussen, S. A., Price, L. H., Larson, M. J., Murphy, T. K., & Goodman, W. K. (2010). Development and psychometric evaluation of the Yale-Brown Obsessive-Compulsive Scale—second edition. *Psychological Assessment, 22*(2), 223–232. https://doi.org/10.1037/a0018492

Substance Abuse and Mental Health Services Administration. (2014). *SAMHSA's Concept of Trauma and Guidance for a Trauma-Informed Approach. HHS Publication No. (SMA) 14-4884.* Rockville, MD: Substance Abuse and Mental Health Services Administration.

Twohig, M. P., Hayes, S. C., Plumb, J. C., Pruitt, L. D., Collins, A. B., Hazlett-Stevens, H., & Woidneck, M. R. (2010). A randomized clinical trial of acceptance and commitment therapy versus progressive relaxation training for obsessive-compulsive disorder. *Journal of Consulting and Clinical Psychology, 78*(5), 705. https://doi.org/10.1037/a0020508

Twohig, M. P., Abramowitz, J. S., Smith, B. M., Fabricant, L. E., Jacoby, R. J., Morrison, K. L., & Ledermann, T. (2018). Adding acceptance and commitment therapy to exposure and response prevention for obsessive-compulsive disorder: A randomized controlled trial. *Behaviour Research and Therapy, 108,* 1–9. https://doi.org/10.1016/j.brat.2018.06.005

Van Kirk, N. (2017, April). OCD and its spectrum disorders: What is it really? [Presentation]. McLean hospital's behavioral health partial program practicum seminar, Belmont, MA.

Wadsworth, L. P., Potluri, S., Schreck, M., & Hernandez-Vallant, A. (2020). Measurement and impacts of intersectionality on obsessive-compulsive disorder symptoms across intensive treatment. *American Journal of Orthopsychiatry, 90*(4), 445–457.

Wetterneck, C. T., Little, T. E., Rinehart, K. L., Cervantes, M. E., Hyde, E., & Williams, M. (2012). Latinos with obsessive-compulsive disorder: Mental healthcare utilization and inclusion in clinical trials. *Journal of Obsessive-Compulsive and Related Disorders, 1,* 85–97. https://doi.org/10.1016/j.jocrd.2011.12.001

Wilhelm, S., Steketee, G., Reilly-Harrington, N. A., Deckersbach, T., Buhlmann, U., & Baer, L. (2005). Effectiveness of cognitive therapy for obsessive-compulsive disorder: An open trial. *Journal of Cognitive Psychotherapy, 19*(2), 173e179. https://doi.org/10.1891/jcop.19.2.173.66792

Wilhelm, S., & Steketee, G. (2006). *Cognitive therapy for obsessive-compulsive disorder: A guide for professionals.* Oakland: New Harbinger Publications.

Wilhelm, S., Berman, N. C., Keshaviah, A., Schwartz, R. A., & Steketee, G. (2015). Mechanisms of change in cognitive therapy for obsessive compulsive disorder: Role of maladaptive beliefs and schemas. *Behaviour Research and Therapy, 65,* 5–10. https://doi.org/10.1016/j.brat.2014.12.006

Williams, M. T., Domanico, J., Marques, L., Leblanc, N. J., & Turkheimer, E. (2012). Barriers to treatment among African Americans with obsessive-compulsive disorder. *Journal of Anxiety Disorders – Special Issue, 26,* 555–563. https://doi.org/10.1016/j.janxdis.2012.02.009

Williams, M. T., Rouleau, T. M., La Torre, J. T., & Sharif, N. (2020). Cultural competency in the treatment of obsessive-compulsive disorder: Practitioner guidelines. *The Cognitive Behaviour Therapist, 13,* e48. https://doi.org/10.1017/S1754470X200000501

Psychotherapy Training 13 of Predoctoral Psychology Interns, Postdocs, and Psychiatric Residents

Kathryne S. Marinchak, Suzanne Spinola, and Howard R. Steinberg

Introduction

In comparison to the general population, military veterans and active-duty service members (ADSMs) have been shown to have increased rates of mental health conditions including but not limited to PTSD and major depressive disorder (Ursano et al., 2014). Service members are less likely to seek out and engage in treatments that may lead to an alleviation of symptoms and improvements in functioning (Kehle et al., 2010), and they are also at greater risk for attempting and completing suicide than those who have not served (U.S. Department of Veteran Affairs, 2021b). Given such challenges, the importance of identifying and disseminating efficacious mental health interventions among veterans and ADSMs is vital (Karlin & Cross, 2014). The ongoing provision of high-quality psychotherapy services to this population requires preprofessional training that includes exposure to the unique experiences and potential treatment challenges among veterans and ADSMs engaged in mental health services. The VA, as the largest provider of mental health services to this population, is uniquely poised to train the next generation of service providers, and this chapter will focus on these training issues and will highlight the supervisory and contextual factors that support the development of competent, compassionate, and culturally aware mental health providers.

Considering the vast amount of information that must be consumed by an individual early on in training, making determinations regarding the key ingredients to provide in this development is an important step towards establishing a framework within which trainees may progress (Rocco et al., 2019). This task increases in complexity when considering the various training approaches across graduate programs (e.g., models of supervision and theoretical orientations) that may affect selection of treatment interventions and supervisory discussions. However, a focus on cultural and other client characteristics that may impact the course of psychotherapy is essential regardless of programmatic differences. Though client factors such as age, race, gender, sexual orientation, and disability status (and potential intersectionalities) are frequently noted to be points of attention, the military service experiences of those veterans and ADSMs are often overlooked (Zwiebach et al., 2019). As these military experiences are unique to this population, it is vital that those engaged in the provision of psychotherapy services to these individuals are provided with the necessary knowledge and tools to enhance their clinical competency (Strom et al., 2012).

Clinical Supervision

In direct-care settings with vulnerable populations, special consideration must be given to factors that influence both the supervisory relationship and process, as well as the therapeutic alliance. Within this novel setting, training plans should identify and address specific competencies related to working with veteran and ADSM populations, including risk assessment, differential diagnosis, and functioning as a member of a large interdisciplinary care team. Additionally, supervisors should emphasize principles of multiculturally competent practice by encouraging the integration of military culture and an individual's unique service with the other facets of their identity.

The process of developing a training plan for supervisees working with veteran and ADSM populations is in many ways similar to the process when working with other groups; however, there are distinct aspects of training with veterans and ADSMs that should be included. The "supervision contract," or agreement, is a widely practiced and highly supported mechanism to formalize supervisor and trainee agreement on goals, tasks to achieve those training goals, and roles and responsibilities of each member of the supervisory dyad. It is a collaborative task that helps in the establishment of the initial supervisory alliance, and aids to maintain rapport and a positive working relationship by providing a blueprint for navigating decisions about patient care, training duties, and any issues with performance (Falender & Shafranske, 2004).

The supervision agreement starts with an assessment of trainee strengths and past experiences relevant to the current setting. In working with veterans and ADSMs, an exploration of trainee familiarity with military culture is a key aspect of this initial discussion. As discussed earlier, trainees present with varying levels of exposure to treatment at large, and to working with veteran and ADSM populations specifically. For trainees with little or no knowledge of military culture, a training goal of increasing awareness of military structure, values, and language should be a central focus of early training (Strom et al., 2012). For trainees with previous experience, training goals can be adjusted to reflect developmentally appropriate opportunities to specialize within the larger "military culture" and focus on specific experiences of subgroups (i.e., female veterans, special forces, combat veterans, veterans who identify as members of an oppressed group, veterans with PTSD, TBI, substance use, etc.). It is essential that training goals reflect the abilities of the trainee at a developmentally appropriate level, which may vary based on training year (i.e., psychology extern vs. intern, psychiatry resident), and based on previous experience (amount of exposure to clinical work or familiarity with military culture) (Sanders & Steinberg, 2012). Ensuring agreement on training goals allows for the mutual identification of tasks through which these goals will be achieved. Tasks should be directly related to training goals, as well as reflective of the practices and needs of the setting of care and patient population (Falender & Shafranske, 2004). These tasks will likely involve a variety of clinical activities (i.e., individual and group psychotherapy) but may also include conducting intakes that explore a traditional biopsychosocial history, and include a history of military service, experiences within their service, identification and discussion of service-related conditions, and experiences of reintegration to civilian life following discharge from the military.

The supervision agreement not only specifies goals, tasks to achieve these goals, and expectations of the trainee and supervisor in regard to risk assessment and timely communication, but also makes explicit the supervisor's responsibility to address factors that may affect the supervisory alliance, and therefore the quality of care of the veteran or ADSM. In supervision, as in therapy, alliance is a core competency crucial to effective practice (Falender & Shafranske, 2004; Falender et al., 2014). A strong supervisory relationship that specifically includes issues of diversity has a direct impact on trainee development and clinical work (Inman & Ladany, 2014; Nilsson & Anderson, 2004; Wilbur et al., 2019). Supervisors not only model specific skills (empathy, transparency, understanding, a nonjudgmental stance, flexibility) (Falender & Shafranske, 2004; Ladany et al., 2013) to form and maintain this alliance, they also identify and address factors which may strain the working relationship. These include the inherent power differential in the dyad (Falender & Shafranske, 2004), as well as cultural differences, differences in personal experience of privilege, identity factors, and diversity issues within the supervisory relationship (Falender & Shafranske, 2004).

Falender et al. (2014) note that "Supervisor willingness to discuss cultural and diversity issues in supervision has been associated with a stronger supervisory alliance," (Duan & Roehlke, 2001; Gatmon et al., 2001), and when trainees perceive the supervisory alliance to be strong they report higher levels of satisfaction with supervision, as well as more comfort disclosing concerns about their own performance and therapeutic challenges (Falender et al., 2014). Satisfaction with clinical faculty and supervisors has been linked to overall satisfaction with training sites and increased willingness to consider future training and employment at the same site (O'Neil et al., 2015). Thus, enhancing the supervisory relationship strengthens the quality of clinical care provided, increases trainee satisfaction with the training experience, and makes it more likely the training setting may retain talented up-and-coming psychologists who might otherwise seek careers elsewhere. Given the high number of trainees and the dearth of providers to fill open mental health slots (Cencirulo et al., 2021), this becomes even more crucial when training in a VA or DoD setting. A primary supervisory task for those working with veterans and ADSMs, therefore, must be the ongoing discussion of cultural issues that impact both the supervisory work and the therapy, with the aim of improving cultural competence of both supervisor and supervisee.

Developing Cultural and Military Competencies

APA guidelines define multicultural competence as a necessary part of ethical and effective practice (APA, 2017), regardless of the setting. As a core competence in clinical work, and as an essential factor in forming and maintaining a strong supervisory alliance, discussions of culture, identity and background should be introduced early on, and infused into ongoing supervisory work.

Multicultural competence is particularly important when working with members of an oppressed group, or those who make up part of an underserved population, such as members of the military.

Multiple studies have shown that members of oppressed and minoritized groups seek therapy at rates lower than their majority culture peers and terminate therapy far earlier (Sue et al., 2009). This is equally true for the military (Hoge et al., 2004), a specialized and underserved population. Veterans and active-duty service members form a numerical minority group within the United States, with approximately 7% of the total population currently or previously serving in the military (Atuel & Castro, 2018). This means that veterans and ADSMs are navigating multiple contexts and systems that likely have few individuals who intimately understand the lived experience of having served. Factors that have been shown to contribute to veterans and ADSMs either declining to seek mental health treatment or terminating treatment early include harboring negative views of mental health services and providers (Kulesza et al., 2015), perceiving a "poor fit" between mental health treatment and "warrior culture" (Bryan & Morrow, 2011), a feeling of responsibility to others over the self (a collectivistic mindset) (Atuel & Castro, 2018), emphasis on personal responsibility (Zwiebach et al., 2019), and feeling frustrated and alienated by a treatment provider who lacks experience with military culture (Tanielian et al., 2014). The onus to bridge that gap and create culturally competent practitioners often falls on clinical supervisors.

Developing competency in working with the military culture is even more important as the VA will train 50% of all U.S. psychologists at one point or another in their careers (Veterans Health Administration, Office of Academic Affairs, 2018). Most trainees, like the majority of providers in the community, have little to no previous experience working with current and former members of the military (Tanielian et al., 2014). When veterans do present for care, they are likely to do so at the VA, and their first encounter with mental health treatment may therefore be with a trainee. Trainees must be prepared to work collaboratively and intentionally with their patients to create an environment in which veterans and ADSMs feel that their experiences, perspectives and presenting problems are understood, and where they are likely to remain engaged in care. As noted earlier, the health-care systems that primarily treat veterans and ADSMs have placed considerable effort into the dissemination of evidence-based treatments for a variety of mental health conditions. Trainings are typically intensive and many have been made available to trainees within these systems. These training programs often allow for an introduction to military culture through the lens of a structured treatment approach specific to this population.

Indeed, issues of identity disruption and difficulties reentering civilian culture are often cited as factors contributing to veteran psychological distress. In a 2011 study, (Demers, 2011) male OEF/OIF service members reported "feeling out of place in civilian society, feeling misunderstood by others, and experiencing a crisis of identity in which they felt caught between military and civilian cultural norms" (Orazem et al., 2017). This experience cannot be recreated in the therapy room if trainees hope to succeed in the task of building rapport and framing therapeutic goals and interventions in a manner congruent with the individual's military identity. As with any cultural membership, distinct patient experiences within this culture will be impacted by overlapping identity groups, including but not limited to gender, sex, sexual orientation, religion, spirituality, race, ethnicity, and socioeconomic status, all of which "affect how they move about in their communities, families, the world and the military" (Zwiebach et al., 2019). Familiarity with military culture at large, as well as a stance of cultural humility and awareness of intersectionality, is a two-pronged approach that will help trainees to build an understanding of an individual patient's experience of these overlapping identities and inform case conceptualization. Supervisors must provide resources on both the structure and salient cultural features of the military. Additionally, they should prepare their trainees to ask questions and collaboratively explore individual experiences with their veteran and ADSM patients as they would in working to guide supervisees generally in developing skills of multicultural competence, cultural humility and self-reflection.

Demonstrations of a commitment to developing an understanding of identities and cultural contexts significant to the individual in question are significant factors impacting both the therapeutic and supervisory alliances, and thus, clinical outcomes (Chopra, 2013; Kilmer et al., 2019). In both cases, issues of identity and culture must be raised by the individual in the position of relative power; in supervision by the supervisor, and in therapy by the clinician. The best way to guide supervisees to embrace a stance of cultural humility is to demonstrate these values, attitudes, and skills in the supervisory dyad. These skills can then be flexibly applied to explore the intersectionality of identities in the military and veteran culture (see Atuel & Castro 2018; Hall et al., 2018; Zwiebach et al., 2019).

Given that every individual experiences their intersection with military culture in a unique manner, there are, broadly speaking, consistent elements that frequently present therapeutically with regard to cultural beliefs, practices, and norms following military training. Understanding and working within this cultural context allows supervisors and trainees to foster greater buy-in to the therapeutic process. These factors include, but are not limited to;

stigma against seeking mental health treatment, avoidance of emotion, the high value placed on stoicism, an orientation to hierarchy and authority, and mission-focused and all-or-nothing thinking that can manifest as frustration with themselves and the therapeutic process (Morse, 2020; Tanielian et al., 2016; Zwiebach et al., 2019). Understanding these factors is key to bridging the gap between military culture and the language of mental health treatment. Mistakenly assuming buy-in to treatment pillars (emotional vocabulary, identification, exploration) projects a lack of familiarity with military culture that may signal to the veteran or ADSM a lack of safety in the therapeutic space. Working to identify intermediate steps and the nonlinear path of recovery from trauma, substance use, depression, anxiety, etc. is fundamental to helping veterans step back from harsh self-critical assessments of their progress in therapy and maintain hope in the relationship and the process to result in measurable improvements in their lives. Equally important is the ability to frame therapeutic goals in a manner congruent with the individual's values, including values formed during their time in the military, such as service to others and the importance of their community.

Training in Current Assessment Approaches

In their work with both ADSMs and veterans, residents in psychiatry and psychology interns will need to learn to hone their clinical assessment skills. Identifying comorbid conditions seen at higher rates in this population will be important in informing case conceptualization, treatment planning, and in making referrals to additional treatment resources. Such assessment is not limited to mental health conditions, but should also include psychosocial and medical problems such as homelessness, unemployment, and traumatic brain injury. As the clinical settings within which clients are seen vary, so will the choice of assessment modalities and strategies implemented. Treatment plans will naturally develop based upon the results of initial intakes or ongoing assessment, in a collaborative, client-centered fashion. This collaboration is an opportunity for the trainee to develop a working alliance that encompasses some of the important clinical competencies discussed earlier in this chapter. Learning how to match an individual's assessment data with the most appropriate evidence-based psychotherapy is a skill that should be developed in the context of supervision. Identifying such opportunities to provide individualized collaborative treatment planning with these clients through shared decision-making is of growing interest due to the potential for improved treatment outcomes (among other factors), especially for veterans and ADSMs diagnosed with PTSD (Etingen et al., 2019; VA/DoD Clinical Practice Guidelines, 2017).

To enhance shared decision-making, there is a push across VA systems to utilize measurement-based care as a tool to support frequent and ongoing conversations between provider and patient regarding the progress of treatment. Through repeated use of patient-reported outcome measures over the course of treatment, providers and clients track changes in relative symptom severity to aid in the collaboration of goal setting and treatment planning (Resnick & Hoff, 2020). Unfortunately, the use of validated symptom rating scales to measure change over the course of therapy continues to be limited (Fortney et al., 2017; Oslin et al., 2019). Across the VA system, implementation of measurement-based care started in 2016 and continues to grow with access to enhanced measurement platforms, however, the use of measures across the system remains lower than expected (Resnick et al., 2020). When working with trainees within these large systems, it is imperative that they learn to incorporate measurement-based care into regular clinical practice. This can be reinforced throughout supervisory contacts across multiple treatment settings within the VA, both through supervisor modeling of this practice, and by incorporating this expectation into the supervisory agreement at the onset of training.

Training in Reduction of Risk

There has been increased understanding of the unique ways in which veterans and ADSMs are vulnerable to suicide, and increased focus on suicide prevention within this population. Given the specific risk factors present in a military population, trainees should be made aware of the standards for risk identification currently in use and required within large systems such as the VHA and the DoD. Screening measures such as the Columbia-Suicide Severity Rating Scale (C-SSRS) and item 9 of the Patient Health Questionnaire (PHQ-9) have been widely used and have been found to be effective in identifying individuals at risk for suicide (Gutierrez et al., 2021; Bahraini et al., 2020). However, use of multiple methods (e.g., patient self-report and clinical interview) to assess for suicide risk was recommended over the reliance on one tool (Sall et al., 2019), meaning that direct discussions of suicidal thoughts and exploration of risk and protective factors must be encouraged throughout the episode of care. Trainees need to be knowledgeable of how to best help higher risk veterans and ADSMs to reduce their risk of suicide, and to possibly engage them in higher levels of care. They also need to have a clear understanding of when to contact their supervisors to bring them into the session to aid in these decisions, as well as how to contact backup coverage should the primary supervisor be unavailable. These conditions should be spelled out explicitly in the supervision agreement and reviewed collaboratively on a regular basis.

Due to their relative familiarity with and access to firearms, veterans and ADSMs are more likely to choose this method of suicide over other methods (U.S. Department of Veterans Affairs, 2021a), and this choice is the deadliest by far. Helping clients address access to firearms is the most effective way to reduce this risk (Lemle, 2020; Sall et al., 2019; Simonetti & Brenner, 2020). Reducing access through lethal means counseling is an imperative with this population and incorporating this early on in a training program cannot be overlooked. As a regular part of their clinical work, trainees should be encouraged to engage with their clients about safe storage options of firearms, including temporary transfer of weapons or the use and distribution of gun locks for those noted to be at risk. Trainee comfort with initiating these conversations, and awareness of available resources through the VA (i.e., the option for VA policy to assume temporary custody of weapons or to supply gun locks) must be assessed at various points throughout their training to ensure this crucial intervention is not overlooked, or avoided due to discomfort.

Finally, large health-care systems such as the VHA and the DoD continually work towards improving methods to identify those that are at highest risk for suicide, though this is not an easy task. The DoD (Kessler et al., 2017) and the VA (Kessler et al., 2017; McCarthy et al., 2021) have utilized predictive modeling to target high-risk individuals who might be appropriate for enhanced mental health services. REACH VET (Recovery Engagement and Coordination for Health-Veterans Enhanced Treatment), a risk-identifier system, integrates predictive modeling and other methods of risk stratification to identify potential at-risk patients and notify suicide prevention coordinators and mental health providers. Within the VA, patients thought to be at greater risk also may carry a high-risk flag in their electronic medical record, indicating the need for heightened attention to presentation, increased frequency of visits, and safety planning. With these indicators, trainees must be aware of their responsibility for more frequent patient contacts and their need to reach out to licensed staff for additional direction, as well as the appropriate documentation regarding the care provided and the risk status. Trainees should also be made aware of each facility's Suicide Prevention Coordinator as an added resource when caring for an at-risk individual and be encouraged to engage with that coordinator as indicated.

Training within Large Systems of Care

Training in a federal agency should include a review of the structure of integrated health-care systems and how they operate and interact to impact patient care. For example, with 200,000 military members transitioning out of the service each year, these individuals have access to the transitional assistance program (TAP) to help them engage with a variety of resources, one being VA health care if eligible (U.S. Department of Veterans Affairs, 2021b). This period of transition is often challenging for many individuals and may involve heightened stress when attempting to navigate the various services. It is a time when acclimation to post-service experiences may be threatened, and the motivation to engage in treatment may wax and wane over time. Helping trainees recognize the importance of engaging these patients at each opportunity is vital. To make matters more complex, the issue of military service connection may also be a part of the transition from active-duty service. Service-connected disability benefits are compensation for social and vocational impairments that are incurred from or exacerbated during service (U.S. Department of Veterans Affairs, 2015). This application process is complex and lengthy (Sayer et al., 2004) and can impact the therapeutic alliance. Therefore, time in supervision should provide some education regarding the differing roles that the mental health clinician, patient, compensation and pension examiner, benefits office, and others may have in the process, and the potential impacts of this experience upon treatment.

The emphasis on interdisciplinary practice allows health-care systems to engage in patient-centered treatment approaches to provide the highest quality care possible. This collaboration is facilitated using the electronic medical record, which serves to enhance communication regarding patient care across the different disciplines involved. A unique result of this collaborative effort is to have multiple mental health providers working with one patient simultaneously, with each provider offering a unique service to the collaborative effort. It may take some time before trainees in these settings learn to work within these seemingly complex systems, and to develop the skills to actively participate, and at times, coordinate care within this model. This team approach facilitates the practice of peer supervision and allows for varying perspectives and knowledge of resources to be shared among providers. It is important for supervisors to help trainees understand what role they are playing, as their level of engagement and decision-making with regards to treatment planning may need to be adjusted accordingly.

Conclusion

Training psychiatry residents and psychology interns and fellows in the provision of psychotherapy to veterans and ADSMs involves attention to the best general practices in supervision combined with the population-specific information described in this chapter. Developing competencies that go beyond the practice of novel treatment approaches to include cultural and military understanding, as well as the intersection of complex person-level and systems-level factors, is vital to the growth of trainees working with these individuals. Additionally, learning to adapt and expand clinical practice to include tools such as video-based telehealth is an opportunity for trainees to apply new skills that will generalize across different treatment settings in their future practice. The role of the clinical supervisor in all of this is large, but this work helps to ensure the development of clinical professionals who will provide much needed clinical services to these individuals who have served.

References

American Psychological Association [APA]. (2017). Multicultural guidelines: An ecological approach to context, identity, and intersectionality. Retrieved from: http://www.apa.org/about/policy/multicultural-guidelines.pdf

Atuel, H. R., & Castro, C. A. (2018). Military cultural competence. *Clinical Social Work Journal, 46*, 74–82. https://link.springer.com/article/10.1007%2Fs10615-018-0651-z

Bahraini, N., Brenner, L. A., Barry, C., Hostetter, T., Keusch, J., Post, E. P., Kessler, C., Smith, C., & Matarazzo, B. B. (2020). Assessment of rates of suicide risk screening and prevalence of positive screening results among US veterans after implementation of the veterans affairs suicide risk identification strategy. *JAMA Network Open, 3*(10). https://doi.org/10.1001/jamanetworkopen.2020.22531

Bryan, C. J., & Morrow, C. E. (2011). Circumventing mental health stigma by embracing the warrior culture: Lessons learned from the Defender's Edge program. *Professional Psychology: Research and Practice, 42*(1), 16–23. https://doi.org/10.1037/a0022290

Cencirulo, J., McDougall, T., Sorenson, C., Crosby, S., & Hauser, P. (2021). Trainee experiences of racism, sexism, heterosexism, and ableism (the "ISMs") at a Department of Veterans Affairs (VA) healthcare facility. *Training and Education in Professional Psychology, 15*(3), 242–249. https://doi.org/10.1037/tep0000312

Chopra, T. (2013). All supervision is multicultural: A review of literature on the need for multicultural supervision in counseling. *Psychological Studies 58*, 335–338. https://doi.org/10.1007/s12646-013-0206-x

Demers, A. (2011). When veterans return: The role of community in reintegration. *Journal of Loss and Trauma, 16*(2), 160–179. https://doi.org/10.1080/15325024.2010.519281

Duan, C., & Roehlke, H. (2001). A descriptive "snapshot" of cross-racial supervision in university counseling center internships. *Journal of Multicultural Counseling and Development, 29*(2), 131–146. https://doi.org/10.1002/j.2161-1912.2001.tb00510.x

Etingen, B., Hill, J. N., Miller, L. J., Schwartz, A., LaVela, S. L., & Jordan, N. (2019). An exploratory pilot study to describe shared decision-making for PTSD treatment planning: The provider perspective. *Military Medicine, 184*(1), 467–475. https://doi.org/10.1093/milmed/usy407

Falender, C. A., & Shafranske, E. P. (2004). Clinical supervision: A competency-based approach. *American Psychological Association.* https://doi.org/10.1037/10806-000

Falender, C. A., Shafranske, E. P., & Ofek, A. (2014). Competent clinical supervision: Emerging effective practices. *Counselling Psychology Quarterly, 27*(4), 393–408. https://doi.org/10.1080/09515070.2014.934785

Fortney, J. C., Unützer, J., Wrenn, G., Pyne, J. M., Smith, G. R., Schoenbaum, M., & Harbin, H. T. (2017). A tipping point for measurement-based care. *Psychiatric Services, 68*(2), 179–188. https://doi.org/10.1176/appi.ps.201500439

Gatmon, D., Jackson, D., Koshkarian, L., Martos-Perry, N., Molina, A., Patel, N., & Rodolfa, E. (2001). Exploring ethnic, gender, and sexual orientation variables in supervision: Do they really matter? *Journal of Mulitcultural Counseling and Development, 29*(2), 102–113. https://doi.org/10.1002/j.2161-1912.2001.tb00508.x

Gutierrez, P. M., Joiner, T., Hanson, J., Avery, K., Fender, A., Harrison, T., Kerns, K., McGowan, P., Stanley, I. H., Silva, C., & Rogers, M. L. (2021). Clinical utility of suicide behavior and ideation measures: Implications of military suicide risk assessment. *Psychological Assessment, 33*(1), 1–13.

Hall, K. G., Garland, A., Charlton, G. P., & Johnson, M. (2018). Military culture and the civilian therapist: Using relational-cultural theory to promote the therapeutic alliance. *Journal of Creativity in Mental Health, 13*(4), 451–466. https://doi.org/10.1080/15401383.2018.1470951

Hoge, C. W., Castro, C. A., Messer, S. C., McGurk, D., Cotting, D. I., & Koffman, R. L. (2004). Combat duty in Iraq and Afghanistan, mental health problems, and barriers to care. *New England Journal of Medicine, 351*(1), 13–22.

Inman, A. G., & Ladany, N. (2014). Multicultural competencies in psychotherapy supervision. In F. T. L. Leong, L. Comas-Díaz, G. C. Nagayama Hall, V. C. McLoyd, & J. E. Trimble (Eds.), *APA handbook of multicultural psychology, Vol. 2. Applications and training* (pp. 643–658). American Psychological Association. https://doi.org/10.1037/14187-036

Karlin, B. E., & Cross, G. (2014). From the laboratory to the therapy room: National dissemination and implementation of evidence-based psychotherapies in the U.S. Department of Veterans Affairs Health Care System. *American Psychologist, 69*(1), 19–33. https://doi.org/10.1037/a0033888

Kehle, S. M., Polusny, M. A., Murdoch, M., Erbes, C. R., Arbisi, P. A., Thuras, P., & Meis, L. A. (2010). Early mental health treatment-seeking among U.S. National Guard soldiers deployed to Iraq. *Journal of Traumatic Stress, 23*, 33–40. https://doi.org/10.1002/jts.20480

Kessler, R. C., Stein, M. B., Petukhova, M. V., Bliese, P., & Bossarte, R. M. (2017). Predicting suicides after outpatient mental health visits in the Army Study to Assess Risk and Resilience in Servicemembers (Army STARRS). *Molecular Psychiatry, 22*(4), 544–551. https://doi.org/10.1038/mp.2016.110

Kilmer, E. D., Villarreal, C., Janis, B. M., Callahan, J. L., Ruggero, C. J., Kilmer, J. N., Love, P. K., & Cox, R. J. (2019). Differential early termination is tied to client race/ethnicity status. *Practice Innovations, 4*(2), 88–98. https://doi.org/10.1037/pri0000085

Kulesza, M., Pedersen, E., Corrigan, P., & Marshall, G. (2015). Help-seeking stigma and mental health treatment seeking among young adult veterans. *Military Behavioral Health, 3*(4), 230–239. https://doi.org/10.1080/21635781.2015.1055866

Ladany, N., Mori, Y., & Mehr, K. E. (2013). Effective and ineffective supervision. *The Counseling Psychologist*, *41*(1), 28–47. https://doi.org/10.1177/0011000012442648

Lemle, R. B. (2020). Veterans, firearms, and suicide: Safe storage prevention policy and the PREVENTS roadmap. *Federal Practitioner*, *37*(9), 426–433. https://doi.org/10.12788/fp.0041

McCarthy, J. F., Cooper, S. A., Dent, K. R., Eagan, A. E., Matarazzo, B. B., Hannemann, C. M., Reger, M. A., Ladnes, S. J., Trafton, J. A., Schoenbaum, M., & Katz, I. R. (2021). Evaluation of the Recovery Engagement and Coordination for Health-Veterans Enhanced Treatment suicide risk modeling clinical program in the Veterans Health Administration. *JAMA Network Open*, *4*(10). https://doi.org/10.1001/jamanetworkopen.2021.29900

Morse, C. (2020). Training for a new environment: Using military operational concepts in counseling veterans. *Journal of Clinical Psychology 76*, 841–851. https://doi.org/10.1002/jclp.22919

Nilsson, J. E., & Anderson, M. Z. (2004). Supervising international students: The role of acculturation, role ambiguity, and multicultural discussions. *Professional Psychology: Research and Practice*, *35*(3), 306–312. https://doi.org/10.1037/0735-7028.35.3.306

O'Neil, J., Chaison, A. D., Cuellar, A. K., Nguyen, Q. X., Brown, W. L., & Teng, E. J. (2015). Development and implementation of a mentoring program for Veterans Affairs psychology trainees. *Training and Education in Professional Psychology*, *9*(2), 113–120. https://doi.org/10.1037/tep0000065

Orazem, R. J., Frazier, P. A., Schnurr, P. P., Oleson, H. E., Carlson, K. F., Litz, B. T., & Sayer, N. A. (2017). Identity adjustment among Afghanistan and Iraq war veterans with reintegration difficulty. *Psychological Trauma: Theory, Research, Practice, and Policy*, *9*(Suppl 1), 4–11. https://doi.org/10.1037/tra0000225

Oslin, D. W., Hoff, R., Mignogna, J., & Resnick, S. G. (2019). Provider attitudes and experience with measurement-based mental health care in the VA implementation project. *Psychiatric Services*, *70*(2), 135–138. https://doi.org/10.1176/appi.ps.201800228

Resnick, S. G., & Hoff, R. A. (2020). Observations from the national implementation of measurement based care in mental health in the Department of Veterans Affairs. *Psychological Services*, *17*(3), 238–246. https://doi.org/10.1037/ser0000351

Resnick, S. G., Oehlert, M. E., Hoff, R. A., & Kearney, L. K. (2020). Measurement-based care and psychological assessment: Using measurement to enhance psychological treatment. *Psychological Services*, *17*(3), 233–237. https://doi.org/10.1037/ser0000491

Rocco, D., Gennaro, A., Filugelli, L., Squarcina, P., & Antonelli, E. (2019). Key factors in psychotherapy training: An analysis of trainers', trainees', and psychotherapists' points of view. *Research in Psychotherapy*, *22*(3), 415. https://doi.org/10.4081/ripppo.2019.415

Sall, J., Brenner, L., Millikan Bell, A. M., & Colston, M. J. (2019). Assessment and management of patients at risk for suicide: Synopsis of the 2019 U.S. Department of Veterans Affairs and U.S. Department of Defense clinical practice guidelines. *Annals of Internal Medicine*, *171*(5), 343–353. https://doi.org/10.7326/m19-0687

Sanders, K. A., & Steinberg, H. R. (2012). Supervision and mentoring of clinical psychology predoctoral interns and postdoctoral residents. *Journal of Cognitive Psychotherapy*, *26*(3), 226–235. https://doi.org/10.1891/0889-8391.26.3.226

Sayer, N. A., Spoont, M., & Nelson, D. (2004). Veterans seeking disability benefits for post-traumatic stress disorder: Who applies and the self-reported meaning of disability compensation (2004). *Social Science & Medicine*, *58*(11), 2133–2143. https://doi.org/10.1016/j.socscimed.2003.08.009

Simonetti, J. A., & Brenner, L. A. (2020). Promoting firearm safety as a suicide prevention strategy within health care systems: Challenges and recommendations. *Psychiatric Services*, *71*(3), 298–300. https://doi.org/10.1176/appi.ps.201900286

Strom, T. Q., Gavian, M. E., Possis, E., Loughlin, J., Bui, T., Linardatos, E., Leskela, J., & Siegel, W. (2012). Cultural and ethical considerations when working with military personnel and veterans: A primer for VA training programs. *Training and Education in Professional Psychology*, *6*(2), 67–75. https://doi.org/10.1037/a0028275

Sue, S., Zane, N., Nagayama Hall, G. C., & Berger, L. K. (2009). The case for cultural competency in psychotherapeutic interventions. *Annual Review of Psychology*, *60*, 525–548. https://doi.org/10.1146/annurev.psych.60.110707.163651

Tanielian, T., Farris, C., Batka, C., Farmer, C. M., Robinson, E., Engel, C. C., & Jaycox, L. H. (2014). *Ready to serve: Community-based provider capacity to deliver culturally competent, quality mental health care to veterans and their families*. Santa Monica: RAND Corporation. https://www.rand.org/pubs/research_reports/RR806.html

Tanielian, T., Woldetsadik, M. A., Jaycox, L. H., Batka, C., Moen, S., Farmer, C., & Engel, C. C. (2016). Barriers to engaging service members in mental health care within the US military health system. *Psychiatric Services*, *67*(7), 718–727. https://doi.org/10.1176/appi.ps.201500237

U.S. Department of Veterans Affairs. (2015). Federal benefits for veterans, dependents, and survivors: Chapter 2 service-connected disabilities. [VA office of public and intergovernmental affairs website]. April 21, 2015. Accessed at https://www.va.gov/opa/publications/benefits_book/benefits_chap02.asp

U.S. Department of Veterans Affairs, Veterans Benefits Administration. (2021a). Transition and economic development: Your VA transition assistance program (TAP). Accessed at https://www.benefits.va.gov/transition/tap.asp

U.S. Department of Veterans Affairs, Office of Mental Health and Suicide Prevention. (2021b). *National veteran suicide prevention annual report*. Accessed at www.mentalhealth.va.gov/docs/data-sheets/2021/2021-National-Veteran-Suicide-Prevention-Annual-Report-FINAL-9-8-21.pdf

Ursano, R. J., Colpe, L. J., Heeringa, S. G., Kessler, R. C., Schoenbaum, M., Stein, M. B., & Army STARRS collaborators. (2014). The Army Study to Assess Risk and Resilience in Servicemembers (Army STARRS). *Psychiatry*, *77*(2), 107–119. https://doi.org/10.1521/psyc.2014.77.2.107

VA/DoD Clinical Practice Guideline for the Management of Posttraumatic Stress Disorder and Acute Stress Disorder. (2017). Accessed at www.healthquality.va.gov/guidelines/MH/ptsd/VADoDPTSDCPGFinal012418.pdf

Veterans Health Administration, Office of Academic Affiliations (2018). Academic year 17–18 statistics: Health professions trainees. Retrieved from https://www.va.gov/OAA/docs/OAA_Statistics_2018.pdf

Wilbur, R. C., Kuemmel, A. M., & Lackner, R. J. (2019). Who's on first? Supervising psychology trainees with disabilities and establishing accommodations. *Training and Education in Professional Psychology*, *13*(2), 111–118. https://doi.org/10.1037/tep0000231

Zwiebach, L., Lannert, B. K., Sherrill, A. M., McSweeney, L. B., Sprang, K., Goodnight, J. R. M., Lewis, S. C., & Rauch, S. A. M. (2019). Military cultural competence in the context of cognitive behavioral therapy. *The Cognitive Behaviour Therapist*, *12*(5), 1–13. https://doi.org/10.1017/S1754470X18000132

Index

Pages in **bold** refer to tables.

acceptance and commitment therapy 188
ACT 188
affirming care 5, 26–34, 134–135
African Americans 47, 91, 185
AHI 106
alcohol misuse 6–7, 76, 79–80, 83–86
alcohol problems 41, 83
alcohol use disorder 6, 75–78, 80, 82–84, 92, 144
anhedonia 40
apnea-hypopnea index 105
Asian Americans 48, 136, 185–186
AUD 6–7, 75–76, 83, 85

BBT-I 103
BCT 81–82, 121, 147
BDD 183
behavioral couples therapy 118, 120–121, 147
BEP 16
BFI 148
BFRBs 183
binge drinking 83
BIPOC 6, 14–15, 56–59, 62, 64–69
bipolar 15
black, indigenous, and people of color 6, 14, 56
body dysmorphic disorder 183

body focused repetitive behaviors 183
brief behavioral treatment for insomnia 103
brief eclectic psychotherapy 16, 60
brief family intervention 148
BSRF 141
Building Strong and Ready Families 141

cannabis 6–7, 76, 78, 90–96
case conceptualization 17, 68, 114, 199–200
CBCT 121–122, 142
CBT 16, 32, 78, 82–83, 94–95, 103–105, 168, **172**–173, 188–189
Chaplains Religious Enrichment Development Operations 139
CM 80, 95
cognitive-behavioral conjoint therapy 121, 142
cognitive behavioral therapy 9, 16, 32, 94, 103, **171**–173
cognitive behavioral therapy for insomnia 103
cognitive processing therapy 6, 15–16, 41, 62, 148
cognitive therapy 187–189
combination treatment 9, 168, 173
communication 30, 79, 81, 121, 139–140, 146, 148–149, 196, 203
community reinforcement approach 79

comorbidity 12, 93, 181, 183–185
compensation and pension 203
compulsions 178–180, 182–184, 186–187, 190
compulsive sexual behavior 43
contingency management 80
couples therapy 8, 113–115, 117–123, 143, 146–148, 151–152
CPT 15–16, 41, 60–64
CRA 79–81
critical interaction therapy 147
CUD 7, 90–96
cultural betrayal 15
cultural competence 4, 19, 197–199
cultural humility 10, 30, 199
culturally responsive care 1, 5, 10, 13, 18–19, 26–27, 34, 49

DBT 32
Δ9-tetrahydrocannabinol (THC) 91
Dialectical Behavioral Therapy 32, 122
differential diagnosis 9, 183, 188, 195
Dimensional Obsessive Compulsive Scale 182
discrimination 15, 18–19, 26, 30, 60, 63, 68, 103–105, 117, 130, 136, 150, 185
diversity 4, 8, 66, 77, 107, 119, 122, 130–133, 136–137, 140, 144, 149–150, 152, 197
DOCS 182
drug use disorder 75, 121
dual military 117, 133, 139
dysphoric arousal 40

EBPs 60–61, 63–64, 66–67
EFCT 147
EFMP 140
EFT 120
EMDR 16–17, 60, 150
emotion focused couples therapy 147
emotion focused therapy 120
ePREP 142
ERP 187–190
ERRT 105
ethnocultural 7–9, 130, 140, 142–146, 150, 152–153, 166, 174–175, 184
ethnoracial 2, 6, 8, 48, 57, 59, 61–62, 64–66, 68, 130, 140, 142–145, 149–150, 152–153, 166, 184
evidence-based psychotherapies 58, 60

evidence-based treatment 2, 8–9, 13, 19–20, 49, 79, 121, 130, 164, 166–167, 175, 198
Exceptional Family Member Program 140
exposure and response prevention 187
exposure, relaxation, and rescripting therapy 104
eye movement desensitization and reprocessing therapy 60, 150

Families Over Coming Under Stress Program 140
FOCUS 140–141

Gender dysphoria 28
gender expression 29
gender identity 25, 28–31, 117, 130, 151
gender minorities 47, 131

historically marginalized group 13
HMGs 15, 18–19
hormone therapy 48–49, 134

IBCT 119–120, 122
identity groups 199
imagery rehearsal therapy 104
immigrant 131, 136–137
Insomnia 7, 94, 101–107, **169**
institutional betrayal 4, 14, 19–20
integrative behavioral couples therapy 147
interdisciplinary practice 203
internalized homophobia 15, 31
intersectionality 17, 58, 68–69, 117, 122, 131, 137, 184, 186, 199
intersectional theory 4, 13
intimate partner violence 18, 26, 31, 40, 116
intimate relationships 8, 45, 113–116, 145
IPV 116, 122, 151
IRT 104–105

Koa 149

Latinx 61, 186
lethal means counseling 202

LGBTQ 5, 14–15, 25–34, 38, 46–47, 118, 139, 141, 146
LGBTQ Relationally-Based Positive Psychology 31

MAP 149
map of the adaptation process 149
marginalization 5, 26, 32–34, 130
MarriageCare 140
Marriage Checkup 143
measurement-based care 201
medical cannabis 92
mental health disparities 5, 14, 26
MET 76–78, 83, 95
MHS 138
Military Crisis Line 150
military culture 4, 10, 19, 32, 83, 114, 137–138, 195–196, 198–200
Military Health System 138
military sexual trauma 3–4, 13–14, 27, 39, 42–43, 46, 63, 84, 113
military treatment facilities 166
minorities 33, 47, 55–56, 61–62, 65, 68, 131, 134–135, 141, 144, 146, 151
minority stress model 27, 120
models of supervision 195
moral injury 43, 139
motivational enhancement therapy 76, 94
motivational interviewing 76–77, 189
MST 3–5, 13–19, 39–40, 43, 84, 117
multicultural competence 197–198

narrative exposure therapy 16, 60
National Transgender Discrimination Survey 30
nightmares 7, 101, 103–105, 107

obsessions 178–179, 182–183, 185–187, 190
obsessive compulsive disorder 178
obstructive sleep apnea 7, 101, 105, 164
OCD 9, 178–190
OSA 106–107
OurRelationship 123, 142

PAIRS 148
PE 16, 41, 60–61, 63–64, 67
pharmacological treatments 6, 49, 94, 168
pharmacotherapy 9, 48, 59–61, 147

physical health 7, 40, 43, 49, 67, 84, 104, 117
power differential 57, 197
Practical Application of Intimate Relationship Skills 148
PREP 139
Prevention and Relationship Enhancement Program 139
prolonged exposure therapy 15
psychotherapy treatments 167–168
psychotic 15, 168

RCT 32, 61–63, 68, 168–173
REACH VET 202
Relational-cultural Theory 32
repetitive transcranial magnetic stimulation **172**
risk assessment 195
risk identification 201
rituals 178–179, 187, 190
rTMS **172**, 174

Safe Actions for Families to Encourage Recovery 150
SAFER 150
self-directed violence 14
sexual assault 12, 14, 18, 26, 40, 61, 132
sexual harassment 14, 117
Sexually Transmitted Infection 40, 43
sexual orientation 5, 8, 15, 17, 25–26, 28, 30–31, 69, 85, 118, 130, 186, 195, 199
shared decision-making 200–201
social locations 8, 130
STI 43
stigma 14–15, 19–20, 27, 32, 48, 141, 150, 166, 175, 184, 200
stigmatization 18–19
Strength at Home Couples Program 122
Strong Bonds Program 139
structured approach therapy 147
substance abuse 6, 14, 75, 77, 79, 81, 83, 85–90, 92, 189
substance misuse 3, 79, 83–85
Substance Use Disorders 3–4, 12, 41, 75, 80, 85–86, 90, 94–95, 113, 144, 188
SUDs 68, 76, 78, 82–83, 86, 144–145, 147
suicide 1, 3–4, 10–11, 14, 67, 102, 150, 166, 185, 194, 201–202

supervision 10, 33, 60, 67, 173, 189–190, 195–197, 199–200, 202–204
supervision contract 196
supervisory alliance 196–197, 199
supervisory relationship 195, 197

TBCT 120–121
TBI 1, 85, 94, 102, 113, 116, 196
TeleFOCUS 141
telehealth 16, 33, 67, 81, 123, **169–170**, **172**–174, 204
TF-CBT 16
therapeutic alliance 28, 30, 63, 67, 120, 195, 203
tolerance 90, 92, 94, 180, 189
trainee satisfaction 197
training goals 196
training plan 195
transgender care teams 29
traumatic brain injury 4, 94, 113, 139, 141, 183, 200

TRICARE 134, 167
triggers 78–79, 120, 179, 187
Twelve-Step-Oriented Therapy 82

underserved population 198

VCIIR 148
veteran-centered care 144
Veteran Couples Integrative Intensive Retreat 148
Veteran Crisis Line 150
veteran family interventions 148

Warrior to Soulmate 148
withdrawal 15, 90, 93, 115
working alliance 200

Yale-Brown Obsessive Compulsive Scale 182
YBOCS 182

For Product Safety Concerns and Information please contact our EU representative GPSR@taylorandfrancis.com
Taylor & Francis Verlag GmbH, Kaufingerstraße 24, 80331 München, Germany

www.ingramcontent.com/pod-product-compliance
Lightning Source LLC
Chambersburg PA
CBHW061347300426
44116CB00011B/2024